Arthur Chichester

The Radical Cure for Ireland

A letter to the people of England and Scotland concerning a new plantation

Arthur Chichester

The Radical Cure for Ireland
A letter to the people of England and Scotland concerning a new plantation

ISBN/EAN: 9783337323646

Printed in Europe, USA, Canada, Australia, Japan

Cover: Foto ©ninafisch / pixelio.de

More available books at **www.hansebooks.com**

THE

RADICAL CURE FOR IRELAND

A LETTER

TO

THE PEOPLE OF ENGLAND AND SCOTLAND CONCERNING A NEW PLANTATION

COMMUNICATED THROUGH A LIVING FRIEND

BY

CHICHESTER'S GHOST

WITH TWO MAPS

WILLIAM BLACKWOOD AND SONS
EDINBURGH AND LONDON
MDCCCXC

PREFATORY NOTE.

SIR ARTHUR CHICHESTER, an English Puritan of moderate views, was Lord Deputy of Ireland from 1604 to 1616, and chief organiser of the Great Plantation. He was born in 1563, the second son of Sir John Chichester of Rawleigh, near Barnstaple. He served against the Armada, and afterwards with Henry IV. of France, who knighted him at the siege of Amiens. He was appointed Governor of Carrick-fergus in 1599, and served as a major-general in Tyrone's war. In 1603 he was made a Privy Councillor, and in 1613 raised to the peerage as Lord Chichester of Belfast. He got a grant of the northern coast of Belfast Lough in Tyrone's war, and of the peninsula of Innishowen on the forfeiture of O'Doherty in 1607. On his death in 1625, these estates passed to his brother Edward, whose son Arthur was the first Earl of Donegall.

THE EDITOR.

CONTENTS.

THE

RADICAL CURE FOR IRELAND.

BY

CHICHESTER'S GHOST.

ERRATA.

Page 28, line 8, *for* "former" *read* "future."
  „   33, line 17, *for* "to" *read* "below."
  „   46, line 5, *for* "might he" *read* "may be."
  „   57, line 5, and 66, line 1, *for* "Radicals" *read* "Jacobyns."
  „   88, line 12, *for* "five" *read* "six."
  „   89, line 26, *read* "Lower" *before* "Tyrconnell."
  „   89, line 27, *for* "Donegal" *read* "Upper Tyrconnell."
  „   126, 2d line from end, *for* "worst" *read* "worse."
  „   192, transpose the words "Ida" and "Iverk."

light of old experience. Hear me !

2. Said Mr T. W. Russell, M.P. (who probably knows more about Ireland than any other member of the House of Commons), speaking on the occasion of Mr Chamberlain's visit to Belfast (12th October 1887), "The real solution of the Irish difficulty lies in the fact that the laws in Ulster and the rest of Ireland

A

THE

RADICAL CURE FOR IRELAND.

BY

CHICHESTER'S GHOST.

———◆———

I.

THE MALADY.

1. NEARLY three hundred years ago I lived, and worked, and left my mark in Ireland. Since then I have watched the course of English mismanagement with an ever-growing painful interest. The time is now ripe for me to preach with some hope of prevailing. I speak the words of fresh knowledge in the light of old experience. Hear me !

2. Said Mr T. W. Russell, M.P. (who probably knows more about Ireland than any other member of the House of Commons), speaking on the occasion of Mr Chamberlain's visit to Belfast (12th October 1887), "The real solution of the Irish difficulty lies in the fact that the laws in Ulster and the rest of Ireland

A

are the same, but the people are different. The other three provinces are governed by priests, patriots, and publicans, and between them these have gone far to make mendicancy a virtue and laziness a fine art, and utterly destroyed the self-reliance of the great mass of the people. The greater part of the population south of Dublin lives in a state of Micawberism, waiting for something to turn up; and if the English and Scottish elements could be abstracted from the commerce of Dublin and Cork, those cities would be left wildernesses."

3. Said Lord Rosebery (who probably knows as little about Ireland as any member of the House of Lords), speaking a week earlier at Ipswich, "The Irish have an association (the National League) of which I do not know enough to say one thing or another, to say either good or evil about it, except this, that Sir Redvers Buller, the permanent Under-Secretary for Ireland, said of it in public evidence, that the people of Ireland considered it their salvation. Either the people of Ireland must be very bad, or the association must be very good, that a nation should hold such an opinion about it."

4. The Union party will not be troubled by this imaginary dilemma. Every honest and competent observer will answer without hesitation, that the Irish people—meaning, of course, the Roman Catholics (as does Lord Rosebery)—are very bad indeed. Not altogether bad as human beings. Besides some glittering sham virtues, which are apt to impose greatly on first acquaintance, they have some real virtues,

chiefly of a primitive type, which make them useful as soldiers and constables. They are not bad when under control. But they are thoroughly bad as free citizens of a civilised country. They are destitute of the civic virtues which would qualify them to stand side by side with the solid Saxons of England and Scotland as ruling members of that United Kingdom, which still moves in the forefront of enlightened communities. They have neither the self-control nor the steadiness of purpose, the love of order nor the sense of justice.

5. With the Irishman, as with other semi-savages, " getting justice " means simply getting his own way. Could there be a clearer proof of this than their behaviour about the sliding-scale of judicial rents![1] These were fixed for fifteen years, greatly to their advantage, at a time when prices were lower than they had been for a generation. To everybody's surprise, prices went lower still, and the tenants howled for a further reduction. This was conceded, with the necessary proviso that a corresponding addition should be made, if prices rose. In 1888 they did rise, and the Commissioners could not decently refuse to make some change in favour of the landlords. They did so very slightly, far less than they ought; and instantly there was a storm of protest and invective, led by the national hero O'Brien. In 1889 the rise continued, with the same results; and now there is another dishonest howl, coupled with hopes of evasive chicanery.

[1] Or the behaviour of Captain Vandeleur's tenants in Clare, after assenting to the arbitration of Sir Charles Russell.

6. Another beautiful illustration is found in the anonymous article[1] by an Irish prelate in the ' Contemporary Review ' of August 1889—an inspired communication, whose full significance will be pointed out at a later stage. " Monsignor Persico began to inspire distrust." Why? Because he shamelessly took evidence from both sides before forming an opinion. The Papal Commissioner actually "oscillated between the dinner - tables of landlords and the palaces of the bishops " ! Truly the Irishman's notion of fair play is " Heads I win, tails you lose." He is a being in whom reason, will, and conscience are the mere slaves of his passions ; in short, he is but a child of a larger growth, unstable as water, reckless of his own future, and equally reckless of the rights of others. People who confess that they are not fit for freedom of contract, prove themselves unfit for trial by jury and representative government.

7. The following extract from the Edinburgh 'Scotsman ' (8th October 1887),—by whom written I do not know—is long to quote, but every word of it is worthy to be read and digested. It must carry to every mind the conviction of having been written by an honest man, who thoroughly knows his subject, and desires only to tell the truth about it. He tells us what all Scotsmen who know the Irish really think about them, and what even Mr Gladstone's idolaters would say, if they did not hate the lairds, or the Established Church, somewhat more than they hate the workers of iniquity.

<hr>

[1] The Papacy : A Revelation and a Prophecy, p. 165.

SCOTTISH AND IRISH UNEMPLOYED—A CONTRAST.

It seems to me that we are crazy on the Irish question
—crazy for two reasons, because of the utter hopelessness of
ever improving Irishmen by the conciliatory legislation we
are giving them, and because of the neglect with which it
leads us to treat the suffering at our own doors. And our
legislators are neither more nor less than the direct enemies
of our country, and of Ireland too, who are constantly talking of Irish affairs, to the neglect of everything else. If our
own people were in a state of material happiness and prosperity, if our blast-furnaces were all going and our foundries
busy, if orders were pouring into our shipbuilding yards, if
trade and commerce were prosperous, we might afford to go
on trifling and dallying with Ireland, and bearing with its
wicked leaders and its wretched people as we have been
doing. But when the reverse of all that is the case—when
our engineering shops are silent, and our shipyards closed,
and our commerce languishing, and hundreds and thousands
of the men and families who are the backbone of the
country are in forced idleness and in voluntary semi-star-
vation (I shall explain what I mean by that), and when the
Irish in our own midst are always and everywhere a nuisance—imposing on our churches, sponging on our benevolent societies, living at our expense in our poorhouses, disturbing the peace of our towns and villages, filling our jails
and prisons—it is time that the country took the matter
up, and settled it in a summary and effective fashion. Not
many of us can get to Ireland to see for ourselves the
real condition of affairs, and amid so many conflicting
accounts it is difficult to know what to believe; but all of
us can look at the character of the Irish in our own midst,
and at that of our own working men. I am persuaded that
neither the one nor the other is properly realised by us, or
things would never be allowed to go on as they do. Take
a few facts regarding both. I was lately at Dumbarton,
The state of trade in that town is lamentable. Out of six

large shipbuilding yards only one is working — that is to say, about 5000 men have been thrown idle. The day I was there half the clerks in one well-known shipyard were paid off, until reviving trade (if it ever revives, and they can wait till then) should permit of their being taken on again. Of these 5000 men fully one-third were Irish, the others of course Scottish. Now notice how they respectively acted. Most of these Scotsmen who were unmarried left the town to seek employment elsewhere ; most of the married men remained, and are there now, living as best they can, honestly and independently, as a rule practising self-denial, and often suffering great privation ; bearing their share of the public burdens, and even voluntarily paying their church seat-rents and subscribing to their church funds, but never on any account taking aid from benevolent societies, far less going on the poor-rates. And how did the Irish act ? In a way exactly the opposite of all that. Scarcely one of them has left the town ; but there they are to be seen, day by day, in idleness and in dirt, meanly living at the expense of the town and their neighbours, draining the funds of the charitable societies, and filling the poorhouse and swelling the rates. If the living thus obtained be not sufficient, they add to it by begging and borrowing. Indeed, this latter mode of obtaining what is not their own is universally practised in all circumstances. As a worthy old resident in Dumbarton said to me — " The Irish never lose their desire to possess themselves of other folk's property." They become a source of mischief, too, in other ways. They increase the police rates. Almost every man, woman, and child who figures in the Dumbarton police court is Irish. The other day seven who were fined and imprisoned for being drunk and disorderly were not only Irish, but virtually and absolutely paupers, dependent for every potato they ate and every drop of drink they swallowed, on the benevolence or gullibility of their neighbours. Surely things have come to a pass in Scotland, as well as in Ireland, when we are found supporting and nourishing lawbreakers and criminals. "If thine enemy hunger, feed him," has been long literally obeyed by us, both as a nation and as municipalities, in our dealings with the Irish.

Again, it will be found that what the Irish are in Dumbarton that they are everywhere. In Edinburgh we are not troubled with them to any extent, but in Glasgow, Paisley, Greenock, and industrial centres in the west, they swarm like locusts, and disturb the peace, and eat up every green thing. A friend of mine, a thorough Gladstonian—but that is a thing of the past with him, for like many other Mid-Lothian electors, he has had his eyes opened lately—wanted to show kindness to our Hibernian friends. He had a property consisting of working-men's houses in Glasgow. In an unlucky moment he let several of these to Irishmen. He only regretted it once. Not one ever paid him a farthing of rent. More than that, they lived in such filth and wretchedness, in such idleness and drunkenness, that the whole neighbourhood was deteriorated, and he at last had to choose between keeping them and losing all his other tenants, or parting with them and keeping the latter. He wisely determined on this last course. He had to "evict" them—no easy matter even in Glasgow. If, however, his property had been in Dublin instead of this side the Channel, he would doubtless have been denounced as one of those inhuman landlords of whom we hear so much, and very likely he would have been stabbed or shot by somebody's orders. The meanness of these Irish is also illustrated by this fact. To become entitled to receive aid from the Glasgow poor-rates, one must have lived three years in the city. This was felt to be a great hardship by emigrants from the sister isle. A three years' apprenticeship was rather a long time to serve for the receipt of public bounty. So some years ago a strong effort was made by them to get this law altered, and to make simple residence in Glasgow, irrespective of time, a sufficient qualification for the enjoyment of poorhouse support. One can imagine the droves and hordes of hungry, ignorant, half-civilised beings that

would have been landed by steamer day by day at the
metropolis of the west. That city suffers quite enough from
them as it is. Let any one take up a Glasgow newspaper
and read its police reports, and he will find this—that for
every Scottish and English name that occurs there are a
score of Irish ones. As a Glasgow man said, "They fill our
poorhouses and our jails, and we cannot get even the use of
our own gallows for them."

Again, in contrast to all that, take another illustration of
the conduct of our own countrymen under privations and
sufferings as real and as prolonged as any of those the Irish
are called on to endure. The scene is in Stirlingshire. Between the "Town of the Rock" and Larbert, I found lately
quite a number of "deserted villages." What was the explanation ? They were once inhabited by hand-nailers, men who
made nails by hand. But that trade has declined. Machinery
has almost displaced it. For every score of men once employed at it not a couple are wanted now. In these villages
the long low cottages had a "but and a ben," and served as a
house and shop. The smithy was at one end and the dwell-
ing at the other. What had become of the inhabitants ? For
a long time they endured privations, waiting quietly on, and
hoping for better times, which never came. At last, one by
one, they left their old homes and birthplaces, some to seek
another kind of work elsewhere in Scotland, but the majority
to quit their native land altogether for the colonies and
America. And there stand their silent smithies and homes.
They did not need to be evicted from them. The country
heard nothing of their loss of trade and sufferings. But had
they been low Irish instead of brave Scottish, what an ado
would have been made! They, in the first place, would
have clung to their houses at all costs, and begged, borrowed,
or stolen a livelihood. Then we should have heard of cruel
landlords and heartless evictions of whole families, from bed-
ridden grandmothers to newly born babes, turned out in cold
and hunger to perish on the roadside ; and all this, too, near
the historic field of Bannockburn, where tyranny and oppres-

sion were once gloriously met and vanquished. We should
be told that we want another Bruce to lead us against landlords and landowners, and to champion the oppressed. What
a pity for the cause of the Gladstonians that they were not
Irish! What a capital argument against the Government
and in favour of Home Rule might have been made out of
their wrongs!

And what are most of the Irish at best? What positions
of trust or importance do they fill? In busy times they are
necessary evils. Skilled workmen in shipbuilding yards and
foundries have one or two about them in the capacity of
labourers to carry their tools and materials; but how rarely
do you find them skilled workmen themselves! "Gibeonites,"
that is their normal condition—hewers of wood and drawers
of water. I noticed in Glasgow that very frequently Irish
names appeared above public-house doors, especially in low
localities; but I learned that even these men were not the
owners of these businesses, but the mere tools and agents of
others. They are also largely employed on the tramway lines,
and dirty, ragged enough fellows they are.

Explain it as you may, on the ground of race, or religion,
or upbringing, the fact everywhere holds that Irishmen do
only the lowest kinds of work, and make themselves a nuisance wherever they are into the bargain. It is all very well
for Mr Gladstone to ask in irony and scorn, "Have the Irish
a double dose of original sin?" Whether that be the case or
not, I cannot tell; but this is patent to the world, they have a
double, triple, quadruple dose of actual sin. No matter where
they be, or in what circumstances, in Scotland as in Ireland,
in America as in our colonies, they seem to have the same
nature. As statistics lately showed in the 'Scotsman,' they,
and they almost alone, form the criminal class in Canada.

John Bright has said that no Parliament in the world save
ours would tolerate the anomaly of having sixty of its members paid by a foreign nation; and surely no people in the
world save ourselves would tolerate in their midst such an
idle, mischievous class of men as these Irish are. All who

know their character know that the only way to do them any
real good is to deal with them with a firm strong hand.

8. The evidence of Irish civic incompetence is indeed overwhelming. You in England and Scotland
all know how vastly disproportionate is the number
of Irish-born criminals to that of the Irish immigrants
who have settled among you. As Sir Lyon Playfair
said four years ago, " In England, if the Irish were as
orderly as the rest of the population, there would be
3500 prisoners sent to the jails instead of 22,000."
There are two millions of Irishmen among the thirty-
two millions who inhabit England and Scotland.
That is one reason why Irish crime in Ireland does
not show a very much higher ratio than all crime in
Great Britain. Another is, that in Ireland so many
crimes are never reported for fear of private venge-
ance, or from despair of getting justice for want of
honest and courageous witnesses. They may indeed
argue that here in Great Britain they are almost all
poor townsfolk (which is true) ; and that they live
under an oppressive government and social system
(which they may get ignorant foreigners to believe).
But they cannot set up the same excuses in America.
Yet there statistics tell the same unflattering tale.
Here are the figures for the province of Ontario
(Upper Canada), which is almost entirely rural.
Land is cheap, and labour dear ; Government demo-
cratic, and society of that American type which is the
modern Irishman's ideal. There, if anywhere, the
Irishman ought to be happy and virtuous. What is
the result of all these advantages ? " The census of

1881 showed the population of this province to be
1,923,228. Of these, 130,094, or 6.77 per cent were
Irish by birth, and 320,839, or 16.68 per cent were
Roman Catholics. [Very few of these Upper
Canadian Roman Catholics are French.] The population has increased since then, but the above pro-
portions have been fairly maintained. If anything,
the percentage of persons born in Ireland has de-
creased. In the year ending September 1886, the
convictions for all crimes and misdemeanours in
Ontario numbered 6490. The number of those convicted who were born in Ireland was 2226. 6.77 per
cent of the people contributed 34.29 per cent of the
crime ! No less than 3844 of the convicted persons
were Roman Catholics. 16.68 of the people contributed 59.22 per cent of the crime !"[1]

9. On the other side of the great lakes, again, the
same tale is told. President Adams, of Cornell University, writing in the 'Contemporary Review' of
November 1887, says that in New England "the
tendency to crime on the part of the Celtic foreign
element is twelve times as great as on the part of the
native stock." Throughout America and Australia
they are justly despised by the men of other nation-
alities, though flattered by venal politicians, and
the unscrupulous party-newspapers which hide and
falsify the general opinion. They speak of themselves as an essentially agricultural people, devoured
by a land-hunger, and so incapable of getting a living
otherwise than as tillers of the soil, that " an eviction

[1] Letter from Hamilton (Canada) in 'Times' of 16th Sept. 1887

is a sentence of death." Yet when they reach countries where land is to be got for the asking, they prefer to loaf about the great towns, and try (very often successfully) to live by plundering their neighbours, under the name of municipal taxation. In Ireland itself some town councils and Boards of Guardians have made a very good beginning in the same line of business. The Dublin paving contract is not unworthy of the city-fathers of New York itself.

10. The distinctive character of the Irish Roman Catholics is a fact, explain it how we may — a sensible fact, loud, glaring, and now very rasping. Race and religion have each a share in its formation. Archbishop Trench thought that race had a larger share than religion; and the recent unexpected behaviour of the Scottish crofters and Welsh farmers will be cited as a proof of his penetration. By "race," however, I do not mean (nor do I think that the Archbishop meant) simple identity of blood, but identity of social conditions and moral environment, working through so many generations as to produce a persistent general character in the population of the area affected. Doubtless it will be said that the southern Irish population is by no means purely Celtic; their appearance and the Milesian tradition indeed make it likely that they are less Celtic than Iberian. Language proves nothing to the contrary. The higher will displace the lower, when two are spoken in close proximity by not very unequal numbers. There have been from time to time infusions of Teutonic blood into Leinster,

Munster, and even Connaught, especially along the
coast; but a very large part, if not the majority of
the Danes and other early settlers, were dwellers in
towns. Urban populations inevitably die out in a
few generations, and the towns must be replenished
from the country. In 1731 two-thirds of the 13,000
families in Dublin were Protestant. A century and
a half later we find the Protestants less than a fifth of
the population of the city proper, and hardly a fourth,
if we include Kingstown and the other suburbs. Cork
had more Protestants in 1731 than it has now, though
the total population is twice as great.

11. The rural English settlers before the seventeenth century were too few and too scattered, either
to preserve their own character (except in South Wexford), or to modify that of their neighbours (except in
some portions of the Pale). A knight with a score of
men-at-arms would be the entire colony of a barony.
They adopted native customs, and were absorbed in
the surrounding mass, becoming *ipsis Hibernicis
Hiberniores*. Some indeed were probably of Silurian
(Iberian) rather than Gothic race; for Strongbow
and his followers came from South Wales. Mental
qualities are not so persistent as physical qualities, and
the heredity of moral qualities is weaker still. They
are moulded in a great degree by social conditions and
prevailing opinions. And it must never be forgotten
that the strangers brought few women with them, and
consequently took native wives. Character is formed
more by mothers than by fathers. Even in the Pale,
the natives have had more influence on the English

than the English on the natives. We can see the influence of the larger over the smaller element of the population in the character of the Protestants outside Ulster. We often find in them the fatal defects of the Irish nature, though generally in a less degree. There is the same weak, changeful, improvident disposition; the same specious false ideals of conduct; the same generosity without justice, which is indeed only a disguised form of self-indulgence; the same insensibility to reason; and the same incapacity for accuracy and perseverance.[1]

12. The later settlement of Leinster and Munster by Cromwell was largely evanescent, and was altogether a much slighter thing than is generally supposed. It was very thorough on paper, but only with regard to the south-east quarter of Leinster; and even there it was never really carried out. The war did not end till the middle of 1652, and the Act for the settling of Ireland was not passed till more than a year after. The date of the forfeiture was 27th September 1653, but the old landowners were allowed to remain till 1st May 1654. The survey had still to be made under great difficulties, and the disbandment of the army and assignment of land to the soldiers did not begin, therefore, till September 1655. Cromwell died only three years later. Such a period was absurdly inadequate for so great a project, even if he had been free to devote his whole attention to Ireland. As a matter of fact, the adventurers and the officers of the army were almost the only settlers of Leinster

[1] See Mr Froude's masterly analysis, 'Eng. in Ireland,' p. 20, et al.

and Munster. As Prendergast explains,[1] many of the
common soldiers sold their land-debentures before the
assignment took place, and many others refused to
settle when the time came. The state of the country
was not inviting. Others, again, were cheated when
their land was pointed out. On seeing a bit of bog
they were induced to sell for a song the title to some
really valuable holding. Only a third of the 33,000
debentures were made use of in any manner whatever; and it is doubtful whether even one thousand
of Cromwell's soldiers actually settled as farmers in
the south of Ireland.

13. There was doubtless a great (almost complete)
displacement of landlords, though many recovered their
estates after the Restoration; but there was no such
displacement of the actual tillers of the soil. If they
had gone, the new landlords could have got no rent.
There was nothing like the Plantation of Ulster, and
the deportation of the peasantry was never even intended, except in the five counties of Wexford, Wicklow, Carlow, Kildare, and Dublin (south of the Liffey).
The three latter were, however, like Cork, reserved for
the Government; and only in the two former was
there any serious attempt to plant. All the Irish were
ordered to remove themselves before the 1st of May
1655. But the new landlords and yeomen could not
do without their labour. Consequently, the Government at first granted various dispensations, delays, and
exceptions, and in the end allowed the scheme to drop
out of sight. Here, however, there was some settle-

[1] Cromwellian Settlement, pp. 222-235.

ment of English farmers. Dublin was close, and much of the country had been depopulated by long and ferocious guerilla warfare, ending with the great massacres by Coote. In the next century Lord Fitzwilliam filled the barony of Shillelagh with Protestant tenants for the sake of their votes. Wicklow, with north Wexford and north-east Carlow, forms the most Protestant part of Ireland outside Ulster. The first county is indeed more Protestant than Cavan.

14. As already pointed out, the soldiers who settled as yeomen were few, and the new Protestant tenants outside Wicklow were fewer still. Many even of these disappeared before the Revolution. They were ruined by the suppression of the cattle-trade under Charles II. and by the persecution under his brother. More Englishmen settled in the towns ; but these were impoverished by the Navigation Laws before the Revolution, and after it were depopulated by the suppression of the woollen manufacture. Professor Huxley,[1] indeed, seems to think that there is about as much English blood in Tipperary as in Devonshire. But if so, why is Tipperary one of the most Roman Catholic counties in Ireland ? The Protestants are less than 6 per cent of the population, and a third of them are concentrated in a few north-west parishes adjoining King's County, about Roscrea and in the barony of Lower Ormond. These parts of the county were planted, chiefly by the Earl of Ormond, several years before the outbreak of the great Civil War. If Cromwell's soldiers had ever formed a fourth, a fifth,

[1] Critiques and Addresses, p. 177.

or even a seventh of the population of any barony, they would have kept their faith like the contemporary or earlier settlers of Wicklow, Cavan, and Monaghan. Nor can Tipperary have derived much Teutonic blood from earlier settlers. Few Danes can have stayed so far from the sea. Though it was made shireland by King John, and in the century following became the County Palatine[1] of the Butlers, it was never really an English county like Kilkenny. Few English names appear in the map[2] prepared by Macdermott for the 'Annals of the Four Masters'; and even now the county has quite the average number of Celtic landlords. The difference in stature and complexion between Tipperary and the south-west may be due to the former having not more Gothic and less Celtic blood, but more Celtic and less Iberian. The Gauls, Britons, and Picts were large fair men; and so, according to tradition, was at least one of the old Irish stocks, the tribe of the Dedannans. But no one can look at the common Spaniard without being struck by his resemblance to the typical " Paddy from Cork."

15. Practically Irishman and Roman Catholic are convertible terms in Ireland; and there can be no doubt that the religion has confirmed, if not aggravated, the faults of the race. The Irish never had warmer friends than Mr and Mrs S. C. Hall; but they were compelled to say that the Roman religion

---

[1] This probably was the reason for it being reckoned English in the statutes of Kilkenny (1367).

[2] Reprinted in the larger editions of Trench's 'Realities of Irish Life.'

was less favourable than that of Protestants to industry and improvement, and that anything which
would increase the number of Protestants would be
one of the greatest possible benefits to the country.[1]
Mr Nassau Senior is the *beau ideal* of a dispassionate
philosophic observer.   Visiting the barony of Mourne
(in South Down), where the people are nearly equally
divided between the two religions, and all live under
the same conditions, he saw a distinct superiority in
all the signs of civilisation on the side of the Protestants.[2]   Mr Lecky is a critic by no means un-
friendly to the Roman Catholics.   Indeed Scotsmen
may think that he has an obvious bias against Protestants of their type ; yet he corroborates the Halls,
and cannot help admitting that the Roman Catholic
is a religion of a lower type than the Protestant.[3]
" It produces habits of thought and life not favourable to industrial activity, and extremely op-
posed to political freedom."   And " no country will
ever play a great and honourable part in the world,
if the policy of its rulers or the higher education
of its people is subject to the control of the Catholic
priesthood."

16. In truth the Roman Catholic religion is not
simply Christianity, but a mixture of Christianity with
pagan notions and practices.   This Mr Lecky has well
explained in his ' History of Rationalism in Europe.' [4]
Its composite character is at once the strength and
the weakness of the Roman Church.   Hence its rapid

---

[1] Ireland, iii. 378 and 395.   [2] Journal in Ireland, ii. 72.
[3] History of England, ii. 383, 384, 388.   [4] See i. 36, 211 ; ii. 211.

diffusion in barbarous Europe, and hence the success
of its modern missions. Hence also the stagnation
and comparative decadence of thoroughly Roman
Catholic nations like Spain, which were once in the
van of civilisation. The pagan element renders the
whole more readily acceptable by heathens, and the
Christian element thus gets a fulcrum for the moral
elevation of large masses of mankind. But its elevat-
ing power is soon exhausted, and it then becomes an
obstacle to the human progress, which up to a certain
point it had assisted. Stereotyping what it has done,
it prevents other influences from doing more. The
fatal principles of immutability and sacerdotal authority cause a mental and moral paralysis in those who
really accept them. As soon as men reach a certain
not very lofty stage of enlightenment, such a religion
becomes impossible as a working rule of life. "Believe in the Pope?" said Dr Arnold; "I could as
soon believe in Jupiter." That is just the feeling of
the normal healthy-minded man of the nineteenth
century in every part of the world. Wherever a
nation nominally Roman Catholic is advancing with
the rest of civilised Christendom, we know that the
Church is a Church only of priests, women, and
peasants. The thinking manhood of the country will
not follow guides whom it feels to be intellectually,
and in some respects morally inferior. A Church
which makes a boast of discouraging intellectual
activity must needs be a clog to every kind of progress. Industry it encourages less than mendicity.[1]

[1] Lecky's History of England, ii. 388.

Mendacity it has long regarded as a very venial [1] failing. The maxims of the Jesuits are lineally descended from the pious frauds of the earlier monks. Cleanliness the priest places a very long way after the form of godliness. A Church which in the latter half of the nineteenth century makes a saint of a lazy dirt-encrusted beggar like Jean Labré, is certainly not in harmony with modern civilised society. But can we wonder at it finding favour with the nation which has evolved that wondrous proverb (shall we not rather say motto ?), " There's luck in muck ! "

17. The Irish are the implacable enemies of England. She cannot even mollify them, except by committing the dastardly crime which Mr Gladstone calls conciliation. They are no more open to reason and justice than a mad dog or a man-eating tiger. They are drunk with a blind fury of greed, and nothing will appease them but full licence to plunder and torture their landlords, and the British settlers whose hard-earned wealth inflames their cupidity, and whose orderly industry is a standing reproach to their turbulent idleness.[2] The great political poet of America once wrote in fiery scorn " Conciliate ?—it just means be kicked." [3] Mr Gladstone has done a good deal of that kind of conciliation in his time ; but hitherto he has taken his share of the kicks from Boers and other inconvenient enemies. He evidently does not mind them much, if they do not loosen his hold on office.

---

[1] Notwithstanding the formal classification of perjury as one of the mortal sins.

[2] See the evidence of Mr Biggar before the Special Commission.

[3] Biglow Papers, second series, No. 7.

But his magnanimity in dealing with Ireland is of a still cheaper and more transcendental quality. Most of the kicking is to be suffered by third parties, who have nothing to do with the conciliation beyond being its victims. The kicks go chiefly to the Irish landlords, whose halfpence all go to their Roman Catholic tenants ; while Mr Gladstone's cheap magnanimity and vicarious generosity are to be rewarded with the empty praise of the Irish mob and the solid pudding of English office. To " conciliate " a highwayman by letting him rob yourself, when there is any prospect of successful resistance, is a cowardly abetment of his crime. But what can we say of the man who buys immunity for himself by helping the highwayman to rob a neighbour who might otherwise be able to repel the attack ? Most of us would place him very low indeed in the depths of contempt. Yet Mr Gladstone has reached a lower depth than even this,—he helps the great robber-gang of Ireland, not for immunity, but for advantage ; not to save anything for anybody, but to sate his thirst for place and power. Now let us leave the " old parliamentary hand " to his complacent musing on the moral sublimity of casting other men to the wolves ; ay, and other men's wives and babes. *Revenons à nos moutons noirs.*

18. The Irish are implacable because they have no national feeling except hatred for England. They may plead some historical justification, but their grievances have been removed, and with ample amends. And they really hate England now, not for

the wrong she has done, but for the wrong which she
prevents them from doing. Not because she robbed
their ancestors in the seventeenth century, and oppressed them in the eighteenth ; but because she will
not let them rob and oppress their neighbours in the
nineteenth. " Oppression maketh a wise man mad,"
quote their apologists ; ay, but greed makes a foolish
one madder. And the most barefaced flatterer of the
Irish has never yet ventured to sing the praises of
their wisdom. If there were any real patriotism in
the so-called " National " movement, it would be re-
spected, and might be in some way conciliated ; but
there is nothing half so respectable about it. It is
nothing but a sordid scramble for other people's
money—a thing which would be simply contemptible,
if it were not carried on with so much devilish
cruelty. Call to witness the gallant persecutors of
Ellen Gaffney and Hannah Connell, Finlay's widow
and Fitzmaurice's orphaned daughter ! Bring up the
fiends who mocked the agony of Lady Mountmorres,
and danced in the blood of her murdered husband !

19. There was never any life in this " great
National movement " till it was converted into a
grand joint-stock gang-robbery. Home Rule is nothing but a bumble-bee buzzing on the back of the mad
wolf, Social Revolution. The cry for " self-government " does not mean that the Irish wish to govern
themselves. Nothing is further from their thoughts.
They would not do it if they could. They wish
only to misgovern their neighbours. Government *for*
self is what they mean. Celts and Saxons, Roman

Catholics and Protestants, are robbed and maltreated
with a most practical and cosmopolitan absence of
national or sectarian partiality, if they have the
common misfortune to be owners of Irish land.
Ancient Irish chiefs meet with no more respect
or forbearance than Cromwellian intruders. The
O'Donoghue and the O'Conor Don have been hunted
out of political life. The memory of the Liberator
has not prevented the grateful peasantry of Derrynane
from driving Mr O'Connell into the bankruptcy court.
The O'Grady is one of the most viciously persecuted
men in all Ireland ; and Mr Dillon takes special de-
light in going down to insult him before the fat
farmers of the Golden Vale of Limerick. The kindest
landlords find no more gratitude than the harshest.
The blackest vials of malignity are emptied on the
heads of philanthropists like Mr Brooke and Mr
Bence Jones, who have spent more on their estates
than they have ever got from their rents. Truly
there is no redeeming or mitigating element in this
agitation. There is nothing more despicable in history,
since the days of the Jacobins.

20. You have to deal not only with irreconcilable
enemies, but with irreclaimable semi-savages,—irreconcilable and irreclaimable for the self-same reason.
The demon of unscrupulous greed has taken full
possession of their souls, and their religion has become naught but a cloak for their cupidity. Priests
are possessed like people. Let him who expected
anything else ponder the weighty words of Archbishop Whately, who, even more than my royal

master, deserves the title of the British Solomon. "A priest solely dependent on his flock is, in fact, retained by them to give the sanction of religion to the conduct, whatever it be, which the majority chooses." [1]

21. As to the Plan of Campaign, it bears theft writ large on its very face; for it makes a man withhold the portion of rent which he admits to be fairly due, as well as the portion which he declares to be in excess. The landlord is always willing to accept anything in part-payment and to give a receipt on account.

22. I do not say that they are irreclaimable absolutely and for ever; but irreclaimable by England and Scotland within measurable time, and without intolerable cost. Ireland is the great drag upon British progress—the millstone round England's neck, which may enable other nations to catch and pass her in the race of improvement. England can never have peace, can never have time to do her own business, till the English garrison is strong enough to take care of itself. Sanitary reform, fiscal reform, legal reform, educational reform, are all hopelessly delayed by Irish turbulence, intrigue, and obstruction. She cannot afford to reclaim the Irish. She has many much better uses for her time and her energy. If they were fewer, and if they were diffused, there would be a prospect of their absorption or assimilation within a reasonable length of time. Two or three millions of them scattered among thirty millions you

[1] Life and Remains, p. 333.

might bear with, and even find useful as soldiers and constables ; but four millions concentrated in one corner of the United Kingdom are beyond influence or management. It would be a mere flea-bite on North America, where in another generation the solid Teutonic population will exceed a hundred millions. And the Americans may very fairly be asked to undertake the reclamation of the race for which they publicly profess so much esteem and affection. But Britain is too small to stand the drain of so large an open sore upon her flank. She cannot afford to wait through centuries of inflammation and debility for the chance of a cure by tonic treatment. The ulcer must be closed by determined surgery. The surgeons of the body politic must cut away the morbid surface, and graft a healthy skin upon the wound.

23. To sum up, the Irish are too many to be tolerated so near. They are enemies massed within your gates. You cannot make them your friends, even in name, without betraying your real friends, and covering yourselves with disgrace. This is a case in which there can be no peace with honour ; nor, indeed, is it at all likely that you can have peace even with dishonour. Judas will be rightly scorned by his purchaser. The Irish tiger has tasted blood. The daughter of the horse-leech will still cry " Give." As Mr Russell tells you, the people are " utterly demoralised, . . . debauched by a conspiracy the most baneful that ever cursed any country." They loaf about, drinking their rent and half as much again

in whisky.[1] The popular heroes, the chosen spokes-
men of Ireland, tell you that they hate England with
an undying hatred, and accept Home Rule only
as a lever for separation and the formation of a
hostile republic. As Mr Sexton told you in 1881,
" the unchangeable feeling between Ireland and
England is the passion of hate." The Corporation
of Dublin takes every opportunity of insulting the
Queen's representatives. The great town of the
south delights in the name of "Rebel Cork"; and
its people lately paraded their disloyalty at the Irish
Exhibition in a way which can never be forgotten or
forgiven. British soldiers cannot walk the streets
of Limerick without insult and imminent danger of
broken bones. The Mayor and Corporation of Waterford have declared that rebels they were born and
rebels they will remain.[2] On this one point we may
be sure that the agitators speak the truth. As their
present apologist said with unwonted terseness, when
he too had his reasons for telling the truth, their aim
is to "march through rapine to the dismemberment of
the empire."

[1] So says their French friend Philippe Daryl, on page 120 of 'Ireland's Disease.' See also Hurlbert, 382.

[2] See Colonel Saunderson's speech in the House of Commons, 14th
February 1889.

II.

THE REMEDY, AND PROBABLE OBJECTIONS.

24. WHAT, then, is to be done? Ireland is an intolerable nuisance and menace to England and Scotland, simply on account of its present inhabitants. You cannot change the Irish people. But you can change the people of Ireland. And only by so doing can you save Great Britain from ruin. She can never have peace—can never have time to do her own business—till the British garrison in Ireland is made strong enough to take care of itself. That is the key-note of the only Irish policy which can do any real good. The one great and lasting benefit which Ireland has got from the English connection, is the Plantation of Ulster. It is the one good work which can never be undone; the one source of hope for Irish order and progress; the one secure base for the advance of British culture and enlightenment. The solid half-million of Protestants in Down and Antrim is the impregnable fortress of Irish liberty; the rock which will for ever beat back the waves of Irish savagery and

superstition.   This is the immortal work of my
master King James the First, of whose wisdom I was
privileged to be the humble instrument.

25. Mr Balfour has done admirable work of its
kind.   No one could have done better within the
limits set by himself or by the Cabinet of which his
illustrious uncle is the head.   I yield to none in
respect for your present and former Prime Ministers,
but they have done no lasting good to Ireland; for
they have done nothing which cannot be undone.   As
Mr Chamberlain said lately at Glasgow,[1] "a merely
negative policy of resistance will certainly fail."   The
energy of Government is spent in writing on the
sand, which the tide, now dyked out, will sweep into
oblivion when it is once again let loose.   The conditions of Ireland have been changed very slightly—
only by Lord Ashbourne's Act—and whether in the
end for the better is very doubtful indeed.   The
character of the Irish has not been changed at all.
"Twenty years of resolute government" will not do
that; no, nor fifty years, if you could count upon
so much.   But you cannot count upon even twenty
years in a country like Britain, where party spirit is
venomous, and the strength of parties nearly evenly
balanced; where government may be brought to a
standstill by parliamentary obstruction; and where
the wisest policy is liable to reversal in six or seven
years at the furthest, by the caprice of a fluctuating
section of the most ignorant electors.   Five per cent
or less of the British electorate, two hundred thousand

[1] February 12, 1889.

weather-cocks, of the sort likely to be greatly impressed by the discovery of Pigott's trickery, and quite unmoved by Mr Hurlbert's crushing exposure of the whole fabric of Parnellite falsehood,—these are the arbiters of England's destiny, and hold in their hands the fate of modern civilisation. Even if the pendulum of popular irresolution does not swing to the other side at the next general election, there is very grave danger that the Union majority will be so reduced as to be practically impotent. No Government will long be resolute under such a precarious tenure of power. Party considerations are prone to lead to neglect of duty, in the hope of escaping trouble, catching stray votes, and checkmating the intrigues of opponents. Continuous resolute government is possible, only if delegated once for all to a body of men whose resolution will be stiffened by their deepest personal feelings and strongest personal interests ; men to whom resistance of the traitors is a matter of life and death ; men who can laugh to scorn the caprice of the English elector, because they have at their back, not only a nation, but an army of their own.

26. There is only one policy of safety and honour in this time of terrible danger. *Suspend the Union. Organise Ulster as the citadel of the empire, and the base of operations for a golden conquest, a new Plantation of Leinster and Munster.* " Upon the future of Ireland hangs the future of the British empire," wrote Cardinal Manning to Earl Grey in 1868. More than that : the decisive battle of human

progress may be fought in the valley of the historic Boyne. The men of Ulster have to quench the first burst of a fiery eruption of barbarism more ruinous than the irruption of Huns and Vandals which destroyed the civilisation of the ancients. Attila and Genseric, Tamerlane and Gengis Khan, were not such foes of human progress and enlightenment as Henry George and Michael Davitt. If Britain fails in the fight, there is small hope of successful resistance in any other country of Europe.

27. A new Plantation ! Every British patriot will say that it is the best thing possible for Ireland, and almost every one will say that it is the last thing possible. "It can never be more than a dream. It has been tried, and failed. The task is superhuman. We cannot get rid of four millions of people. To drive them out would be cruel; to buy them out would be too costly. What Cromwell failed to do, with all his despotic power and ruthless temper, surely cannot be done in this age of supersensitive humanity and administrative impotence."

28. Part of this cry of despair is true, but immaterial; most of it is not true, for want of the special study requisite for understanding the question. No living man has had my special experience of the old Plantation. Few men, if any, I am sure, have made a serious study of the problem under modern conditions. The Hill Difficulty is never so steep or so high as it looks to the doubting heart at a far distance. Each step of the ascent becomes clearer and easier to the single-hearted will, resolute to find a way, or to

make it. The imaginary magnitude of this task of curing Ireland's disease has turned many a good man, like Lord Spencer, into a gibbering captive of Giant Despair. If he were to look facts and figures closely in the face, and take up the task bit by bit, the difficulties would disappear one by one. So it is with every good work that ought to be done—hard, and huge, and hopeless as it may seem in the mass.

29. At the outset I must demur to the common sweeping statement that previous attempts have been failures. There is some truth in it, but far less truth than falsehood. I did not fail in Antrim : Belfast is my monument. Hamilton, Hill, and Montgomery did not fail in Down. The great plantation of the six counties was not a failure. It is true that only Armagh and Londonderry can be called Protestant by count of noses, and that Cavan never recovered from the blow of 1641, when nearly every settler was expelled ; but in Tyrone, Fermanagh, and East Donegal, the Protestants are certainly strong enough to hold their own in any contest but that of the polls. They are a social force too strong to be uprooted; and in fair fight, where quality could tell against quantity, they would be found to have the preponderance of physical force. They are more than 40 per cent of the population. They own nearly all the land, cultivate at least four-fifths of it (in value), and pay at least nine-tenths of the local rates and direct imperial taxes. Boycotting, rent-stealing, and intimidation of juries and witnesses, are no more possible there than in Down and Antrim. And the Protestants could, if

they chose, soon turn the scale in brute numbers, by getting rid of their Roman Catholic dependants, and replacing them with Protestants.

30. Cromwell certainly did not fail in Ulster, where he planted the only real colony of his soldiers in the valleys of the Lagan and the Bann. The country between Lisburn and Armagh is the most English in Ireland, and the most sternly Protestant in all Europe. There sprang the Orange Society, and there is still its living centre. Elsewhere Cromwell made no serious systematic attempt to plant large bodies of Protestant farmers and labourers. In Leinster and Munster there was only a transfer of land-ownership, not a transformation of the people, except in the corporate towns. These urban colonies were ruined by the later Commercial Restraints, and must in any case have died out for want of a rural population on which to indent for fresh supplies of Protestant blood.

31. Study of Irish local history and geography makes it evident that the failures of Cromwell and the earlier Undertakers were due, not to the inherent impossibility of the task, but to their setting about it in a wrong way, and to the hostility or mismanagement of later Governments. The work was carried on in a desultory way, and its parts were discontinuous. The rural colonies were too scattered to help each other, and too small to maintain themselves against the pressure of surrounding hostile hordes in times of disturbance, or to resist the absorbing influence of the larger body on the smaller in times of peace. Many of the settlers, if not most, were un-

married; as we learn from the outcry about their perversion through Popish marriages.

32. Next, it must be explained that there is no need to get rid of four millions of Irishmen. All that is necessary is to secure Protestant control of a majority of Irish constituencies, local and imperial. The judicious removal of one-fifth of the enemy, and the substitution of rather less than half a million of Protestants, will secure all Ulster and Leinster, except the city of Dublin. The Protestants, if united, would have a slight majority in the British Parliament, and be able to hold their own under any system of local government. Even this state of things would be an immense gain to England. She could with a clear conscience shift the burden of managing Ireland to other shoulders. There would be an end of the dark possibility of English political parties descending to the American level of baseness, and bidding against each other for the support of England's deadly enemies. But you ought to aim at something better still. After the conquest of Leinster the Protestants would still be much less than half of the total population. This would give plausibility to an outcry against their ascendancy; which would also be in danger from the defection of a few thousand traitors, corrupted by American gold or personal jealousies and ambitions.

33. The perfect security of an overwhelming Protestant predominance would be secured by a very easy additional Plantation. The removal of half a million more, making up in all just a third of the

Roman Catholic population, and only a fourth of the total population, would soon make Cromwell's great idea a living reality. It would leave room for 350,000 Protestants, who would soon transform fertile rural Munster into the likeness—not indeed of Down and Antrim, but at least of Derry and Armagh. Clare, being on the other side of the Shannon, ought to be restored to its old and natural connection with Connaught.

34. The Roman Catholic population of Ireland in 1881 was 3,960,000. The removal of one-third (1,320,000) would reduce it to 2,640,000; while the substitution of two Protestants for every three Roman Catholics removed would raise the number of the former to nearly 2,100,000. But this is not all : these figures do not give a sufficiently favourable view of the case. The population of Ireland is now decreasing at the rate of 1 per cent per annum. The average excess of births over deaths is only 28,000. The average number of emigrants since 1881 has been over 80,000. There is no immigration, except a little into Belfast from Scotland and Lancashire. The population is already less by 400,000 than it was in 1881 ; and in the course of a generation we may expect a further decrease of at least half a million. The decrease, taking Ireland as a whole, will be almost entirely among the Roman Catholics. Since 1861 they have lost 12 per cent, while the Protestants have lost only 7 per cent. The latter have grown from being $22\frac{1}{4}$ per cent of the population in 1861 to be $23\frac{1}{3}$ per cent in 1881. In the rural districts

the proportion of loss is nearly the same for each religion. In Dublin, which was slowly increasing up to 1881 (if we include the suburbs), the Protestants have slightly lost ground. Since then the agitation has stopped its progress, if not caused a decline. Belfast, on the contrary, has been growing with enormous strides—just now, it is believed, at the rate of 5000 a-year; and the Protestants have been increasing faster than the Roman Catholics. The latter were two-sixths in 1861, but only two-sevenths in 1881; and in 1891 they will probably be only two-eighths. The great riots caused many to leave the town, and have kept away others who might have come. The increase of Protestants in Belfast even now almost counterbalances the rural decrease; but when a new Plantation is set up as a counter-attraction to America and Australia, Protestant emigration will almost entirely cease and the birth-rate will rise enormously. We may reasonably hope that in 1921 there will be considerably more than two millions of Protestants to face rather less than two millions of Roman Catholics.

35. The Plantation cannot begin before 1891, when the number of Roman Catholics in Ireland will not exceed 3,600,000, and the number to be removed will therefore be in reality not 1,320,000, but only 1,200,000. Still even this, it will be said, is a mass which it would be absurd to think of moving. So it would, if you tried to move them all at once; but I do not ask you to do anything so tremendous. The work may be spread over thirty years. The average

extent of the clearance to be made in any one year
will be only 40,000 persons—just half as many as
are got rid of by voluntary emigration.   In fact, the
new Plantation, at first sight so appalling and appa-
rently impracticable, resolves itself on nearer view into
an addition of 50 per cent to the annual emigration
now carried out by private enterprise with a little aid
from some of the British colonies.

36. But it will be objected reasonably enough, " If
twenty years of resolute government of the present
type are not to be expected, how can you reckon on
thirty years of a policy which will excite more bitter
fury in the enemy and more piteous appeals to the
sentimental British elector ? "   Certainly we cannot
hope for any such continuity of purpose and practice
in a Government at London ; but we can be perfectly
sure of it in a Government at Belfast.   The work
must be delegated once for all by the British Parliament to a Parliament of Ulster.   An Orange Government will be unmoved by the wildest hurricanes of
sound and fury on either side of St George's Channel.
These can signify nothing to a power broad-based on
the steadfast constituencies of Protestant Ulster.   All
the howling and whining, all the cursing and reviling,
will only stiffen its back and quicken its hands.   It
will simply laugh at agitators so long as they keep
their distance, and make very short work with them if
they ever come to close quarters.   Mischief-makers,
English or Irish, who attempt to interfere with the
great work, will be turned out with more vigour than
ceremony.   If they dare to come back, they will

spend the rest of the thirty years reflecting on their
folly in solitary cells at Belfast or Londonderry. The
Irish Protestants will be spurred and kept to their
duty by the very instinct of self-preservation. They
know their Roman neighbours far too well to be taken
in by smooth words and fine promises. They have
nothing to lose by carrying out the work, and everything to gain. Failure cannot put them in a more
dangerous position. Success means not only security,
but a vast increase of prosperity. Their hopes and
their fears, their sympathies and their antipathies,
their private feelings and their public spirit, their
personal interests and their political aspirations, will
all combine to make them carry out the Plantation
with unrelenting vigour and invincible determination.

37. Now is the fulness of time arrived. The Protestants of Ulster are united as they never were
before. They have been welded together by a common danger, and they will stick together for their
common safety and their common hope. There is
now nothing to divide them, nothing to check their
mutual sympathies. Old bones of contention have
been swept away; old founts of bitterness have
dried up. There is no longer an Established Church
to excite the jealousy of unwise Methodists and
Presbyterians. The new security of tenant-right
has removed the apple of discord between farmers
and landlords. The farmers are disposed to look
more kindly on the landlords as fellow-soldiers bearing the brunt of the attacks of the common enemy.
The landlords are now alive to the value of a sturdy

Protestant tenantry, which they did not rightly appreciate in the days of their unshaken security. They cherished, if they did not avow, a weak preference of serfs to tenants; and were easily ensnared by the polite profuse improvident, Roman Catholic, with his low bow, his wheedling words, and his large offers of rent. All went well so long as he remained politically helpless; but now he knows his power, has thrown off the mask of subservience, and stands confessed the insolent robber. The landlords whose ancestors made room for him, as so many did in the time of the Peep-of-Day Boys and the Hearts of Steel, by turning out the less plausible and flexible Protestants, now bitterly regret the short-sighted greed and vanity of their order. They have found that the man who is less ready to cringe is also less likely to insult, and that the man who promises least is the one who pays best. They will be properly thankful now for Protestant tenants, if they can get them. Lord Rossmore in Monaghan has given earnest expression to their repentance. Let us hope that it will bear fruit. Even under the new land laws, much can be done by a large landlord, who will have none but a Protestant, for every vacant farm over which he can exercise any control.

38. Lastly, it may be urged that, even if England could be brought to allow wholesale confiscation and expatriation, the Government of Ireland would not and could not drive out a quarter of the population of Ireland. They need not, if by driving out is meant what Cromwell is supposed to have done, expulsion

without compensation. What I ask you to do is to buy them out without any more compulsion than is involved in making a railway or improving a town for general public interests. You need not use Cromwell's methods, for you can use better ones : you have resources which he had not. England and Scotland have now a surplus of population, ready if not eager to emigrate. In his day they had not. Sending the men of Leinster and Munster into Connaught was useless. If they had gone, they could easily have come back. You can send them to America, whence it is not so easy to return ; and can do it under conditions which will prevent them from desiring to return. Cromwell had a practically uncontrolled power of physical compulsion. You have a practically unlimited power of the purse. You can cause Irish labourers to leave Ireland with alacrity ; and Irish farmers to leave it, not indeed without sentimental reluctance, but without being able to convince impartial spectators that they have suffered any real hardship or substantial injustice. England has become accustomed of late years to spend money freely on Ireland without good security for reimbursement. She has been spending for Ireland's advantage ever since the famine. Mr Gladstone lately proposed to advance £50,000,000 or more to Irish tenants for buying out Irish landlords. Lord Salisbury will, it is expected, gradually repeat this proposal in another form, in addition to the £10,000,000 already advanced under the Act of Lord Ashbourne. What is here proposed is, that instead of buying out Irish landlords, the money should go to buy out Irish tenants, and to fill their places with Protestants from Ulster, England, and Scotland.

39. In the absence of the necessary statistics, I cannot say, with any pretence to accuracy, how many of the 1,200,000 would be landless labourers; probably not more than one-sixth. The cottier-tenants supply much, if not most of the labour on the farms proper. One million persons are equivalent to 200,000 families—that is, more than one-third of the whole number of Irish agricultural tenants.[1] The average rent of Irish farms was put at £15 by Dr Erck at the meeting of landlords in Dublin in the summer of 1887. This estimate is confirmed by the return of 183,820 judicial rents, fixed by the Land Commissioners up to the end of July 1887. Doubtless the average for Leinster and East Munster is a good deal higher—probably between £20 and £25. But on the other hand, we must remember—1st, that the best parts of Ulster will not be within the scope of the Plantation; and 2d, that the average rent of Protestant farmers is much higher than that of Roman Catholics. Under the old £12 franchise, half or more of the electors were Protestants in such counties as Wicklow, Monaghan, and Donegal, where three-fourths or more of the inhabitants are Roman Catholics. A large part of Leinster is farmed by Protestants, and an appreciable part even of Munster. We may, therefore, safely take £15 as the average judicial rent of the Roman Catholic farmers who must be bought

[1] 560,000.

out for the new Plantation.   Each will of course get the value of his interest, which will not, I believe, on the average exceed twelve times the judicial rent. The minimum will be seven, as in the existing law of compensation for disturbance.   The reasons for this estimate, and the arrangements for a just valuation, will appear hereafter.   Meanwhile I need only caution the reader against drawing conclusions from isolated instances of fancy prices, given in a time of excitement and expectancy.   In the south, many purchasers hope that Home Rule will some day give them the fee-simple for nothing.   Moreover, most of the farms in the Protestant parts of Ulster, where we hear most about the high prices of tenant-right, have good houses, with barns, gardens, orchards, and other improvements made by the tenants.   The case is very different with the ordinary Roman Catholic farmer.   His improvements will seldom be worth more than the rent for five years.   Mr Bence Jones,[1] whose tenants near Clonakilty were much above the average of county Cork, found, on inquiry, that very few, even according to their own valuations, had made improvements worth more than the rent of a single year.

40. The cost of buying the tenant-right will be £36,000,000, at the average rate of £180 for each of 200,000 farms.   This money will simply be invested, almost as safely as if lent to the Bank of England. The incoming Protestant tenant will probably pay it up, to get the full advantage of the Irish land laws.

[1] Life's Work in Ireland, p. 81.

If he does not, 4 per cent on the amount can be added
to the judicial rent. The whole will probably be less
than the economic rent of a farm managed on the
English principle outside the Land Act of 1881.

41. Some further payment will, however, be necessary to gild the pill of expropriation. A free passage
to North or South America, needs not cost more than
£5 a head—in all £5,000,000 ; and an average allowance of £20 to each family for loss on forced sale of
stock, and for miscellaneous expenses before departure,
would absorb £4,000,000 more. In fine, £45,000,000
will suffice for removing, without any real hardship,
a million of England's inveterate enemies—the average
cost being £45 a head and £225 a family. The remaining £5,000,000 will be ample for all the expenses
incidental to this removal, and to the substitution of
firm friends of England in the vacant farms. The
chief items of expense will be agency, valuation,
travelling of Scottish and English settlers, and loss of
rent between dates of removal and new occupation.
As boycotting will be impossible under an Orange
Government, few farms will be vacant for more than
six months. Proper arrangements must of course be
made for the early despatch of intending settlers
previously registered. Many vacant farms will, however, be instantly taken by Protestants already in the
neighbourhood. After all, it is only doing publicly,
on a larger scale, with ampler means and more
facilities, what practical Mr Russell is now doing
by private effort—what has indeed already been done
at Collon and Coolgreany. Practical Prince Bismarck

is doing the same thing in a quiet way with the Poles
of Posen.

42. You need not put in so many tenants as you
send away. It will be easy and in every way desirable to combine the vacant holdings into farms of
double the former average size. These will be more
attractive to emigrants, as well as more profitable to
landlords, and more conducive to agricultural improvement. In fine, what is wanted is a body of
100,000 Protestant families (which may, but need
not, include 500,000 souls) to fill 100,000 farms,
having an average judicial rent of £30, and an
average area of probably fifty acres. There will be
no lack of applicants in Ulster from the beginning,
and when they have shown the way, we may expect
an influx of enterprising men from England and
Scotland. Merely to stop the emigration of Protestants from Ireland would be by itself almost enough
to supply what is wanted. In the rural districts they
are decreasing as fast as the Roman Catholics. The
low rate of natural increase of births over deaths
(only 28,000 for nearly 5,000,000, little more than
$\frac{1}{2}$ per cent *per annum*), is itself a result of the emigration which takes away so many of the healthiest
young men and young women. Very few emigrants
are over fifty, and only one in five is a child. To stop
the emigration of Protestants, by opening new fields
to them in Ireland, would in a very few years cause
a great increase of marriages and births. In thirty
years the mere retention of intending emigrants,
without taking into account the higher birth-rate,

would provide Ireland with an additional Protestant population of 300,000 souls, equivalent to at least 100,000 families. This is on the very safe supposition that the average number of emigrants would be not less than 10,000, as during the decades before 1881 ; at present it is much greater. The emigrants are 80,000 a-year, and the Protestants are nearly a quarter of the population ; except in Belfast, Derry, and other manufacturing towns, they are decreasing quite as fast as the Roman Catholics. After deducting the population of these towns, and allowing for what they draw from the country, it is still likely that the Protestant emigrants are not less than a sixth of the whole—let us say 13,000. Probably at least a third of these are cottiers or younger sons of farmers, who would never think of leaving Ireland if they could get a farm with safety.

43. Lastly, let us remember that England and Scotland send away yearly more than 100,000 men and women in the prime of strength. If even a tenth of these were diverted to Ireland, the problem would be solved. The number of immigrants required for Ireland, in any single year, counting labourers as well as farmers, would not exceed 30,000 souls or 6000 families.

44. A further sum of £10,000,000, must be spent on removing 40,000 families of Irish labourers (200,000 souls), and replacing them with 60,000 families of Protestants. The reason why there must be three immigrants for two emigrants is this : one in five of the agricultural holdings in Ireland is a

mere croft or allotment, with an area of less than
five acres, and a rental less, generally much less, than
£4 ; the occupants are really labourers, necessary for
the cultivation of the adjoining farms. To get the
total number of labourers displaced, we must therefore add 200,000 of the 1,000,000 already provided
for under the name of tenants. Making every allowance for the superior efficiency of the new men, the
farmers will probably need three of them to replace
four of the old stock ; indeed, the demand for labourers may be increased by improved cultivation.
The expense of inducing 40,000 Irish labourers to
leave Ireland with their families, will not exceed
£3,000,000—£75 each. This will send him to
America with a cheque for £50 in his pocket.
There will be competition for expatriation under
these circumstances. To make sure of getting 60,000
families of Protestant labourers, we must allow for
a similar expenditure, though it may not be necessary
after the first few years. In the beginning it will
cost £25 to convey an English labourer's family to
Ireland, and settle him comfortably with a little
cash in hand. Decent cottages must be provided
in place of the Irish hovels. This duty will fall
upon the Guardians ; but the Government will have
to do something more than making advances for
their assistance. Cottage-building is not a paying
investment, and it will be safe to allow £25 as
irrecoverable expenditure on housing each immigrant
family. A further inducement and security will be
necessary at first—viz., a gift of £25 on completion

of an engagement to reside five years in Ireland. In case of the man's death within five years, the amount ought to be paid to his widow or children. The Government must of course guarantee a pension to the family of any man who might he murdered, and liberal compensation for malicious injury to person or property; but this would be recovered from the rates of the guilty locality, and would be very rare under an Orange Government. There would remain £2,500,000 as a reserve for contingencies. Part might be devoted to giving personal allowances (contingent on good behaviour), to priests and bishops, whose incomes might be seriously lessened by the enforced emigration of their flocks. As a rule, however, these ought to be granted for not more than five years; the object being merely that the Pope should have time to arrange for the transfer of any superfluous priest to America or Australia, after reorganising the staff of his Church in each planted diocese and province, in accordance with its reduced necessities. In special cases, pensions might be granted for life to aged clergy.

45. In all, £24,000,000 would be expended without any prospect of direct recovery. This is a poor enough compensation for the harm done by the English Commercial Restraints, and indirectly it would be repaid many times over, even in money. The prosperity, and, consequently, the revenue of Ireland, would increase steadily, and after a time with great rapidity; while the special expenditure caused by her poverty and turbulence would undergo an equally

steady diminution. There would be a rush of capital to develop the neglected resources of the country. Leinster and Munster are for the most part naturally much richer than the eastern side of Ulster, which Scottish industry has changed from a wilderness to a hive of industry, wealth, and comfort. Arthur Young[1] said that the soil of Tipperary and Limerick was the richest he ever saw. Meath is little if at all inferior. "In the elements of natural fertility," says the famous modern farmer M'Combie,[2] "only the richer parts of England, and very exceptional parts of Scotland, approach to it. Under the treatment the soil of Ireland receives, great part of that of Scotland would long ago have ceased to produce any crops at all—would have lapsed into sterility. It is only the natural richness of the soil of Ireland which has averted a like result." Put a south Irish farmer in Ayrshire or Galloway, and he would starve; put a Scottish farmer in Limerick or Tipperary, and he would make his fortune in the term of a judicial rent. England and Scotland may well say to the farmers of the Golden Vale, "Why cumber ye the ground?" Let them make room for those who can make a better use of mother earth and her bounty.

46. The economic advantages of the change will indeed be enormous; but they are almost thrown into the shade by the social, moral, and political advantages. £60,000,000, spent under Lord Ashbourne's Act, would put no friends in the place of

---

[1] Travels in Ireland, i. 485.
[2] Quoted in Thom's Almanac (Agricultural Statistics).

foes. It would, for the most part, go to strengthen and multiply your implacable enemies — men who pride themselves on being essentially aliens, and whose religion alone will for ever prevent any real sympathy or co-operation with England or Scotland. And the security would be far from good. The Irish will not soon cease to regard the British as oppressors, and will not scruple to spoil the Egyptians if they get a chance. And the expulsion of the landlords would be a gravely retrogressive step, fatal to the progress of the country in the manners and notions, the arts and the comforts, of modern civilised society. It must be confessed that many, if not most, of the Irish landlords have hitherto taken little trouble to discharge their functions of leadership and fulfil the ends of their existence as members of an enlightened progressive community; but they are always an element of hope, and a great latent power for good, which may hereafter be evolved into action with great blessing to their neighbours. Farmers and peasants who never see anybody superior to themselves in mode of life, standard of behaviour, and width of intelligence, are apt to remain, or become, either boors or conceited churls. Rural England without its resident gentry (of whom the clergy are practically a part) would never have risen above the rudeness and narrowness which are so characteristic of rural America. And that is not the only reason for retaining the Irish landlords in their present position. Their expropriation means the removal of the only effective check on the deadly evil of over-population, whose necessary consequences are squalid poverty and desolating famine. The large landowner has a direct and immediate interest in preventing the endless subdivision and wasteful cultivation, so dear to the Roman Catholic peasantry of Ireland. And nobody else can be relied upon to perform this indispensable service to the common-weal. This, as Mr Senior has so well explained in his ' Irish Essays,' is the economic justification of the landlord's existence.

47. Money spent under Mr Gladstone's bill, or Lord Ashbourne's Act, would only fill Ireland with more and stronger enemies of England. The same money spent on a new Plantation will fill Ireland with fast friends of England, turn a Roman majority into a Protestant majority, and make three-fourths of Ireland practically an accretion to Great Britain. She might then have Home Rule for the asking ; for instead of being the plague-spot of Western Europe, she would be the citadel of resistance to anarchy and retrogression.

48. The cost of this Revolution, not less urgent than that of 1688, would be nominally £60,000,000 in all—a shilling in the pound of one year's national income — but not half £60,000,000 in reality, as we have seen, and nothing like £60,000,000 all at once. Spread over thirty years of steady work, it would be only £2,000,000,—only another penny of income-tax at the worst. But there is no fear of even that amount of pressure on the struggling tax-payers of the United Kingdom. £1,200,000 would go either as an investment at fair interest, or as mere advances to be soon repaid ; and might therefore,

without fear of financial criticism, be provided by temporary additions to the national debt. The remaining £800,000 would require only a special tax of a penny on incomes exceeding £400. This, indeed, will yield far more than is needed ; and if the necessary statistics could be got, it would probably appear that the limit of exemption might be raised a good deal higher, perhaps even to £800. At least three-fourths of the payers of direct taxation, contributing more than nine-tenths of the whole amount, belong to the Union party. Few of them have so little public spirit that they would not back their votes with their money ; and in the Gladstonian remnant the mouths of the great majority would be shut by getting the benefit of the exemption. Thus ever vanishes the spectre of difficulty from the path of duty, when the single-hearted patriot, *vir justus et tenax propositi*, looks it sternly in the face, with a clear determination to take it by the throat.

III.

THE CONDITIONS OF SUCCESS.

49. CROMWELL and the Undertakers failed to plant the south, as I have shown before, partly because their work was undone by the misgovernors who followed, and partly because their plans were not based on sound principles. The main principles of an effective and durable Plantation are these:—

50. 1*st*, That the colonies must be mainly, and in the beginning altogether, rural. It is useless to fill a town with Protestants unless it is surrounded by a Protestant country.

51. 2*d*, That each colony must be strong enough to resist absorption by the surrounding Irish, and also to secure its own local self-government. Cromwell never dreamed of the danger of universal suffrage. In each unit of plantation, such as a barony of the average size in Leinster (with about 10,000 inhabitants), there must be a decided majority of Protestants, including male and female in the usual proportion. They ought to form not less than 55 per cent of the population, and to have such control over the land

as will enable them to prevent an increase of Roman
Catholics, by over-breeding and subdivision of holdings. In fact, every farm ought, if possible, to be
held by a Protestant,—Roman Catholics remaining
only as tradesmen and labourers.

52. 3*d*, That the colonies must be continuous and
compact, not in scattered sections. The progress of
the Plantation ought to be like the march of an army
of occupation into a hostile country. There must be
a gradual advance from an impregnable base. Each
step must be made secure before the next is taken.
Each colony must be linked, on one side at least, to an
older colony, and so to the solid core of Protestant
Ireland, the great north-east corner comprising Antrim, Down, North-east Derry, and North Armagh.
In this way whatever is done is done once for all,
and cannot be undone. If the enterprise be inter-
rupted or abandoned before completion, nothing will
be lost—the work will not be thrown away. What
is gained has been gained for ever. The planted
barony or parish or estate will be indissolubly jointed
to Protestant Ulster.

53. 4*th*, Subsidiary to the last principle is the
following. The line of advance ought to be chosen
with a view to the grouping of colonies so as to command not only baronies, but counties and parliamentary divisions.

54. 5*th*, That plenty of time must be taken for
deliberation and preparation, as well as for the exe-
cution of the work, and no more attempted in any

one year than can certainly be carried out with the means available. Thirty years will be needed for all that is here proposed.

55. 6th, Consequently, that the work must be intrusted for that period, by an irreversible Act of the Legislature, to an absolute Government, not liable to overthrow except by force of arms from without, and not liable to change of purpose by any force of entreaty or abuse or intimidation. They will have hard work to do—sometimes, it may be, very stern work—work which could not be done by an overburdened English Parliament, or an ever-badgered English Government, but which must be done for the safety and welfare of England herself, no less than Ireland. The only fit government that can be created is one formed and controlled by a Parliament of Ulster, holding a strong and sure Protestant majority. The Ulster Protestants will be steeled to the work by all their interests, their sympathies, and their antipathies. Every motive, public and private, will converge to the same end. They thoroughly understand their enemies, and will not relent or be deceived. They will never dream of treating the National League as a body of misguided friends and fellow-citizens, to be set right by appeals to reason and enlightened conscience. They know that they might as well apply sarcasm to a rabid rhinoceros. They will have no hesitation in dealing with the Leaguers as natural and mortal enemies, to be crushed according to the laws of war.

56. 7*th*, The Planting Government must have an assured command of the necessary money, by being invested with the exclusive power of collecting taxes over a part of Ireland sufficient to yield a revenue of at least £3,000,000, according to the present rate of taxation.

IV.

PARTICULARS OF TREATMENT.

57. SUCH are the general principles. Now for the
practical application. If you adopt the findings of
the Special Commission in condemnation of the Irish
leaders, you are logically bound to make some change
in the constitution of the United Kingdom. The
Queen's judges have in effect found that the majority
of the Irish nation is deliberately engaged in a criminal conspiracy, of which outrage and assassination are
essential elements. They have given a judicial stamp
to Mr Gladstone's assertion that " the ultimate sanction
of boycotting is murder." It never has succeeded,
and never can succeed, except through a well-grounded
fear that past outrage will be imitated in the future.
To allow such a nation to have any longer any share
in your Government and Legislature is the height
of folly, if not absolute wickedness. It is simply
cherishing a disease, which must prove fatal to the
British body politic, if not cast out by prompt treatment of the most vigorous type. You must hang up
the Union to save its life. The Government ought

to force through the House of Commons, with the least possible debate, a short Act suspending the Act of Union for thirty years, and providing that during that period, the Parliament of Great Britain shall have the same legislative powers over Ireland as over England and Scotland. Peers of the United Kingdom ought, of course, to be considered peers of Great Britain, for the time being. This will at once rid the House of Commons of its worst elements of discord and degradation, double the patriotic majority, and render it almost impossible for the Destructives to get a majority at the next general election. Even if they do, the majority will be so small that they will not dare to repeal this Act, or the next, against the almost unanimous opposition of the Upper House. But the election ought, of course, to be postponed till the last moment—June or July 1893. Every minute is precious for getting a good start in Ulster. To dissolve a year earlier would be a wicked waste of a golden opportunity; to dissolve at any other season would be a gross tactical blunder; to do so in winter would simply be throwing away at least a score of seats. Midsummer is the only time for a Conservative general election, for two reasons: first, canvassing is much easier and pleasanter, especially to ladies; secondly, as everything is done by daylight, there is less risk of successful personation at Liverpool and other places where there are many Irish on the register.

58. The House having been cleared of the great body of Obstructives, an Act for the government of

Ireland during the suspension of the Union ought to be passed in the same session—if possible, that of 1890. Prompt suspension for the rest of the session will soon put an end to obstruction by English Radicals. It is amazing to outsiders that certain outrageous brawlers have not been so suspended, or expelled, in many former sessions of the present Parliament. The Act ought to enact—

59. (a) That Ireland (except that portion of it hereinafter described as the Grand Duchy of Ulster) shall be governed as a Crown colony,[1] the sovereign having sole and absolute legislative, judicial, and executive authority, which he may delegate as he pleases; provided that he shall do nothing in contravention or evasion of this Act and its spirit.

60. (b) That no legislative body, if wholly or partly elective, shall be established by the Crown in Ireland, and that no change shall be made in the present constitution and powers of the superior courts of justice at Dublin, without the consent of both Houses of the Parliament of Great Britain. [The object of this and succeeding sections is to prevent possible mischief from the influence of a Radical Cabinet.]

61. (c) That all municipal councils, boards of guardians, and other elective local authorities, now existing or hereafter to be established in Ireland or Ulster, shall be elected by the ratepayers voting according to their rates, in the manner hereinafter prescribed (in section j) for such elections in the

---

[1] As proposed by Sir M. E. Grant-Duff in his speech at Banff, Nov. 2, 1858.

Grand Duchy of Ulster. All local rates shall in the first instance be paid by the occupier, whether the premises belong to him or not; but he may deduct one-half of the amount from the next payment of rent made by him to the owner. The liability of the occupier for the other half shall be personal, and it cannot be levied from the owner or any succeeding occupier. An owner of rated property let to another person shall not be liable for any portion of the rate, unless he has received rent for the period in question, and then only to the extent of the rent actually received. No rate shall be levied on any land, whose owner or occupier has been prevented from cultivating it, or feeding cattle on it, or gathering or selling the produce, or selling the cattle, by any conspiracy on the part of other persons, such as the practices commonly called boycotting : provided that, if the loss sustained has been only partial, a proportionate deduction shall be made from the valuation, and the rate be levied on the remainder. No rate shall be levied on land left vacant during the six months of grace allowed for redemption by an evicted tenant, unless the said tenant redeem, in which case the whole rate shall be levied from him. All municipal corporations and other local authorities shall be subject to the control of the Local Government Board, as regards audit of accounts and otherwise, in the same manner as boards of guardians at present. The Local Government Board shall remove any member of a local authority, and declare him incapable of re-election for life or a fixed period, if he make himself wantonly offensive to any other member, or impede the despatch of business by excessive talking or otherwise. The provisions of this section shall apply to Ulster also. [They will cut at the root of many of the most nefarious devices of the League for the ruin of landlords and honest farmers. The present law as to levy of rates is scandalously unreasonable and unjust.]

62. (d) That coroners shall no longer be elected, but they and justices of the peace shall be appointed only by the Court of Queen's Bench for life, or such periods as it may think proper, and may be dismissed by the said Court for any reason which it may think sufficient. No person shall be eligible for election as mayor or alderman in Dublin, Cork, and Limerick, unless he has previously been appointed a justice of the peace. In other municipal corporations no person elected to such offices shall exercise any magisterial functions, unless already a justice of the peace. The police may refuse to execute any coroner's warrant, until the Court of Queen's Bench has considered and passed orders on the proceedings. [No one can doubt the need of this provision who remembers the proceedings of these courts of malice against Mr Brownrigg at Mitchelstown, Ellen Gaffney at Philipstown, Captain Hamilton at Coolgreany, and Messrs Dudgeon and Empson at Collon.] This provision shall also apply to Ulster, substituting the words "High Court of Ulster" for "Court of Queen's Bench."

63. (e) If in any civil suit or criminal trial, either party asserts that the jury is likely to give an untrue

verdict under the influence of corruption, intimidation,
party feeling, religious sympathy, personal antipathy,
or any other improper motive, and the judge is satisfied
that there are reasonable grounds for the assertion, the
suit or trial shall be heard and determined by the
judge exclusively, discharging the functions of a jury
in addition to his own. This provision shall also be
applicable to Ulster.

64. (*f*) The police shall be bound to eject any
person whom they have reason to suppose a trespasser,
when requested by any person whom they may reasonably suppose to be the owner or lawful occupier of the
premises, or a member of his family, or his representative, agent, or servant. The burden of proving excess
of force in ejection shall be on the trespasser. No
force shall in any case be deemed excessive, unless it
causes death, fracture of a bone, loss of any joint or
member, privation or serious permanent impairment
of any sense or bodily function, serious permanent
disfigurement, or incapacity to move about or attend
to ordinary business for the space of a whole month.
No force whatever shall be deemed excessive, if the
trespasser shows by words or otherwise an intention
of using any deadly weapon, or a stone, or any hot,
poisonous, or otherwise dangerous substance, after
being warned by the police officer. Whatever may be
done to eject a trespasser may be done to prevent his
entrance under similar circumstances. The powers of a
constable under this section may be conferred by the
lord lieutenant of a county on any respectable householder not objected to by the chief police officer of the

county, and may be at any time withdrawn. This also shall be applicable to Ulster.

65. (g) That the Grand Duchy of Ulster (as defined in the annexed Schedule I.) shall be incorporated with the kingdom of Great Britain for purposes of external defence, foreign relations, the regulation of commerce, the management of the telegraphs and post-office, and legislation relating to the above matters. It shall be represented in the House of Lords by twelve peers of Ireland possessing land of the annual value of £1000 within the Grand Duchy, to be elected by all the peers having the said qualification. It shall be represented in the House of Commons by two members for the University of Dublin, and 26 members to be elected according to the present law for the 26 territorial constituencies described in Schedule IV. [The number is fixed with reference to the taxation of Ireland as compared with that of the United Kingdom. She pays less than a tenth of the whole (£7,000,000 out of £74,000,000), and is absurdly over-represented by 103 members out of 670.] One member for 75,000 inhabitants instead of 50,000 would be a very liberal allowance—especially as the population is decreasing. On that scale Ireland would have 68 territorial constituencies, besides the University of Dublin. She would get very few more, if a new distribution were made according to the population of the United Kingdom, after the census of 1891. Even according to that of 1881 she has a dozen too many.

66. It will be seen that the temporary disfranchisement of Ireland will not affect two-fifths of the coun-

try from the very beginning. Another fifth, Leinster and Dublin city, will be brought into the pale of representation after ten or twelve years, as I shall hereafter explain. And another fifth, Munster (except Clare), will be re-enfranchised after about twenty years, when Leinster has been so assimilated to Ulster as to contain a majority of Protestants. Only Connaught and Clare will remain a Crown colony for the full period of thirty years.

67. (*h*) That the supreme legislative, judicial, and executive authority in and over the Grand Duchy of Ulster, for all purposes except those already specially excepted, shall be vested for thirty years in a great Council of 368, to be elected for five years at a time. Trinity College shall be represented by its two members of Parliament. Of the remaining 366, half shall be elected by the adult male inhabitants of the 145 rural baronies and 16 urban wards, who have attained the age of twenty-five, are able to read and write, and are not disqualified by conviction of felony, defect of intellect, or receipt of public relief. The other half shall be elected by the ratepayers of each barony or ward. Each ratepayer shall have one vote for every pound of valuation on which rates are paid by him either as owner or occupier; consequently, a man living in his own house shall have two votes for every pound rated. There shall be separate valuation lists of owners and occupiers; the name of an occupying owner of course appearing in both. A landlord paying rates for a tenant, rated at £4 or less, shall have a corresponding number of votes in the occu-

pancy-roll. The exemption of tenements under £8 (and not under £4) in certain boroughs shall cease, and (after the first election) the tenant having an interest in his farm shall be rated as an occupying owner upon its market value. That part of this section which relates to rating shall apply to the Crown colony of Ireland as well as the Grand Duchy of Ulster. [As the tenant having an interest in his farm is really a joint-owner, it is not fair that he should, as at present, escape taxation on all his property, and on a great part of what he occupies. The real letting value of an Irish farm is the landlord's rent, *plus* about 5 per cent on the capital value of the tenant's interest. This just and necessary reform in rating will be an invaluable aid to the work of plantation, furnishing a simple, sure, and self-acting method of checking valuations of tenant-right for purposes of compensation. Few men will overstate the value of property on which they will have to pay pretty heavy rates. And thus the value of farms belonging to Roman Catholics, who may have to be expropriated, can be correctly gauged by the value set on adjoining farms by Protestants, who have no temptation to deceive the Government. As the valuation of tenant-right cannot be made quickly, the first election must take place on the present rate-books. After the new system of rating has been established, and barony councils elected, the members of the Great Council may be chosen by these local bodies, instead of by the ratepayers directly.]

68. (*i*) Belfast shall be the seat of government. In

the cities of Belfast, Londonderry, and New Dublin, each ward shall return one ratepayers' member and one inhabitants' member for every 10,000 inhabitants, or fraction thereof exceeding two-thirds. But no voting-paper may contain the name of more than one candidate. [The wards of Derry herein contemplated are those now existing. The wards of Belfast are the present five, together with Lisburn, Lurgan, Newry, Dundalk, and Drogheda. The wards of the new city of New Dublin will be found described at the end of the Schedule of Baronies, No. II.] The remainder of Ulster shall be divided into baronies, with an average population of nearly 11,000 according to the last census, and probably little more than 10,000 according to the next. Each of these shall return one member for the ratepayers, and one for the male inhabitants. The Great Council may allot additional members to the cities after each census, and may create new wards, or alter the boundaries of those now existing; but except in this respect, it shall have no power to alter its own constitution without the consent of Parliament. [Twenty-three members of each class have been allotted to Belfast in anticipation of the census of 1891, which will undoubtedly show a population exceeding 240,000. It was 208,000 in 1881, and is said to be increasing at the rate of 5000 a-year.]

69. (*j*) That all municipal councils, barony-moots, boards of guardians, and other elective local authorities now existing or hereafter to be established in Ulster (or Ireland), shall be elected by the ratepayers voting according to their taxation, as above explained

with reference to the Great Council; except the grand juries of counties, which shall be elected by the councils of the cities and baronies over which their jurisdiction may extend.

70. [As a body like the Great Council, having supreme legislative power, controls a man's life and liberty, it is right that mere humanity (if it can be called civilised) should be considered, as well as pecuniary support of the State, in determining the State's composition and proceedings. But local boards are merely managers of contributions for the common advantage, and it is simple justice that each contributor should control the outlay in exact proportion to the income derived from his pocket. What he does pay can always be known with accuracy enough for substantial justice. We may fairly leave out of sight tolls, harbour-dues, and similar items of local revenue, which come largely, if not mainly, from outsiders, and are generally spent with strict regard to the special benefit of the payers. In the homely language of the honest Scottish proverb, "Those who pay the piper ought to choose the dance." The good old Whig maxims, that "taxation without representation is tyranny," and that "taxation and representation should go hand in hand," have in late years been sometimes honoured in the letter, but nearly always outraged in the spirit. Representation of taxation is a sham unless the one is proportioned to the other. All justice is a matter of proportion. There is no approach to such proportion except in the election of guardians of the poor and sanitary boards; and even

there its existence is threatened by the Radicals and
Parnellites, whom it prevents from pampering their
idle friends at the expense of their industrious neighbours. The present arrangement of equal control and
unequal contribution to the maintenance of police,
roads, schools, drains, and even water-supply, is a
system of the grossest iniquity. It is neither more
nor less than downright Communism — systematic
plunder under the form of law and the name of taxation. Equal voting power could be just, only if the
money to be spent were raised by an equal poll-tax
on every elector. Few of the Destructives in the
present House of Commons have an equitable right to
their seats in an assembly which has absolute control of the whole revenue and expenditure of the
country. They seldom represent a majority—generally not even a quarter—of the taxes paid in their
constituencies.

71. You have now a grand opportunity of firmly
cementing those things which the God of justice has
joined together, and which men's folly and wickedness
have put asunder. The most visionary Radical on
the side of the Union will admit the inexpediency of
extending local self-government on the English model
to the savage hordes of rebel Ireland. And the im-
pudent iniquity of " one man one vote " will win no
applause among the hard-headed hard-working men
of Belfast and the Protestant counties. They know
that equality means the tyranny of their idle and
ignorant enemies ; and feel that their only safety lies
in political recognition of natural inequality. They

need no political Darwin[1] to teach them that " quality before quantity " is the first principle of civilisation, even as it is the fundamental law of progress in every department of the universe.

72. Belfast, happily, is safe under any possible municipal franchise ; but Derry is not ; Newry is not ; the Dublin townships are not. Bandon, Kingstown, and Strabane have already fallen into the hands of the Philistines. Vigilance is needed even in Armagh. Outside the four Protestant counties, Cookstown and Rathmines are the only places deserving the name of town which can boast of a Protestant majority. In historic Enniskillen the Roman Catholics are now nearly 60 per cent of the population. In Tyrone and Fermanagh Protestants pay more than nine-tenths of the rates, but county councils on the new English model would certainly be ruled by the mere Irish. Protestants pay more than half of the rates of Dublin, yet they have only five representatives in a town-council of sixty members. Even this paltry representation they will probably lose at the next election. But if they had votes according to their taxes, they would have a good prospect of electing a majority of the council. And the defeat of the Parnellite pirates would be certain, if the many respectable Roman Catholics, who hate the League as an honest man must, should simply abstain from going to the poll. They pay probably half of the rates not

---

[1] Professor Huxley's recent exposition of natural inequality encourages a hope that he will thoroughly play this part in the history of human progress.

paid by Protestants. In many rural districts similar results would follow; and even in Cork and Limerick there would be a great change for the better in the character and condition of the elected. Local government may be granted to Ireland on this principle, with a fair prospect of good and little danger of evil. Introduced on the present English plan, it would soon turn the country into a wilderness of wasp-nests. It would be disguised State-socialism of the lowest type. One set of citizens would pay nearly all the taxes, to be spent in opposition to their wishes by another set, who would pay little or nothing.

73. There is an appearance of complication in the great reform proposed, but it is a delusive appearance. There would be no confusion, and not much more trouble, either in polling or registration, than there is at present. The rate-books would show at a glance how many votes could be claimed by each elector, and it would only be necessary to give him a corresponding number of voting-papers. Further simplicity and better representation of minorities would be secured by enacting that no voting - paper should be available for more than one candidate. This system would have the effect which cumulative voting is intended to have, but in a surer and simpler manner. Women, infirm persons, and non-resident ratepayers ought, of course, to be allowed to vote by proxy, minors by their guardians, corporations by their agents, and the Crown by the Lord Lieutenant of the county.]

74. (k) That the Great Council shall continue to

levy all taxes now levied in Ulster by authority of the Parliament of the United Kingdom, and shall not remit or reduce them without consent of the Parliament of Great Britain. It may, however, enhance such taxes, or impose new taxes. No tax shall be levied in Ulster by Parliament, or any authority except that of the Great Council and bodies subordinate thereto. All taxes raised in Ulster shall be collected and disposed of by the Great Council and its subordinate bodies, subject to the provisions of this Act : Parliament and the Government of Great Britain having no power to interfere except for enforcing the said provisions. All questions as to the interpretation of this Act shall be decided finally by the High Court of Ulster, sitting jointly with an equal number of judges of the High Court of England, chosen by lot, and with one judge of the Scottish Court of Session, chosen in the same manner. No money raised by general taxes shall be granted in aid of local rates, except according to present rules and practice, or for special expenditure made necessary by the Plantation, or for other purposes, with the consent of Parliament. The Great Council shall defray all charges now incurred in Ulster by the Government of the United Kingdom, except for the army, navy, and national debt. It shall also defray the cost of the new superintending civil staff and departmental offices, which must be established at Belfast when the present officers at Dublin cease to have control over Ulster ; also its own expenses and those of the separate Privy Council—provided that no payment shall be made to any member of the Great Council, unless he is a member of the Privy Council ; also the expenses of the new High Court of Ulster, and any other new court of justice which may be established. The remainder of the revenue received from taxes, corresponding with those levied in Great Britain, shall be spent for the purposes of the Plantation in any year when it may be required, and shall be accounted for at the end of the thirty years, when the surplus, if any, shall be applied to the reduction of the national debt. All revenue from new or enhanced taxes may be spent on the volunteers, or for purposes of the Plantation, as hereinafter explained.

75. (*l*) That the Government of Great Britain shall manage the telegraphs and post-office, and collect the income therefrom ; but the Great Council shall have power to forbid the nomination of any person for employment in any such work in Ulster, and may transfer, punish, or dismiss any person so employed, whenever it thinks fit. It may search for, intercept, or forbid the despatch of any letter or telegram. It may establish telegraphic or postal communications of its own, or make special use of the regular establishment by means of its own officers for emergent purposes of the Plantation.

76. (*m*) That the Great Council may delegate its executive authority to a Privy Council of not more than eleven members, whom it may appoint and remove at pleasure.

77. (*n*) The Great Council may delegate its judicial authority to such courts as it may think fit to establish,

including a High Court of not more than seven judges, which shall have exclusively (except in regard to the interpretation of this Act as provided in section *k*) all the jurisdiction now possessed in Ulster by the House of Lords, the Judicial Committee of the Privy Council, and the superior courts of every kind at Dublin. The decisions of a full bench shall be final throughout England, Scotland, and Ireland, and no court outside Ulster shall at any time entertain any suit or complaint on account of anything done by any person while resident in Ulster, whether the consequences of such action shall occur in Ulster or Ireland or Great Britain. [This provision is designed to prevent harassment of members or agents of the Ulster Government who may have property, or may afterwards reside outside Ulster, by such proceedings as Mr Parnell's action against the ' Times ' in Scotland.]

78. (*o*) Except at the instance of the Great Council, no person shall be liable to a civil suit or criminal prosecution, and no court shall issue process or take any proceedings whatever, on account of anything done by the Privy Council of Ulster, or under its orders, or with its previous or subsequent approval, for the purposes of the Plantation. A written declaration by the Privy Council, or an officer empowered by it to give such declaration, shall be conclusive proof that the Act referred to was done for the purposes of the Plantation. [The work cannot be done within the allotted time, unless the managers have despotic power, and are not liable to be harassed by chicanery, or impeded by technicalities. They must have the

resources of martial law at instant command, without the trouble and delay of special legislation.]

79. (*p*) The Privy Council may forbid any person or class of persons to enter Ulster; and any person disobeying such an order shall be an outlaw.

80. (*q*) The Privy Council shall have power to forbid any suit or prosecution, or to stay proceedings if already begun, for a time not exceeding six months, pending special legislation by the Great Council if considered necessary.

81. (*r*) The Privy Council may forcibly deport any person from Ulster to any other part of Ireland, or to any other Crown colony, or to any other country which does not object to receive him : and it may confiscate his property. [Tenants in some cases will not emigrate voluntarily, unless they get far more than the market value of their interests. This provision is necessary also for the suppression of boycotting].

82. (*s*) The Privy Council may compel the sale of a tenant's interest in the premises which he occupies at what they consider the real market value in ordinary times and circumstances. They may confiscate his interest wholly or in part if he delays to remove himself and his family when ordered, or resists forcible removal or deportation, or in any way obstructs the work of the Plantation. A tenant under orders to remove may, however, make a private sale of his interest to any person approved by the Privy Council. [This approval would, of course, be given only if the purchase were made in good faith by a Protestant

intending to cultivate the farm in person or by means of other Protestants.]

83. (*t*) In any barony or ward where 46 per cent or more of the inhabitants are Roman Catholics, in the barony of Enniskillen, and in the baronies of Portlough and Lower Tirkeeran adjoining the city of Londonderry, the Privy Council may compel any owner to sell or lease to them any premises from which they desire to remove a tenant, or which they require for controlling the influx of new inhabitants into a town. If sold, the price shall be twenty-five times the net average judicial rent. If leased, the landlord shall receive the net judicial rent, less 5 per cent for expenses of management. If the tenant's interest remains in the hands of the Government at the end of the lease (which shall in all cases run to the expiry of this Act), the owner must either purchase that interest at the price paid, or sell the farm to the commissioners appointed by the Government of the United Kingdom of Great Britain and Ireland to wind up the accounts of the Government of Ulster. [It is highly improbable that this last provision will give much trouble. In most cases the tenant's interest will be bought by the Protestant settler. In the rest the landlord will be glad to get it, the general improvement of the country having greatly increased its value. This and some previous provisions may seem unnecessary, as they could be enacted by the Great Council itself. They may well, however, be inserted in the Act of Parliament to save the Council from spending time in discussions which

is urgently needed for the active work of the Plantation.]

84. (*u*) The Privy Council shall have authority to call upon the militia and all regular troops stationed in Ulster to enforce its orders and prevent or repress crimes and disturbances, when it may think that the constabulary need such aid. It shall have absolute and exclusive authority to raise, disband, and control volunteer forces within the Grand Duchy. For the expenses of such forces the Great Council may impose special taxes. [The inhabited-house-duty, from which Ireland is now exempt, may be imposed for this purpose without causing many murmurs. Comparatively few Ulster Roman Catholics live in houses rated at £20.]

85. (*v*) The Grand Duchy of Ulster shall, if the Great Council so desire, at any time after the lapse of five years from the date of this Act, be enlarged by the addition of one or more of the counties of Meath, Kildare, and Wicklow (as described in Schedule III.) Each county so added shall then become entitled to send a representative to the British House of Commons at the next general election, and two representatives for each barony (as provided in section *i*) to the Great Council of Ulster. After twelve years, or, if the Great Council so request, after ten years, all the counties of Leinster (including the city of Dublin, the city of Kilkenny, and the town of Wexford), together with the urban counties of Clonmel, Queenstown, and Waterford in Munster, shall be incorporated with Ulster, and shall

be represented in the House of Commons and Great Council (according to Schedules III., IV., and V.) in the same manner as the original counties, baronies, and wards of the Grand Duchy. Six additional peers of Ireland shall be elected as members of the British House of Lords. The Great Council may increase the High Court of Ulster by four judges, and make such other changes in the public establishments as it considers necessary. Belfast shall continue to be the seat of the Government and Great Council of the Grand Duchy. The Government of the Crown colony of Ireland shall be removed from Dublin to Galway. After twenty years from the date of this Act, the counties of Munster (except Clare, but including the counties of the cities of Cork and Limerick and the town of Tralee) shall be added to the Grand Duchy, Belfast still remaining the capital. The same results shall follow as from the incorporation of Leinster.

86. (*w*) The Government of the Grand Duchy shall within twelve years, and if possible within ten, remove from the counties of Armagh, Cavan or East Brefney, Down, Fermanagh, Fingal, Monaghan, Oriel, and Tyrone not less than 45,000 families (or separate occupants of farms), on whose loyalty it cannot depend, and put in their places 30,000 families (or adult males living separately), on whose loyalty it can depend. Not less than half of the removals and replacements shall be in Oriel and Fingal. It shall within twenty years remove at least 80,000 families (or separate occupants of farms) from the ten rural counties of Leinster (as described in Schedule III.),

and replace them with 54,000 families (or adult males living separately). It shall further, before the expiry of this Act, remove at least 90,000 families (or separate occupants of farms) from the rural counties of Munster (excluding Clare), and replace them with 60,000. It shall also remove 14,000 from the county of Tyrconnel in Ulster and replace them with 7000.

87. (x) The towns of Lisburn, Lurgan, Newry, Dundalk, and Drogheda shall from the date of this Act form part of the municipal borough of Belfast, each being a ward returning two (and in the case of Newry three) members to the municipal council, and each having a resident alderman or deputy-mayor nominated by that council. The county of New Dublin (as described in Schedule III.) is hereby incorporated as a municipal borough under the Municipal Corporations Reform Act of 1840 (3 & 4 Vict. cap. 108). It shall be governed by a council of twenty-one members elected for the three wards described in Schedule II.—nine for Kingstown, and six for each of the others; and by a mayor and seven aldermen elected by the Council. The township of Drumcondra Glasnevin and Clonliffe is hereby incorporated with the Mountjoy ward of the city of Dublin; and those parts of the parishes of Donnybrook and St Mark lying within the township of Pembroke, which are included in the Dublin Harbour Parliamentary Division, are hereby incorporated with the South Dock ward of the same city. The premises of Trinity College shall cease to be part of the said

city, and shall form a separate barony and county in the Grand Duchy—the governing body of the University being the local authority of the said county and barony. The Great Council shall as soon as possible organise local authorities for the other baronies and counties of Ulster.

88. (*y*) This Act shall come into force from the date of receiving the Royal assent, but until the date of the first meeting of the Great Council, which shall be not later than July 1st (let us hope 1891), all the powers vested in that Council by this Act shall be exercised by the present Viceroy of Ireland. Arrangements for the first election shall be made by him in accordance with section *h* of this Act. He shall create the new counties and baronies described in Schedules II. and III., by Order in Council, and appoint the officers requisite for their administration under the present law. And he is hereby empowered to create such new townlands as may seem necessary. He shall also make such new arrangements of townships (Navan to wit), poor-law unions and electoral divisions, and other areas under local authorities, as may be rendered necessary by the separation of the Grand Duchy from the rest of Ireland. He shall also arrange for the transfer of men and functions, from the Local Government Board and other departmental authorities at Dublin, to the new offices at Belfast. He shall make provisional rules for the conduct of business in the Great Council. The existing law courts shall continue to exercise jurisdiction until new courts have been established by the Great Council,

and shall then transfer to the High Court of Ulster all suits and trials which may be claimed by the latter as properly within its jurisdiction. [Arrangements made in consultation with present Conservative and Union - Liberal members of Parliament for Ulster would doubtless be ratified at the first meeting of the Great Council. Most of the judges of the new High Court would simply be transferred from Dublin, where the present staff would obviously be too large for three-fifths of the present territorial jurisdiction. Their places need not be filled up till Parliament has fixed the future number.]

V.

THE COURSE OF THE CURE.

89. Let us now take a forecast of the probable working of the machinery thus to be set up, after a preliminary survey of the field of operations. Before making plans for the consolidation and extension of the Protestant element in Ireland, one must have clear notions as to its present strength and distribution. Map No. 1 will illustrate the facts and simplify the exposition. Antrim and Down, as every one knows, are overwhelmingly Protestant. In rural Down the Protestants are 70 per cent, and in rural Antrim nearly 80 per cent. In the city of Belfast they are more than 70 per cent, and the proportion is steadily rising. Most of the Roman Catholics in rural Antrim are massed in three corners. The largest body is in the mountainous north-east corner, the barony of Lower Glenarm, with the adjoining half of Cary, and the eastern parishes of Kilconway. Many of these are Scotch Highlanders, brought in by the Macdonnells, Earls of Antrim, who were of the same stock as the Macdonalds of Kintyre. Of the 6036 inhabi-

tants of the four parishes in the extreme north-east only 832 (14 per cent) are Protestant. Another body of Roman Catholics is on the swampy shores of Lough Neagh and the Bann, between Randalstown and Lough Beg. They are numerous along the Bann as far as Finvoy. The third body is also on the shore of Lough Neagh in the south-west corner of the county, and the barony of Upper Massereene. This distribution is typical of most of Ulster. Where there has been immigration, the Protestants occupy most of the arable land ; the Roman Catholics occupy the hills, the bogs, and the rocky coasts. Lough Neagh lies almost in the heart of Protestant Ireland, yet the people of its marshy shores are mostly Roman Catholic. Between Crumlin and Antrim the land is higher and drier, and there the people are mostly Protestant. The greater part of Antrim is Scotch, but there is a compact English colony in the valley of the Lagan, with Lisburn as its centre.

90. In Down the Roman Catholics prevail all along the south coast from Portaferry to Newry. Their density is greatest between Newry and the Mourne Mountains. Eastward it gradually lessens as we go inland. North of Killyleagh and Ballynahinch the people are almost entirely Scotch. In the west the English element prevails among the Protestants, but there is a strong Scotch colony at Dromore and another about Rathfriland. South-east Antrim and North-east Down were settled shortly before the great confiscation of 1607 opened the way for the great Plantation. The country on the shores of Belfast

Lough, vaguely called South Clandeboye, was held forfeited on the attainder of Shane O'Neill in 1569. After unsuccessful attempts by the Earl of Essex and Sir T. Smith, Castlereagh and the Lower Ards were planted by Hamilton and Montgomery, while I settled Belfast and Carrickfergus. Scotland is very near, and the success of these settlements attracted a stream of immigration, which was afterwards encouraged to spread northward by the Macdonnells of Antrim and O'Neills of North Clandeboye. West Down was opened up by the forfeitures consequent on the rebellion of Magennis and other chiefs in 1641, but Bagenal had formed an earlier settlement at Newry. Shortly after the Civil War, North-west Down and South-west Armagh were planted with Cromwell's soldiers and other English settlers, who soon spread into North Armagh.

91. Antrim and Down are a solid block of 2148 square miles, with nearly 700,000 inhabitants, of whom 500,000 are Protestants—two-thirds of them Scotch. This only is Protestant Ireland strictly so-called, if we reckon by whole counties. Adjoining it on the east lies half-Protestant Ireland—Armagh, and the three counties forming the great central block of Ulster. It has an area of 3302 square miles, and a population of 610,000, in which the rival creeds have almost equal followings. The last census shows a Roman Catholic majority of 1500, which has probably now disappeared. The Protestants are holding their own in Tyrone and Fermanagh, while gaining ground

F

slowly in Londonderry and rapidly in Armagh. In a diminishing population their majority rose from 5000 in 1861, to 12,000 in 1881—a change caused chiefly by the growth of manufactures in Bessbrook and other towns. The percentages are 55 in Londonderry, 53½ in Armagh, 45 in Tyrone, and 44 in Fermanagh. They are chiefly English in Armagh, East and South Tyrone, and Fermanagh. In the last county the Scotch are almost unknown ; they are, however, much the stronger section throughout Londonderry and the valley of the Foyle. On the whole there are about three of English to two of Scotch descent. The Protestants are by no means evenly distributed. In the north-east corner the barony and liberties of Coleraine are even more Scotch than the adjoining part of Antrim. The northern and eastern parts of Armagh (quite half of the county) are as English as the adjoining parts of Down. Protestants slightly predominate on the shores of Lough Erne and Lough Foyle, in the valley of the Blackwater and the main valley of the Foyle, under its various names from Londonderry to Six Mile Cross; but as we rise, receding from the loughs and main streams, we find more and more Roman Catholics. The hill-slopes and highland valleys are peopled much as they were three centuries ago. The parish of Upper Bodoney, in North Tyrone, furnishes a striking illustration. In the lower half, which is included within the new parliamentary division of North Tyrone, nearly half of the people, 1021 out of 2321, are Protestant ; in the upper half only about a twelfth, 192 out of 2378. In the great upland block of South-central Derry and North-central Tyrone, stretching from Maghera nearly to Omagh, and from Dunnamannagh and Dungiven nearly to Dungannon, hardly one man in four is a Protestant. The proportion is as bad at the two ends of Fermanagh, in much more fertile country. It is far worse in the extreme south of Armagh, beyond Newry and Newtown - Hamilton. This region was never planted, and differs little from the adjoining parts of Louth. The great barony of Dungannon, lately trisected in a very clumsy manner, is typical of the four counties. There is a small majority of Roman Catholics. They occupy the western uplands on the slope of the watershed of the Bann, and the low wet lands on the shores of Lough Neagh. In the populous parish of Clonoe, at the mouth of the Blackwater, nine out of ten are Roman Catholics. The Protestants occupy the central strip, which was more fertile and easy to drain. They are in great force in the north, about Cookstown ; whence their compact colony stretches beyond Magherafelt in the adjoining county. About Dungannon settlers and natives are nearly equal ; but in the south, on the upper reaches of the Blackwater, there is the strong Protestant colony of Caledon and Aughnacloy, planted on the forfeited estates of Sir Phelim O'Neill.

92. The remaining two of the six counties of the great Plantation are the mere fringe of Ulster. They were not so well planted in the beginning, and the work in Cavan was almost obliterated in the great Rebellion of 1641. The less inviting country

of Donegal has lost greatly by the emigration of Presbyterians to America; and the Protestants are still losing ground. They are less by 11,000 than in 1861, and are now only 23½ per cent instead of 25. The Roman Catholics are actually increasing in the great rocky congested parishes of the west—Templecrone (Dunglow) and Tullaghobegly (Gwec-dore). The Protestants are mostly concentrated in the eastern parishes in the valley of the Foyle, and along the shores of the upper part of Lough Swilly, and the upper part of the Bay of Donegal. They are Scotch to the north of the Finn, and English to the south. The barony of North Raphoe, with some adjoining parts of South Raphoe, of Kilmacrenan (as far as Millford), and of Innishowen (as far as Moville), forms a half-Protestant tract whose natural connec-tions are with Derry and Tyrone. Most of it was included in the ancient territory bearing the latter name. In the south, the country from Donegal town to Lough Erne is almost up to the average level of Fermanagh. In the parishes of Drumhome and Templecarn the Protestants are 45 per cent, but the equally good country near Ballyshannon shows a great falling off to less than 20 per cent. They are more numerous about Dunfanaghy and be-tween Donegal and Killybegs. I blame myself and my successors greatly for not thoroughly clearing and planting Innishowen. For want of a Pro-testant peasantry in the neighbourhood, there is now a majority of Roman Catholics in the Maiden City.

93. In Cavan the Protestants are pretty evenly distributed at the rate of nearly 20 per cent. They rise to 40 round Bailieborough and the shores of Lough Oughter (Cavan and Killashandra), but sink to the level of Longford and Leitrim in the baronies of Clanmahon and Tullaghaw, and almost disappear in the hills about Stradone. They are nearly all English except at Bailieborough.

94. Fertile Monaghan is for our present purpose the most interesting, and as regards the work to be done, by far the most important of the nine counties of Ulster. It is the "Gap of the North," a Roman Catholic wedge running into half-Protestant Ireland, and cutting off Armagh from Fermanagh. Its history is peculiar. It was made shire-land before the west of Ulster, and was confiscated before the six counties— most of it in 1589, by an act of gross injustice to the Macmahon. Having been previously granted away without conditions, it was not included in the scheme of the great Plantation. Indeed, the baronies of Dartrey and Trough (with parts of the others) re-mained in the hands of the Macmahons and Mac-kennas till after the great Rebellion, into which they were led by their neighbour Sir Phelim O'Neill; but its fertility afterwards attracted settlers, and the Protestants are now 26 per cent. The great southern barony of Farney lies in a separate river-basin, and differs from the rest of the county in his-tory. It was at one time considered part of the Pale, and was granted by Queen Elizabeth to the Earl of Essex in 1569, but was never planted, and

is still like an ordinary part of Leinster. The still larger barony of Cremorne in the centre is in nearly the same plight, except at the Scotch settlements of Ballybay and Castleblayney. The two northern baronies, Trough and Monaghan, have strong settlements of Scotch and English round Glaslough and Monaghan, but are on the whole not much better than Cremorne —only as 29 per cent is better than 26. Only the western barony of Dartrey comes up to the level of Tyrone and Fermanagh. The Protestants are nearly 44 per cent, and might be nearly 50 if the north-east corner were cut off.

95. Obviously the first great object of the New Plantation must be to consolidate half - Protestant Ireland, by levelling up the "Gap of the North" to the standard of Armagh and Londonderry. Farney and nearly a third of Cremorne (in the south-west) lie outside the necessary line of the first Protestant ring-fence, and may be transferred to the adjoining southern county, with which they are naturally and historically connected. They were part of the old principality of Oriel. Monaghan proper would then be Protestant to the extent of one-third. Hence the arrangement on the map of counties and baronies (No. 2).

96. Outside Ulster there are nearly 300,000 Protestants, a third of whom are in Dublin and its suburbs. They have been gradually leaving the city, where they are now only 20 per cent. In the suburbs (including Kingstown) they are 40 per cent; in both together 25 per cent. In the suburban

township of Rathmines they have a small majority of the 24,000 inhabitants. There is no considerable mass of them anywhere else in the three provinces. Few can be found among the poorer classes. The Protestants of the middle class are mostly towns-people. Protestant farmers are, with few exceptions, found only in those counties of Leinster and Munster which were partly confiscated before the Confederate War, and partially planted by Boyle, Coote, Parsons, and the other southern "Undertakers." They are rare in the Pale and Kilkenny, but comparatively numerous in King's County Queen's County, and especially Wicklow, with the adjoining parts of Wexford and Carlow. There are also many in South Cork, North-east Tipperary, East Sligo, and about Carrigallen and Manorhamilton in County Leitrim. These two latter counties of Connaught were finally confiscated when Leinster and Munster were found insufficient for the payment of Crom-well's army, and were afterwards partially settled. Much of South Leitrim had, however, been granted away before the war on the report of the iniquitous Commission of Defective Titles. Wicklow is by far the best rural county outside Ulster; it is even better than Cavan — the Protestants being 20 per cent instead of 19, and occupying a larger pro-portion of the land. One reason is that the free-booting native tribes of O'Byrnes and O'Tooles were almost exterminated in a long series of bloody wars. The settlements in West Leinster during the seventeenth century were rather urban than agricultural. Maryborough and Mountmellick, Portarlington and Parsonstown, even Athlone and Tullamore, still have a notable Protestant element.

97. When the Protestants are 15 per cent, we may safely assume that they pay half of the rates; and experience shows that boycotting, the Plan of Campaign, misappropriation of poor-rates, and intimidation of juries are not easy to carry out, and can be successfully resisted. There is therefore a marked difference between such places and the rest of Roman Catholic Ireland. On the map of creeds (No. 1), the five considerable oases of civilisation have been demarcated. The largest is the rough triangle extending from Dublin to Carlow, Newtown Barry, Ferns, and Ballaghkeen. It includes, besides the city and suburbs, nearly all Wicklow, half of Carlow, and a third of Wexford (in area though not in population). There are 115,000 Protestants among the 485,000 inhabitants. The second includes the north-western half of Queen's County, (five baronies), with part of Cullenagh, the baronies of Clonlisk and Ballybritt with parts of Eglish and Upper Philipstown in King's County, and about half of the baronies of Ikerrin and Lower Ormond in the county of Tipperary. Its population is about 75,000, of whom 12,000 are Protestant. Another is the valley of the Bandon river in South Cork, from Inishannon upwards, a tract containing about 30,000 inhabitants, of whom nearly 5000 are Protestant. All along the south coast, from Kinsale to Crookhaven, the Protestants are generally 10 per cent or more of the population; and about

Skull nearly 20 per cent. In four parishes,[1] with 14,500 inhabitants, there are nearly 2800 Protestants; but they have not the same social strength there as further east. Many are not settlers, but native peasants converted by the Trenches during the Famine. The fourth large oasis is the town of Sligo, with the surrounding parishes, as far as Lissadill and Ballysadare, and the country about Manorhamilton and Drumahaire, in the adjoining county of Leitrim. There are about 8000 Protestants among the 45,000 inhabitants. A much smaller one consists of the town of Longford, with the valley of the Camlin up to Ballinalee. There are 2500 Protestants with 12,500 Roman Catholics. The early settlers of this county were nearly exterminated in the Civil War.

98. Supposing the Act to be passed before the end of 1890, we may expect that the Irish Government will complete its arrangements in six months, and that the Great Council will meet in the middle of 1891; it will probably contain at least 259 Protestants against 109 Roman Catholics. If illiteracy is made a disqualification, there will be half-a-dozen fewer of the latter. Almost all of those elected by the ratepayers will be Protestants; Roman Catholic candidates can succeed only in one barony of Tyrconnell (West Innishowen), four baronies of Donegal (Outer Banagh, South Boylagh, North Boylagh and Cloghaneely), in one barony of Cavan or East Brefney (Stradone), in eleven baronies of Oriel (all ex-

[1] Durrus, Skull, Kilcoe, and Kilmoe, nearly conterminous with Ivahagh, the ancient territory of the western O'Mahonys.

cept Bailieborough and Clankee), and in five baronies
of Fingal (all except Coolock and Kilmainham); also
in the ward of Drogheda, in the city and county of
Belfast. Twenty-three representatives are probably
quite as much as they deserve for their direct taxation, local and imperial. The division of inhabitants'
members would be closer. The Roman Catholics would
have nearly half of the rural baronies, and the Protestants would have to depend on Belfast for their
superiority. Sixty-nine baronies will certainly return
Roman Catholics ; and they may hope for fifteen from
the cities — viz., two from Derry, four from New
Dublin, and nine from Belfast. Every ward of
Belfast, except Lisburn and Lurgan, might return
one, and St George's might even return two out of its
five. On the other side, if the Protestants are united,
there will be 72 members for baronies, and 23 for
wards of cities. In four rural baronies, Middle Orior,
Upper Dungannon, Clanawley, and Kilmacrenan, the
results are doubtful, the two parties being probably
nearly equal, though the exact numbers cannot be
ascertained. The census-returns do not give the
necessary information for townlands. If we add
two of the doubtful seats to each side, we shall have
in all 97 Protestants against 86 Roman Catholics
in that part of the Great Council which would form
the Lower House, if each kind of members sat
separately.

99. That traditional arrangement would work
well enough under ordinary peaceful conditions;
provided that direct and indirect taxation were

separately controlled. Dead-locks could be averted by the Norse plan of a joint sitting, after a dissolution had shown that neither House was likely to give way to the other. In this case so cumbrous a constitution would defeat the very object of its creation. When a great task of vital moment—in fact, a revolution, is to be accomplished within a given time, constitutional checks and formalities cannot be allowed to tie the hands of statesmen. The Legislature of Ulster must decide every question once for all by a single division; and its decision must have the support of a secure and overwhelming majority.

100. It would of course be possible to provide something better than a weak and not perfectly safe majority of 12 in a house of 184,[1] by restricting the area of the Grand Duchy. That would be right enough if we had only to consider the safety of the Protestant population of Ulster proper; but it would defeat or greatly delay all the other objects of instituting a separate government. The Protestants of the North, instead of joining hands with their endangered brethren in Dublin and Wicklow, would be cut off by a wide fertile block of the most Romish part of Ireland. This very expanse of Meath, Oriel, and Fingal, is the most hopeful and attractive part of all Ireland for settlement. Moreover, without taking in the suburbs of Dublin and the intervening counties, Ulster could not secure the surplus of revenue required for carrying out the Plantation. The boundary has been chosen to effect all these

---

[1] Including Trinity College.

purposes, taking care also to have the area sufficiently compact, and at least half of the population
Protestant.

101. Let me therefore explain and justify the
Schedules.   No. I. defines the Grand Duchy in
terms of existing counties and other local divisions.
It includes the whole of the present province, except
a few townlands of Donegal and Fermanagh (transferred to Connaught for the better arrangement of the
latter county), the greater part of the hilly barony of
Tullaghaw in West Cavan (also transferred to Connaught), and a large group of Roman Catholic
parishes in South Cavan, which are transferred to
Leinster.   The total population of the excluded parts
is 52,933, of whom only about 5241 are Protestant.
On the other hand, the Grand Duchy takes from Connaught most of the exceptional parish of Carrigallen
in Leitrim, with 1277 Protestants (30 per cent) among
its 4151 inhabitants.   This fits in well enough with
the new county of Cavan, or East Brefney.   Leinster
yields up a large area, containing about 243,965 inhabitants, of whom about 50,091 are Protestants.   Thus
the total population is 1,938,001, in which, according
to the last census, the Roman Catholics exceed the
Protestants by more than 26,000.   As, however, the
Protestants of Ulster proper have been gaining on the
Roman Catholics since 1861, at the rate of nearly
5000 a-year, there can be little doubt that in 1891
we shall find the majority on the other side.   In
1861 the Roman Catholics of Ulster were more by
20,000 than the Protestants; in 1881 they were less

by 76,000. The change is mainly due to the enormous growth of Belfast, now the corner-stone of Ireland. The annexed rural portions of Leinster comprise the whole of Louth, more than half of Meath, and all County Dublin north of the Liffey, except the parish of Leixlip.

102. These rural districts will form a solid junction between the sturdy North and the polished Protestant colony of the Dublin suburbs. Dublin city we cannot take in, saving only the site of Trinity College, which is made a new county in itself, so that the University may not be left in the outer darkness. The southern suburbs are formed into a rather straggling borough of New Dublin, also a county in itself. It includes Kingstown, Dalkey, and Blackrock, Rathmines (less the parish of St Catherine), and Pembroke (less that poor section of it which forms part of the present parliamentary division of Dublin Harbour). The Protestants in the excluded part will not be more than 20 per cent of the 5000 inhabitants—probably a good deal less. To round off the new borough, I have added the parishes of Kilmacud and Stillorgan, with some north-east townlands of Kill and Tancy. In the total population—75,123—there will be about 31,750 Protestants,—three out of seven. In the north they will be three out of six; in and about Kingstown, three out of nine. Even under the present township-franchise (£4 rating), the council would be controlled by Protestants. As to the other townships, it is only necessary to say that, besides the north end of Pembroke already mentioned, the old city gets the united

town of Drumcondra Clonliffe, and Glasnevin; that
Killiney and Bray go to Wicklow; and Clontarf and
New Kilmainham to the new county of Fingal; and
that the small extra-urban parts of the parishes of St
Catherine, St James, and St Jude, intervening between
Rathmines and New Kilmainham, are joined in one
new barony with the latter.   Dublin is thus girt
with a ring of loyal Ulster, — a precaution which
may be of use in dealing with Fenians and other
firebrands.

103. All the Schedules have been drawn up after
mature consideration for nearly two years, involving
minute and repeated collation of large maps with the
detailed census-lists and other sources of information.
Readers with special local knowledge will of course be
able to point out improvements; but I am reasonably
confident that the arrangements proposed will, on the
whole, work well, and be found worthy of adoption in
permanence.   A few in Tyrconnel are intended to be
only temporary, pending the success of the Plantation
in the localities concerned.   The barony has been
taken as the political unit, and framed by grouping of parishes and townlands on the following
principles :—

First, That it should have an average population of
rather more than 10,600 according to the last census,
which will probably have dwindled to 10,000 before
the next.   The limits are 8000 and 14,000, except
for Kilmainham, which contains 14,500. Those which
approach the higher limit have generally a low valuation, or contain, like Kilmainham, a large class of

persons who cannot vote—such as soldiers, lunatics, paupers, or other inmates of public institutions.

Second, That they should be compact, and, if possible, conveniently grouped round some market-town or central village.

Third, That they should be homogeneous in class of population and economic conditions. The hilly regions have been separated from the plains, and the arable country from the pastoral—a natural distinction which coincides largely with a historical distinction, the local prevalence of natives or settlers.

Fourth, That they should be susceptible of easy grouping to form compact and convenient counties and parliamentary divisions.

Fifth, That as many as possible should contain a majority of Protestants; thus, among other advantages, to narrow the necessary field of operations when the Plantation begins.

104. The counties and parliamentary divisions have been framed on similar principles. Those of Munster and Connaught are only provisional, as I have not yet worked out the baronies; but I do not think that any substantial change will be found necessary. Each parliamentary division contains six, seven, or eight entire baronies. Seventy-five thousand, according to the census of 1881, has been taken as the standard of population for a division; and the counties have been arranged to contain multiples of this unit. To consolidate Protestant Ulster, the county of Londonderry has been merged in that of Tyrone, and the old dominion of the O'Neills restored

to its former greatness, omitting only the awkward peninsula of Innishowen. After taking in East Donegal, and lopping off a few southern parishes (Errigal Trough, Kilskeery, Magheracross, and nearly half of Clonoe), we shall find Protestants and Roman Catholics nearly equal in the great united county. The next census will probably show a small majority on the side of the former. An improvement is necessary at an early date to give compactness to Fermanagh. The border barony of Ballyshannon must be attached to the county of Belfast until it has been planted, since it contains a Roman Catholic majority of more than 7000; but its natural connection is with Fermanagh. That county has been altered so as to contain a small Protestant majority (under 1000), by cutting off its extremities and taking in more-Protestant parishes from Donegal [1] and Tyrone.[2] In any case, Tyrone and Fermanagh will have Protestant county-government. In the latter, the Protestant baronies are at least 4 out of 7, and in the former 19 out of 32.

105. The straggling, awkward, highly artificial county of Donegal has been somewhat reduced by transfers to Belfast, Fermanagh, and Tyrone, as well as Connaught; and the old territorial name of Tyrconnel has been restored. Cavan (East Brefney) is confined to the valley of the Erne, and loses more than half of its area and population for the benefit of Oriel, Meath, Longford (Annaly), and Leitrim (West Brefney); but it gains a barony from Fermanagh,

---

[1] Drumhome and Templecarn.   [2] Kilskeery and Magheracross.

and a parish from Leitrim, besides some townlands from Monaghan. One result of these changes is to raise the Protestants from 19 to 25 per cent. Monaghan is changed to make it fit in more neatly between Armagh and Fermanagh. It loses about a third on the south and east, chiefly to Oriel; but it gets a fragment of a parish from Tyrone on the north, and two small baronies from Fermanagh on the west. In consequence of these changes it becomes more compact, and has 33 per cent Protestants instead of 26. Armagh is shortened and broadened so as nearly to treble the Protestant majority in a rather smaller population. The unsettled southern strip is handed over to Oriel, and the towns of Lurgan and Newry to Belfast. About 10,000 Protestants go with about 26,000 Roman Catholics. By way of compensation, Armagh gets the large parish of Muckno (Castleblayney) with some other townlands from Monaghan, and the large parish of Tullylish (Gilford) with Shankill and some adjoining townlands of Donaghcloney from County Down. At the north-west corner, it takes from Tyrone a portion of Clonoe, almost exclusively Roman Catholic. In the end 61 per cent (or more) will be found Protestant.

106. Down is changed only by the aforesaid transfers to Armagh, and by the attachment of Newry, Lisburn, and the new barony of Holywood to the new county of Belfast. This new county includes also the new baronies of Ligoniel in Antrim, and Ballyshannon in Donegal. With these rural additions, and the five outlying wards of the municipal

borough, the population of Belfast will be fully
300,000, even according to the last census; and it
will be fairly entitled to retain its four seats in
Parliament. The county and municipal borough of
Drogheda are of course abolished. The abolition of
the county of Carrickfergus, and the transfer of Lisburn and the new barony of Ligoniel to Belfast, are
the only changes in Antrim.

107. The new county of Oriel, a famous old name
revived, corresponds nearly with the ancient principality in the old kingdom of Ulster. It includes all
Louth (except Dundalk and the southern parish of
Tullyallen), the southern strip of Armagh already
alluded to, the large barony of Farney with most of
the large parish of Aghnamullen in South Monaghan,
the south-east corner of Cavan (with about 25,000
inhabitants), and the north-east corner of Meath (with
about 14,000). Louth is discarded in favour of the
older name, partly because there is a parliamentary
division of Louth in England containing an important
market-town, but chiefly on the general principle
that ancient territorial names are to be preferred
on their own merits. They are well-known to the
people, and their revival will be a legitimate gratification of the national feeling of the so-called National party — if it has any. The present county-
names have seldom any title to veneration. Many
are borrowed from insignificant towns, and half of
them were coined so recently as the last quarter of
the sixteenth century. I have adopted old names, at
least as alternatives, wherever practicable, and have

followed the same rule in naming the baronies. Every one will, I think, welcome the revival of Fingal, as the name of a county formed of Dublin north of the Liffey, with a few suburban parishes on the south, and the south-west portion of Meath as far as Drogheda and the Boyne.

108. The changes in Leinster need no explanation. They are obviously made to create¦ nearly equal counties, each forming a parliamentary division in itself. Dublin gets three members, and the boroughs of Wexford and Kilkenny become urban counties in the Waterford group, along with Queenstown and Clonmel. In Munster the enormous county of Cork has been broken up into its old component parts—Carberry and Muskerry, Desmond [1] and Barrymore. Tralee is carved out of Kerry to form an urban constituency with the city of Limerick. North Tipperary is restored to its natural connection with Limerick, and the whole county of Clare to its natural connection with Connaught. The extremely clumsy counties of the last province have been rearranged in better accordance with history and geography.

109. The Protestants being one-fourth of the population of Ireland, ought to control seventeen of the sixty - eight territorial constituencies. The parliamentary divisions of Ulster have been arranged with a view to this end of justice, which was shamefully neglected in the arrangements of 1885. The wards of Belfast were cut up, and the limits of the borough

[1] In the narrower sense.

extended to secure representation of 60,000 ignorant Roman Catholics; but no change was made in Dublin to secure representation of 90,000 intelligent Protestant taxpayers in the city and its suburbs. This could easily have been effected by the simple expedient of treating the township of Rathmines like Pembroke, which was long ago added to the parliamentary borough. Dublin would then have been entitled to five members, and the fifth could have been provided by abolishing the sham borough of Kilkenny, whose population is made to reach 15,000 only by the absurd addition of several rural parishes. Under the scheme proposed the Protestants can, if united, return members for North Tyrone, West Tyrone, and Fermanagh; though the contests will be close, unless illiteracy is made a disqualification. They are secure in the solid north-eastern block of fourteen constituencies.

110. The revenue of the Grand Duchy cannot be stated with any pretence to accuracy, but will probably be not far from half of the present revenue of all Ireland. It contains two-fifths of the population, and much more than two-fifths of the wealth. Half of the customs-revenue comes from Belfast and other northern ports; and a custom-house at Kingstown would draw away a great part of what is now received at Dublin. The receipts from income-tax, succession-duty, and other direct taxes at New Dublin, would be very large in proportion to the population — it being the place of residence for so many men of business in the old city. On the other

hand, it must be remembered that half of the Irish revenue comes from whisky; much of which, however, is consumed and really paid for in England. Dublin is the chief seat of the trade, and Ulster is by far the most sober part of Ireland. To be on the safe side, let us put the revenue of Ulster at two-fifths of the whole revenue received in Ireland—*i.e.*, £3,000,000. The expenditure in Ireland, exclusive of army, navy, and national debt, is rather less than £3,750,000. Nearly a million is spent on education, and a million and a half on police. The necessary expenditure of Ulster would certainly not exceed two-fifths of the present total, for it has far less than its proportionate number of constables. Rural Ulster, excluding Donegal, contains fully a quarter of the population of Ireland, and little more than one-eighth of the Royal Irish Constabulary. The surplus, indeed, would be only £1,500,000 instead of the necessary average of £2,000,000; but the work would be slower and on a smaller scale in the earlier years. £18,000,000 would be more than enough to remove 300,000 Irish and put 200,000 loyal folk in their places. The annexation of Dublin and Leinster would raise the surplus to nearly £2,500,000 during the most expensive period of the undertaking.

111. Having got the money, what ought the Ulster Government to do with it? First of all, obviously, it ought to round off the Protestant block by planting the county of Monaghan and the barony of Bally-shannon. To do this will involve the removal of 22,000 Roman Catholics in Monaghan, and 5000 in

Ballyshannon (in all 27,000), and the substitution of
17,000 or 18,000 Protestants.   At the same time it
would be easy to ensure a decided Protestant majority in the three doubtful parliamentary divisions,
by planting the new baronies of Glenderg, Upper
Tirkeeran and Upper Strabane in Tyrone, and the
new baronies of Tirhugh, Magheraboy, and Clanawley
in Fermanagh.   This would involve the removal of
11,000 more Roman Catholics,[1] and the introduction
of 6000 or 7000 more Protestants; the totals thus
reaching 38,000 and 24,000.   This first campaign
would require three years.   No actual planting could
be done in the first.   It must be devoted to legislation
and general preliminary arrangements.   The nature
of these will be described hereafter.

112. The objects of the second campaign will be
to strengthen still further the Protestant element in
Tyrone, so that it cannot by any political intrigues
lose its ascendancy; to bring Cavan within the
Protestant fence ; to prepare the way for the great
southward march, by securing the southern baronies
of Down and Armagh ; and to carry out all these
changes so as at the same time to increase largely the
number of Protestant seats in the Great Council.   To
effect these improvements, the Ulster Government
must remove 26,000 Roman Catholics from Cavan
(East Brefney) ; 7000 from the baronies of Mourne,
Castlewellan, and Rosstrevor in Down ; 5000 from the
baronies of Tiranny, Keady, Middle Fews, and Middle
Orior in Armagh ; 6000 from the baronies of Clogher,

_____
[1] 5000 from Fermanagh.

Fintona, and West Omagh in Mid Tyrone; and 4000 from Mountjoy (Stewartstown) and Upper Dungannon in South-east Tyrone; also 3000 from the city of Londonderry. In all, 51,000 Roman Catholics must make room for about 30,000 Protestants. All of these reckonings, it must be remembered, are based on the figures of 1881, from which in practice a reduction of at least 5, and sometimes 10 per cent will be found feasible in the rural districts. This work ought to be finished in two years. Among the results of the two campaigns would be the gain of two seats in Parliament (Monaghan and East Brefney), and the gain of thirty-four seats in the Great Council. In five years from the institution of the Ulster Government, its essential work in Ulster proper ought to be practically accomplished. Three parliamentary divisions, Mid Tyrone and the two Tyrconnels, will remain to be conquered; but they are out of the line of direct march, and may be assimilated at leisure. They are not very inviting to emigrants from England and Scotland, and must be gradually repeopled from Ulster itself. There will be less difficulty about the Roman Catholic baronies of Maghera and Loughinsholin (Draperstown) in North-east Tyrone. These also ought to be transformed, but the baronies of Glenarm in Antrim and Lower Lecale in Down may be safely left untouched as interesting remnants of old Ireland. The town of Enniskillen, and the barony of Clanawley may be made Protestant by the same piece of work. There is a Protestant majority of about 1000 in the rural part, and an equally

large Roman Catholic majority in the urban. By
sweeping away the latter the whole barony is secured,
along with the whole of the famous Protestant town.
That part of it which lies in the old barony of Tirkennedy and new barony of Enniskillen is already
half-Protestant.

113. The total number to be removed from Ulster
proper is 185,000, according to the last census ; the
total for Tyrone will be 41,000 ; for Fermanagh,
10,000 ; and for Tyrconnel 74,000. A complete
clearance must be made of the great pauper rabbit-
warrens in the north-west of the last-named county.
Cloghancely and North Boylagh cannot support comfortably more than a third of their present population,
and when properly depleted may be consolidated into
a single barony.

114. In five years all ought to be ready for the
decisive battle of the two nations. The men of Ulster
will have gained confidence and skill by success in a
novel but comparatively easy struggle of the same
kind. They will have a broad and impregnable base
for the conquest of the rich country between Newry
and Dublin. That will be the key-stone of the arch.
It will be the most costly, and in many respects the
most difficult portion of the whole enterprise. An
obvious difficulty is the number of large Roman
Catholic landlords, the Norman Lords of the Pale.
But this obstacle is more apparent than real. Their
priests will compel them to make a show of opposition,
but in most cases it will be only a show—their hearts
will not be in it. Even the most Ultramontane land-

owner must in his heart prefer heretic tenants, who
are sure to pay their rents, to "good Catholics," who
will keep it in their own pockets if they get a chance.
A more serious trouble is the existence of a large body
of small Roman Catholic landowners holding the north-
eastern part of the barony of Farney. These are the
late tenants of the Marquis of Bath, who have pur-
chased their farms under Lord Ashbourne's Act. The
great cost of buying them out is not the chief obstacle
—it would all be recovered in time ; but their com-
pulsory expropriation would have an air of bad faith
and hard treatment. Fortunately they cannot sub-
divide for fifty years ; and if this provision is strictly
enforced, the present holders at least may be left undisturbed during good behaviour. The danger of
general expulsion would secure general docility, and
make each man eager to aid the police in detecting
Fenian agents and other criminals. Including their
families and servants, the persons concerned are probably about 8000 souls, nearly all within the new
barony of Farney (Carrickmacross). Another difficulty is the exposed border, liable to be invaded by
secret agitators and nocturnal brigands. It is to
avoid this that provision is made for the early annexation of Meath and Kildare. Yet another difficulty
is avoided by the provision for governing Drogheda
and Dundalk from Belfast. Hostile or even weak
local authorities in these gates of Meath and Louth
might cause not only a good deal of unpleasantness,
but some serious impediment.

115. Another peculiar circumstance is that the new

counties of Oriel and Fingal must be raised to the state of Down and Antrim, in order that the city of Dublin, as well as Drogheda and Dundalk, may be gradually transformed by recruitment from a thoroughly Protestant rural population. The same thing must be done afterwards to Wicklow and part of Kildare : a bare majority will not suffice. The Roman Catholics of Oriel and Fingal, excluding the Dublin suburbs, and such towns as Skerries, Balbriggan, Ardee, and Carrickmacross, are about 180,000. At least three-fourths (135,000) must be removed, and 90,000 Protestants put in their places. As the farms are larger than in most other parts of Ireland, fully 9000 families of Protestant labourers must be imported, chiefly from England and Scotland. Ulster cannot supply nearly so many at once, though it will probably send half or more of the 9000 farmers also required. The total number to be removed from the original Grand Duchy will then be 320,000, according to the census of 1881. These must be replaced by 190,000 Protestants. The population will then consist of nearly 1,100,000 Protestants, and less than 600,000 Roman Catholics.

116. This third and greatest campaign will be conducted under great physical difficulties, and against most furious opposition in Ireland ; but good management and dogged perseverance will ensure success, and success in this campaign will change the course of Irish history. Everything else will become easy. English capital will flow into Leinster and Munster as soon as they are annexed ; and when the Ulster

Government comes to deal with a southern county, it may find much of its work already done for it by private enterprise. Roman Catholic tenants will readily sell when they get a good offer, knowing that they must go later, if they do not go sooner.

117. In the second period of five years, Lower Tyrconnel and Mid Tyrone, as well as Oriel and Fingal, ought to be made Protestant counties; but an extension of two years may be taken by the Ulster Government to make all sure before it annexes Leinster. The name Ulster will not then be fully descriptive of the Grand Duchy; but the United Grand Duchies of Ulster and Leinster would be a far too cumbrous title, and would have to give way after eight or ten years (on the annexation of Munster) to a title still more cumbrous. It is better, on the whole, to keep the first name unchanged through all the thirty years. Little needs be said about the plantation of Leinster. The advance ought to be first southward to Wexford, and then westward to Ossory and the Shannon. The ten counties (excluding Wexford and Kilkenny) have about 810,000 inhabitants, of whom nearly 90,000 are Protestant. The removal of 450,000 Roman Catholics, and the substitution of 300,000 emigrants from England, Scotland, and Ulster will ensure a Protestant majority of nearly 120,000—almost enough to counterbalance the Dublin rabble. It will be possible to treat Wicklow and most of Kildare like Oriel and Fingal, and thus surround Dublin with a thoroughly Protestant country. And the interesting old English colony of South Wexford

may be left undisturbed in Forth and Bargay, if
a clean sweep is made of the Irish in the other
baronies.

118. Twenty years after the first meeting of the
Great Council it may expect to begin the plantation
of Munster. The thirteen rural parliamentary divisions have about 1,000,000 inhabitants, of whom less
than 50,000 are Protestant. To ensure a Protestant
majority of 100,000, or 7500 on the average for each
division, we must remove 600,000 Roman Catholics,
and put 400,000 Protestants in their places ; but
keeping within the limit of one-third for all Ireland
(1,320,000), we can remove only 550,000. West
Carbery, therefore, the least inviting and not the most
troublesome part of the province, must be left out
of the present calculations. As already explained, it
is expected that the census of 1891 will show only
500,000 occupying the places of the 550,000. Perhaps
the census of 1901 will show a further decrease ; and
as the plantation of Munster will not begin before
1911, there is every reason for expecting that West
Carbery also may be planted without exceeding the
gross estimates for the cost of removing 1,200,000 :
but the money might be better spent in Sligo or
Clanricarde. The former contains a valuable seaport,
and even now more than 10,000 Protestants. The
latter contains Ballinasloe, the seat of the great live-
stock market of the kingdom.

119. As to the *modus operandi*, I need only trace
the broad outlines. The Privy Council would do
well to intrust the general management of the Plan-

tation to a first-class man of business, such as the
manager of a great railway or steamship company.
£10,000 a-year or more would not be wasted in
securing his services. Under him ought to be a staff
of local agents qualified for valuation, and another
staff of recruiting agents, who could visit England
and Scotland, and personally conduct parties of
farmers and representative labourers wishing to see
their future homes before closing the bargain. Each
tenant selected for expropriation ought to get notice
for six months, after valuation by the local agent.
During this time he could appeal to the general
manager, who ought to have one or two deputies
specially qualified for this sort of work. They would
also have to check the local valuer's estimate, if it
exceeded ten times the judicial rent. Unless the
appellate authority should think it necessary to give
an extension of time, a fresh notice to remove ought
to be served on the tenant one month before the
expiration of the six. If desired, £10 would be
advanced to him for expenses of removal; and he
would get free railway-tickets for himself and his
family. On presenting himself at Belfast, Derry, or
Kingstown, and producing a certificate that he had
delivered up possession of his farm (in as good condition as when it was valued), he ought to get a cheque
for the price of his interest therein on some bank
in America, or elsewhere outside the British Islands.
Free passages to America would be provided; and the
emigrants would get free lodgings while waiting to
embark. Iron barracks could be quickly put up for

their accommodation. At the end of six months the tenant would forfeit a shilling in the pound of his tenant-right for every day's delay; and at the end of the seventh month he would be forcibly expelled and deported. In towns like Enniskillen and London-derry, the Government ought to buy up all the houses and adjoining fields in order to prevent the influx of fresh Roman Catholics.

VI.

AIDS AND PRECAUTIONS.

120. SOME further legislation would be needed to make resistance and obstruction of any kind a game clearly too dangerous for anybody but a madman. The Government of Ulster must be, before all things, a Government that will "stand no nonsense." Imprisonment with hard labour for six months must be made the minimum of punishment for assault or obstruction of a constable, process-server, sheriff's officer, or other public servant discharging any duty in connection with the Plantation ; and each member of a riotous crowd or occupant of a defended house must be made liable to punishment for the acts of any unknown person in his company. There will be no hardship in this. Persons who do not want to get into trouble on such occasions have only to restrain their curiosity, keep their distance, and mind their own business. Needless gathering in a crowd ought to be distinctly recognised as a misdemeanour. It is an abetment of violence, by increasing the facility of commission and the difficulty of detection.

121. Penal legislation, however, is hardly the most important part of the work of the Great Council. Prevention is better than cure. The present state of the law as to trespass, insult, and self-defence, can only be described as wickedly perverse. It seems designed to combine the utmost encouragement of malice, disorder, and wanton aggression, with the utmost embarrassment and intimidation of public servants doing their duty, and honest citizens asserting or defending their rights. What can be more absurd than the formalities of an eviction? Can any one show a shadow of a reason why the proceedings should be void, as the Parnellites contend, unless every human being is removed from the premises? It is clear common-sense that the removal of the responsible occupier is all that ought to be required.[1] What can be more unjust than the law that a landlord must account to an evicted tenant, who afterwards redeems, for the profits which the latter might have made during the six months of grace? It is hardly possible for a new cultivator, even if one can be found for such a period, to get any profit in six months, even supposing that he enters on the very first day.

122. In regard to trespass, the law of Ireland is one of the grossest embodiments of unreason that any part of the world can exhibit. The constabulary cannot expel a trespasser or help anybody else to do so. Hence the necessity for section f in the proposed Act for the better government of all Ireland. The

---

[1] There is some uncertainty as to what is really required.

Government of Ulster may be expected to go a good deal beyond that slight instalment of reform. One of the first conditions of a sound system of criminal jurisprudence is, that it should in everything seek to tie the hand of the rough, and give more power to the elbow of the decent citizen. All legal proceedings are evils, though some are necessary evils; and the best laws are those which lessen the need of such proceedings as far as possible, by enabling the good citizen to protect his own rights without the trouble and expense of going to court. Any owner, or other person lawfully entitled to occupy any premises, ought to have the power of expelling a contumacious trespasser without being harassed by nice distinctions as to necessary or unnecessary force. A man who goes or stays where he knows he has no right to be, ought to be regarded as voluntarily incurring anything that happens to him after due warning, and is equitably entitled to no redress whatever; he ought, in fact, to be an outlaw during the continuance of his trespass. On the other hand, it must be distinctly laid down that the trespasser has no right of self-defence against his ejector, unless it is impossible for him to run away; and that no public servant in uniform, or person known to be a sheriff, magistrate, or other public officer can, when acting under colour of his office, be treated as a criminal trespasser. Disaffected persons have contrived to make a malicious use even of the existing law against trespass. Trespass, in order to insult, intimidate, or commit theft or mischief, must be made punishable with a long term of imprisonment with

hard labour. . Every immigrant farmer ought to be
invested with the powers of a constable on his own
premises, and furnished with a short handbook of his
powers and duties, prepared under the authority of
the Privy Council. This will enable the new settlers
to protect themselves, and save much expense for
additional constabulary. It will then be possible to
say in sober earnest, not as now in cruel irony, that
an honest man's house is his castle.

123. Public insult must be made an offence punishable not less severely than the violent acts which are
often only its natural, if not necessary, consequence.
It is the most fruitful source of riots and affrays. If
we check it, we stop disorder at its fountain. A
word is often worse than a blow. " Hard words
break no bones," it is said. No; but they do far
worse,—they cut hearts and poison blood.

124. Besides an amendment of the law of trespass,
a further removal of legal restrictions on the natural
right of self-defence is required for the protection of
soldiers and constables in the streets, and of house-
holders attacked by mobs. Whenever an accused
person raises a plea of self-defence on reasonable
grounds, he ought to be released on his own recog-
nisance, and not to be liable to arrest until after
conviction, unless he absconds. Farmers ought to be
free to use their guns in defence of their crops, cattle,
and buildings. It must be made clear that a shot
is always a lawful answer to a stone endangering the
shooter, or his household, or any person whom he is
protecting, even if he fire without or against the

orders of his superior officer. Discipline can be maintained by official punishment, without the aid of the ordinary criminal law. The law of the land sins grossly in interfering with an honest man's natural right to defend himself in the only effectual way against pain and death and mutilation. Stoning the police is now a very safe amusement for English and Irish roughs. Certainty of getting a shot in return will soon make an end of it; and nothing less will have the desired effect. Severity at the beginning is the only true mercy in the end. "They may talk of punishment as cruel," said the greatest man ever born in Ireland, "but there is nothing so inhuman as impunity."[1] No one in his senses will defy a severe law administered by men whom he knows to be inflexible. And if the Irish are foolish enough to doubt the inflexibility of the Orange Government, one lesson will be enough. Surely it is better, for the greatest happiness of the greatest number, that one turbulent citizen should forfeit his worthless life, than that a dozen policemen should be mangled and tortured in the discharge of their duty, as happens every year under the present system of impotent imbecility. Of course, firearms must be kept out of untrustworthy hands by a strict law of gun-licences.

125. It remains only to provide against the danger of division among the Protestants. Mr Gladstone and his disciples will try hard to stir up Scotch against English, and labourers against farmers. The more their numbers increase—the greater the success of the

[1] Stanhope's Conversations with the Duke of Wellington, p. 251.

Plantation—the greater will this danger become ; for there will be less of the counteracting danger, less pressure from the Irish enemy, to keep them together. There is only one sure preventive—a resource that is, I fear, distasteful, even repulsive, to the fastidious Anglo-Catholic, and to the cosmopolitan philosophic Liberal, anxious, above all things, to avoid the appearance of religious intolerance. The rough Orange Society saved Ireland once, in the end of the eighteenth century, and it must be called in to secure her safety in the end of the nineteenth. Let Lord Salisbury listen to the confession of Archbishop Trench, and be wise in time. " I hate the Orangemen, . . . but I see in them the last hope of Ireland."[1] Let the preacher of cool, not to say cold, universal charity study the organisation of the unpolished Protestants whose " illiberal fanaticism " he despises. He will find, like Mr S. C. Hall,[2] that " in principle the Orange Society cannot be described as even uncharitable." Doubtless it has been unjustly violent in practice, but I do not ask you to encourage such practice. What I pro-pose is that the living force of this great organism should be used to bring rich and poor together—not only as at present by the pressure of a common danger and attraction of a common antipathy, but by a common sympathy in social intercourse and in pursuit of posi-tive social benefits ; in short, to develop it into a vast friendly (and festive) society, divesting it of the secrecy which does no good, and keeps away many good people who have peculiar scruples of religion. It is

---

[1] Life, vol. i. p. 97.   [2] Ireland, vol. ii. p. 468.

essential to the greatest usefulness of the Society, that it should have the hearty support of the gentry and the Presbyterian ministers. It might then take firm root in Scotland.

126. It is also desirable, if not essential, that the Society should be able to go beyond business principles, and show special liberality to its poorer members, more especially to those suffering injury from Roman Catholics. To do this, it must get a good deal more than the regular insurance rates from its wealthier members; it ought, indeed, to have a large special capital for extra-commercial purposes. The rich men of Ireland could do nothing better with their money than subscribe a million sterling as a beginning. There are one or two who could give the whole amount without feeling the loss. Is no one ambitious of raising an imperishable monument to himself in the hearts of his grateful fellow-countrymen?

VII.

GENERAL VINDICATION.

127. THESE last proposals will have brought to a head the objection which must have been simmering in the minds of many readers through the whole course of policy which I have been expounding. Here, at the end, is the place for statement and refutation. It will be said in effect by the objectors that this is a policy founded on religious animosity and intolerance, and therefore both immoral and impolitic.

128. As to the morality. I must first reply that real religious intolerance, even when unjust, is an infinitely more respectable motive than the class-hatred which is now the greatest sentimental force in the political life of your century. It must be to some extent reverent and disinterested, looking above and beyond the creature whom it moves. Whenever, therefore, it displaces or counterbalances the lower antipathy, there is a distinct rise in the moral level of the nation. But religious antipathy is by no means always a wrong feeling. Hatred of evil is the neces-

sary complement of love of right; and no intelligent Protestant can doubt that the Roman Church
is on the whole an element of evil in an enlightened
nation like the British, if not in the world at large.
Here it undoubtedly does more harm than good. It
is the immutable enemy of intellectual and moral
progress beyond its own low standard. Rome is
the mortal foe of England at this very moment,
not less than in the days of the grand Armada
and the glorious Revolution. As Mr Froude has
told us more than once, the wolf has not lost his
teeth, nor the will to use them, though in modern
times it often suits him to whine through sheep's
clothing.

129. " Hate the sin, but not the sinner," you will
say. Well, I do not ask you to harm any individual
Roman Catholic, nor even to harbour any angry feeling against him, merely on account of his faith. I
simply urge you, in national self-defence, to remove
from your very midst a host of deadly enemies, whom
you may best identify by their being Roman Catholics,
who include in practice nearly all the Roman Catholics of the lower and middle classes in Ireland, and
who will remain your implacable enemies so long as
they remain Roman Catholics, and you remain honourable men. Without saying that their religion is a
cause of Ireland's disease, we may certainly say that
it prevents the cure. And it is a handy shibboleth, by
which in practice you may distinguish those who, for
other reasons also, are your real and necessary enemies.
There are doubtless thousands of Roman Catholics in

Ireland who would be loyal and honest, if they dared to stand out against their priests and their neighbours. But as they do not dare to act upon their feelings, it is not practicable to draw any distinction between them and the leaders whom they reluctantly follow. He that is not with you is against you in a mortal struggle like this.

130. Nothing that I have proposed will cause any pecuniary loss, or real injustice of any kind, to any Roman Catholic. And on the other hand, removing him to America will not only improve his worldly prospects, if he is honest and industrious, but will do him a great moral service, by placing him in a new moral atmosphere, to make a new start under a Government whose faults are indeed many and great, but whose written constitution enforces the freedom and sacredness of contract. Moreover, if he goes to America, there is some hope that he or his children will become Protestant. In the rural parts generally most of his neighbours will be Protestant, and the only schools within reach will be free from priestly influence. There can be no such hope if he remains in Ireland. The Irish ought to be dispersed like the Jews, for their own good, as well as for the good of their present country and the sister-kingdoms. Their existence as an organised nation would indeed be an unmixed evil to the whole of Christendom.

131. As to policy. In the first place, as you have all written in your copy-books, "Honesty is the best policy." No policy will ever succeed that is based on shutting your eyes and ears to the main facts of

the situation. It is a great glaring fact that the Irish Roman Catholics are the implacable enemies of all that is good and great in England and Scotland. It is another such fact that they are highly danger- ous enemies, through their alliance with the great mass of folly and ignorance, envy and malice, in Great Britain itself. You have yet three years for raising bulwarks against the destruction of all that makes England worth living in and worth fighting for. If you do not make an effective use of them, you will deserve the punishment which all mankind must suffer.

132. Secondly, Boldness is the best policy. As my old friend Sir Francis Bacon[1] told you long ago, "Boldness hath done wonders in popular States." Many Conservative statesmen are still under the dominion of fixed ideas, engendered in the days of the old narrow electoral system, when individual votes were almost everywhere worthy of special consideration. They still construct flabby election addresses and negative political manifestoes, with a miserable anxiety to avoid displeasing anybody, which of necessity ends in really pleasing nobody. Not so is enthusiasm roused, and without enthusiasm the Union party cannot now hope to carry a general election. The Destructives have the immense advan- tage of being able to rouse all the baser passions by promises of wholesale plunder to the covetous, and gratification of jealousy to the malicious. Mr Frederic Harrison,[2] who ought to know, tells us that the new

---

[1] Essays, xii. [2] Nineteenth Century, May 1889, p. 755.

electors are guided not so much by reason as by feeling. Great masses of men can be moved to vigorous action on the side of right and duty only by a clear, simple, positive, aggressive policy, appealing to some deep-seated general sentiment. The Union party must appeal to the hereditary Protestant instincts of the British nation. That is the only way to gain Scotland: it is, indeed, the only way to keep England. Remember how much of the Conservative predominance in Lancashire, and how much of the greater strength of Union sentiment in the West of Scotland as compared with the East, are due to Protestant disgust at the hordes of Irish Roman Catholics who infest those parts of the great Protestant island.

133. "But it will alienate our Roman Catholic supporters, and prevent us from conciliating others." No; in practice it will not make the slightest difference. The only Roman Catholics, whom you can conciliate, will never need to be conciliated. The land-owners, and those who associate with them, support the Union because it saves themselves or their friends from ruin; and they would do so, even if the Prime Minister were the Orange Grand Master or Mr Johnston of Ballykilbeg. The other Irish Roman Catholics, you know, cannot be "conciliated," except by licence to plunder your friends; while the few English Roman Catholics will generally sympathise with the Irish of the same classes. Having no personal interest in the matter, they will be led by their priests; and their priests, often Irish by birth, are nearly always Irish

by sympathy. There is only one doubtful English constituency where English Roman Catholics are perhaps strong enough to affect the balance of power—that is the Lancaster Division ; and the recent elections there are highly instructive. In 1885, when Mr Parnell and the priests urged them to vote against the Liberal Government, a Conservative was returned by a majority of 857 ; in 1886, when he lost their support, a Gladstonian displaced him by a majority of 195. The Irish alone could not have caused this reverse. For the district is mainly agricultural.

134. The Pope is not worth conciliating. He cannot do any good, and he is too good a man to do any harm. I desire to speak with all respect of Leo XIII. He is one of the few to whom the title of Holiness may be applied without provoking a smile or a frown ; but he is not the Papacy. He has done his best, and his best is nothing ; he has thundered, and his bolt is a *brutum fulmen*. The "most Catholic nation of Europe" treats the Holy Father with undisguised contempt, when he preaches a righteousness which does not suit the passions and the pockets of the majority. Only three bishops out of twenty-eight even ordered the Rescript to be read in their churches ; and only Bishop O'Dwyer of Limerick has taken any step to enforce obedience. Elsewhere nothing has been done to punish contumacious priests ; and Rome will do nothing to punish the contumacious prelates. The Pope cannot even prevent the firebrand of Gweedore from disturbing the parish of his peaceful neigh-

bour. His arm is held in an unseen grip. Behind him lurks the real master of the Church's policy, the General of the Jesuits.

135. The sinister society, which nearly all civilised Governments have at some time had to expel from their dominions, and which even the Pope once felt bound to suppress, does not object to a decent show of regard for truth and justice, honesty and Christian charity. But it will not let the Pope go beyond a show. It will never allow such paltry things to interfere with its own power, or the material grandeur of the ancient hierarchy whose framework it animates and controls. Ireland is the one country of Europe where the priest is pampered and popular. Can any one seriously suppose that Rome will do anything to disgust and estrange the people of a country where a parish priest can, like Father MacGarvey[1] of Millford (in Donegal), save £23,000 out of the fees of his flock? You may be quite sure that the thinly disguised Episcopal author of " The Papacy—a Revelation and a Prophecy,"[2] did not prophesy without knowing, when he told us that the Rescript would remain a dead letter. He gives one reason of much weight—viz., that the Irish are the indispensable missionaries of the Church in English-speaking countries. But there is one still weightier, about which he is discreetly silent. The Irish on both sides of the Atlantic are the great paymasters of the Roman Church. Their own priests are their obedient, if not outwardly humble servants—equally ready to lead or

[1] Hurlbert, p. 398.   [2] Contemporary Review, August 1889.

to follow the multitude to do evil ; "retained to give the sanction of religion to the conduct, whatever it be, which the majority chooses."[1] The Vatican cannot afford to quarrel with the Irish. Without their support it would soon be bankrupt.

136. My Lords of Salisbury and Hartington, listen, I beseech you! To know and to measure rightly the living human forces which may be turned into useful channels—is not this the first and greatest canon of the art of statesmanship ? The Orange feeling of Ulster is a great force, a force which makes up by intensity and persistence for the limitation of its area. It is your Old Guard, that will die but never surrender. The Protestant feeling of England and Scotland is wider and stiller, but it also is deep, and when fairly set in motion its momentum will be overwhelming. The English Roman Catholics are not a force of appreciable magnitude, and if you can gain their support by any means, it must be by means which will disgust a hundred times their number of Scotch and English Protestants. You can do it only by winning over the priesthood of the United Kingdom, through official favour and lavish expenditure in Ireland. The offer of a university is simply ludicrous. Will the taxpayers allow you to give £500 a-year to every Irish parish priest, and £5000 a-year to every Irish bishop ? You could not really "conciliate" them by any smaller provision. And if you did succeed in buying them, you would find that you had not bought a single Irish seat in the House of

---

[1] Whately's Life, p. 333.

Commons. As Sir Henry Blake[1] has so well explained, the Irish priest leads the politics of his flock only as a horse leads the cart in which it is driven.

137. Give up this paltry angling for fractional votes, and trust yourselves to the mighty current of Protestant enthusiasm! You can afford to despise cant about bigotry. Your quarrel is not with the good Pope, but with priests like MacFadden, with prelates like Archbishops Croke and Walsh, and with the anti-Christian Society which now curries favour with tyrant rowdies, as of old with tyrant kings and tyrant nobles. What have you gained by your notable device of choosing a perfectly untried Home Secretary, simply because he was a Roman Catholic? His accession to the Cabinet has been at times embarrassing to his colleagues, and detrimental to the party. Translate Jonah to a screner sphere, if you wish in earnest to prevent the arch - enemy from fulfilling the worst of Lord Palmerston's prophetic alternatives.

---

[1] See the sketch of Father Morrissey in ' Pictures from Ireland,' by Terence Magrath.

APPENDIX.

SCHEDULE I.

THE GRAND DUCHY OF ULSTER.

(*a*) The entire counties of Antrim (including Carrick-fergus), Armagh, Down, Londonderry, Louth (including Drogheda), Monaghan, and Tyrone.

(*b*) The county of Donegal, excluding the town of Bun-doran and the five townlands of Ardfarn, Drumacrin, Ma-gheracar, Rathglass, and Rathmore, in the parish of Innis-macsaint.

(*c*) The county of Fermanagh ; except the three townlands of Agho, Ross, and Tullygerravra, in the parish of Boho ; the eighteen townlands of Aghamuldowney, Barr of Drumgormly, Barr of Slattinagh, Carran West, Cashelnadrea, Dog Big, Dog Little, Frevagh, Garrison, Gortecn, Knocknashangan, Scrib-bagh, Slattinagh, Slisgarran, Stranacally, Tower Beg, Tower More, and Tullysranageega, in the parish of Devenish ; and the fifteen townlands of Cornadarum, Corramore, Drumnas-reane, Garvros, Glen East, Glen West, Killymore, Knockare-van, Leglehid, Meencloyabane, Muckenagh, Muggalnagrow, Slisgarran, Tullyloughdaugh, and Tullymore, with the islands in Lough Melvin, all in the parish of Innismacsaint.

(*d*) In the county of Cavan, the entire parishes of Anna-gelliff, Annagh, Bailieborough, Castleterra, Drumlane, Drung

Enniskeen, Kildallan, Kildrumsherdan, Killashandra, Kilmore, Knockbride, Larah, Moybolgue, Shercock, Tomregan, and Urney; also the parish of Killinkere, except the two townlands of Drumfomina and Drummallaght; the parish of Kinawley, except the four townlands of Dunmakeever, Eshveagh, Tonanilt, and Tullycrafton; also in the parish of Ballintemple, the two townlands of Coolnacarrick and Rabrackan; in the parish of Crosserlough, the five townlands of Aghaconny, Cashel, Gortachurk, Kilmainham, and Mullaghkeel; in the parish of Denn the seventeen townlands of Acres, Aghadreenagh, Ardlougher, Ardvarny, Banagher, Cornamahon, Cornaseer, Corrakane, Corraweelis, Crumlin, Drumavaddy, Drumcrow, Gallon Glebe, Killycannon, Kilnacreevy, Pollakeel, and Shannon; in the parish of Lavey, the twenty townlands of Aghadreenagh, Beaghy, Cargagh, Corragho, Corrawillin, Cuttragh, Derryglen, Drumgora, Drumhillagh, Drumbirk, Feaugh, Gortnakillen, Grellagh, Killyconnan, Kilnavar, Knockanoark, Lateevy, Lavey, Leiter, and Mullymagowan; in the parish of Mullagh, the thirteen townlands of Annagarnet, Ardlow, Crossbane, Crosscarn, Crossreagh, Doon, Enagh, Greaghclogh, Greaghnadarragh, Lenanavra, Lisnabantry, Lisnahederna, and Secharan; in the parish of Templeport, the nine townlands of Bofealan, Burren, Coologe, Crossmakelagher, Drumane, Killynaff, Lecharrownahone, Toberlyan, Duffin, and Tonyrevan.

(c) In the county of Dublin, the baronies of Balrothery East and West, Nethercross and Castleknock; the barony of Coolock, except the town of Drumcondra, Clonliffe and Glasnevin; the barony of Dublin, except the parish of St Mark, and so much of the parish of Donnybrook as is included in the Dublin Harbour Parliamentary Division; in the barony of Rathdown, the parishes of Booterstown, Dalkey, Donnybrook, Kilmacud, Monkstown, and Stillorgan; with the town of Kingstown and the townlands of Galloping Green North, and Newtonpark in the parish of Kill, the town of Rathmines and Rathgar in the parish of Rathfarnham, and the town of Clonskeagh and six townlands of Friarland, Mount

Anville, Mount Merrion, Mount Merrion South, Roebuck, and Trimleston in the parish of Taney; in the barony of Uppercross, the parishes of Donnybrook, St Catherine, St James, St Jude, St Nicholas, and St Peter.

(*f*) In the city of Dublin, the premises of Trinity College.

(*g*) In the county of Leitrim, the parish of Carrigallen, except the townlands of Gortermone and South Tully.

(*h*) In the county of Meath, the baronies of Duleek, Upper and Lower, Dunboyne, Morgallion, Ratoath, Skreen, Slane, Upper and Lower; the barony of Upper Deece, except the parishes of Agher and Rathcore; in the barony of Lower Deece, the parishes of Derrypatrick, Kiltale, and Knockmark; the barony of Lower Kells, except the parishes of Emlagh and Newtown, the town and townland of Carlanstown in the parish of Kilbeg, and the fifteen townlands of Ballintlieve, Baltrasna, Bawn, Billywood, Curraghtown, Donore, Farrana-doony, Glebe, Moynalty, Rathbane, Rathwire, Upper and Lower, Rathstephen, Shancarnan, and Walterstown, in the parish of Moynalty; in the barony of Lower Navan, the parish of Dunmoe, and the parish of Donaghmore, except the town of Navan, and the three townlands of Nevinstown, Rathaldron, and Windtown.

Total area, 8973 square miles.

Total population in 1881—

Present Province,	.	.	1,743,075	Protestants, Jews, &c.,	909,509
Deduct—					
In Cavan .	.	48,422		4,469	
In Donegal	.	1,761		222	
In Fermanagh	.	2,750		550	
			52,933		5,241
			1,690,142		904,268
Add—					
In Dublin		126,264 (approximate)		41,517	
In Leitrim		3,904		1,252	
In Louth .		77,684		6,505	
In Meath .		40,017		2,069	
			247,869		51,343
			1,938,011 (R. C. 982,400)		955,611

Roman Catholic majority, 26,789 [excluding Trinity College.]

I

SCHEDULE II.

NEW BARONIES.

The Arabic figures in dark type indicate the general number.

I.—ANTRIM.

1.   1. *Cary.*—The parishes of Armoy, Ballintoy, Culf-eightrin, Grange of Drumtullagh, Ramoan, Rathlin.   Population 11,993, of whom 6824 are Protestants.

2.   2. *Lower Dunluce.*—The parishes of Ballyrashane, Ballywillin, Billy, Derrykeighan, and Dunluce.   Population, 11,684; Protestants, 11,017.

3.   3. *Upper Dunluce.*—The parishes of Ballymoney, Kildollagh, and Kilraghts.   Population, 10,548; Protestants, 8977.

4.   4. *Kilconway.*—The parishes of Finvoy and Rasharkin, except the three townlands of Dromore, Dunminning, and Killycowan, in the latter.   Population, 10,172; Protestants, 6850.

5.   5. *Route.*—The parishes of Dunaghy, Grange of Dundermot, Killagan, Loughguile, and Newtown Crommelin.   Population, 10,960; Protestants, 6926.

6.   6. *Glenarm.*—The parishes of Ardclinis, the present barony of Lower Glenarm, the parishes of Carncastle, Grange of Innispollan, Grange of Layd, Layd, and Tickmacrevan, with the three townlands of Capanagh, Mullaghsandal, and Skeagh in the parish of Kilwaughter.   Population, 10,696; Protestants, 4200.

7.   7. *Broughshane.*—The parishes of Racavan and Skerry, except the townland of Lower Broughshane in the former.   Population, 9091; Protestants, 7471.

8.   8. *Ballymena.*—The town of Ballymena; the three townlands of Ballyloughan, Brocklamont, and Caruiny, in the parish of Ahoghill; the three townlands of Bottom,

Dunclug, and Town Parks, in the parish of Kirkinriola; the townland of Ballykeel, in the parish of Ballyclug; and the townland of Lower Broughshane, in the parish of Racavan. Population, 10,620; Protestants, 8520.

9. 9. *Upper Clandeboye.*—The parish of Craigs, except the townlands of Ballyconnelly and Fenaghy; the parish of Kirkinriola, except the town of Ballymena, and the three townlands of Bottom, Dunclug, and Town Parks; the townlands of Cardonaghy and Leymore, in the parish of Ahoghill; and the townlands of Dromore. Dunminning and Killycowan

ERRATA IN SCHEDULE II.

For "No. 15," read "No. 19."	For "No. 18," read "No. 15."
„ "No. 16," „ "No. 20."	„ "No. 19," „ "No. 18."
„ "No. 17," „ "No. 21."	„ "No. 20," „ "No. 17."

For "No. 21," read "No. 16."

12. 12. *Toome.*—The parishes of Ballyscullion, Grange of Ballyscullion, and Portglenone; the nine townlands of the parish of Duneane named as excluded from Lower Clandeboye. Population, 10,478; Protestant, 6824.

13. 13. *Connor.*—The parish of Ballyclug, except the town of Ballymena, and the townland of Ballykeel; the parish of Connor, except the townlands of Scolboa, Slaght, Tardree, and Tullaghgarley; the townlands of Ballynulto, Clatteryknowes, Crosshill, Glenwhirry, Greenhill, Kernyhill, and Kinnegalliagh, in the parish of Glenwhirry. Population, 8996; Protestants, 8182.

SCHEDULE II.

NEW BARONIES.

The Arabic figures in dark type indicate the general number.

I.—ANTRIM.

1 1 *Cary.*—The parishes of Armoy, Ballintoy, Culf-

barony of Lower Glenarm, the parishes of Carncastle, Grange of Innispollan, Grange of Layd, Layd, and Tickmacrevan, with the three townlands of Capanagh, Mullaghsandal, and Skeagh in the parish of Kilwaughter. Population, 10,696; Protestants, 4200.

7. 7. *Broughshane.*—The parishes of Racavan and Skerry, except the townland of Lower Broughshane in the former. Population, 9091; Protestants, 7471.

8. 8. *Ballymena.*—The town of Ballymena; the three townlands of Ballyloughan, Brocklamont, and Carniny, in the parish of Ahoghill; the three townlands of Bottom,

Dunclug, and Town Parks, in the parish of Kirkinriola; the townland of Ballykeel, in the parish of Ballyclug; and the townland of Lower Broughshane, in the parish of Racavan. Population, 10,620; Protestants, 8520.

9. 9. *Upper Clandeboye.*—The parish of Craigs, except the townlands of Ballyconnelly and Fenaghy; the parish of Kirkinriola, except the town of Ballymena, and the three townlands of Bottom, Dunclug, and Town Parks; the townlands of Cardonaghy and Leymore, in the parish of Ahoghill; and the townlands of Dromore, Dunminning, and Killycowan, in the parish of Rasharkin. Population, 10,075; Protestants, 9093.

10. 10. *Middle Clandeboye.* — The parish of Ahoghill, except the town of Ballymena, and the five townlands of Ballyloughan, Brocklamont, Cardonaghy, Carniny, and Leymore; the townlands of Slaght and Tullaghgarley, in the parish of Connor; the townlands of Ballyconnelly and Fenaghy, in the parish of Craigs; and the three townlands of Ballymacilroy, Cloghogue, and Downkillybegs, in the parish of Drummaul. Population, 8646; Protestants, 7731.

11. 11. *Lower Clandeboye.*—The parish of Cranfield; the parish of Drummaul, except the three townlands of Ballymacilroy, Cloghogue, and Downkillybegs; the parish of Duneane, except the nine townlands of Brecart, Cloghogue, Drumraymond, Gortgill, Killyfast, Moneyglass, Muckrim, Toome, and Intake. Population, 10,255; Protestants, 5951.

12. 12. *Toome.*—The parishes of Ballyscullion, Grange of Ballyscullion, and Portglenone; the nine townlands of the parish of Duneane named as excluded from Lower Clandeboye. Population, 10,478; Protestant, 6824.

13. 13. *Connor.*—The parish of Ballyclug, except the town of Ballymena, and the townland of Ballykeel; the parish of Connor, except the townlands of Scolboa, Slaght, Tardree, and Tullaghgarley; the townlands of Ballynulto, Clatteryknowes, Crosshill, Glenwhirry, Greenhill, Kernyhill, and Kinnegalliagh, in the parish of Glenwhirry. Population, 8996; Protestants, 8182.

14. 14. *Antrim.*—The parishes of Antrim, Donegore, Grange of Nilltecn, Grange of Shilvodan, and Kilbride; the townlands of Scolboa, and Tardree, in the parish of Connor. Population, 8729; Protestants, 7658.

15. 15. *Lower Massereene.*—The present barony of Lower Massereene, and the parishes of Templepatrick and Bally-martin. Population, 8940; Protestant, 8099.

16. 16. *Upper Massereene.*—The parishes of Aghagallon, Aghalee, Ballinderry, Camlin, Glenavy, and Tullyrusk. Population, 10,573; Protestants, 6686.

17. 17. *Killultagh.* — The parishes of Blaris (outside Lisburn), Derryaghy, Lambeg (outside Lisburn), Magheragall, and Magheramesk. Population, 11,145; Protestants, 9239.

18. 18. *Moylinny.*—The parishes of Ballycor, Ballynure, Grange of Doagh, and Rashee; the six townlands of Brae-town, Douglas, Glenhead, Jockey's Quarter, Mistyburn, and Skerrywhirry, in the parish of Glenwhirry; and the seven townlands of Ballycalket, Ballygallagh, Ballyhowne, Bally-linny, Ballywalter, Bruslee, and Lisnalinchy, in the parish of Ballylinny. Population, 9479; Protestants, 9119.

19. 19. *Carnmoney.*—The parish of Carnmoney, the town of Mossbeg, and the four townlands of Ballycarl, Carntall, Kingsbog, and Straidnahanna, in the parish of Ballylinny; and the three townlands of Ballybought, Ballyvaston, and Ballywonard, in the parish of Shankill. Population, 9236; Protestants, 7641.

20. 20. *Carrickfergus.*—The parishes of Carrickfergus, Kilroot, and Templecorran. Population, 11,770; Protes-tants, 10,504.

21. 21. *Larne.*—The parishes of Glynn, Grange of Killy-glen, Inver, Island, Magee, Larne, and Raloo; also the parish of Kilwaughter, except the three townlands of Capanagh, Mullaghsandal, and Skeagh. Population, 13,682; Protes-tants, 11,865.

(721 ought to be deducted in each case as passengers on an American ship in the harbour.)

II.—COUNTY OF BELFAST (also No. 105).

22. 1. *Ligoniel.*—The parish of Drumbeg (in the present county of Antrim), and the parish of Shankill, excluding the municipal borough of Belfast and the three townlands of Ballybought, Ballyvaston, and Ballywonard. Population, 11,661; Protestants, 9304.

23. 2. *Holywood.*—The parish of Holywood, except the six townlands of Ballycultra, Ballydavey, Ballygrainey, Ballymenagh, Ballyrobert, and Craigavad; also the parish of Knockbreda, excluding the municipal borough of Belfast and the four townlands of Ballydollaghan, Gilnahirk, Gortgrib, and Tullycarnet. Population, 10,712; Protestants, 9631.

III.—COUNTY DOWN.

24. 1. *Bangor.*—The parish of Bangor; the six townlands of Ballycultra, Ballydavey, Ballygrainey, Ballymenagh, Ballyrobert, and Craigavad, in the the parish of Holywood; and the townlands of Ballymoney and Craigogantlet, in the parish of Newtownards. Population, 8614; Protestants, 8134.

25. 2. *Lower Ards.*—The parishes of Ballywalter, Donaghadee, and Grey Abbey; and the seven townlands of Ballyblack, Ballyhaft, Ballywatticock, Crossnamuckley, Cunningburn, Drumawhy, and Loughriscouse, in the parish of Newtownards. Population, 10,217; Protestants, 9960.

26. 3. *Newtownards.*—The parish of Newtownards, except the townlands included in the baronies of Bangor and Lower Ards. Population, 10,688; Protestant, 9792.

27. 4. *Lower Castlereagh.*—The parishes of Dundonald, Kilmood, and Tullynakill; the parish of Comber, except the five townlands of Ballygowan, Clontonakelly, Edenslate, Monlough, and Tullygarvan; and the three townlands of Gilnahirk, Gortnagrib, and Tullycarnet, in the parish of Knockbreda. Population, 9611; Protestants, 9322.

28. 5. *Upper Castlereagh.*—The parishes of Drumbo and Killanney; the parish of Saintfield, except the townland of Lisowen; the five townlands of Comber not included in the barony of Lower Castlereagh; the seven townlands of Augh-nadarragh, Ballycloghan, Ballygowan, Barnamaghery, Carrick-mannan, Drumreagh, and Ravara, in the parish of Killinchy; the townland of Ballydollaghan, in the parish of Knock-breda; and the three townlands of Creevytenant, Glasdrum-man, and Magheraknock, in the parish of Magheradrool. Population, 11,203; Protestants, 10,171.

29. 6. *Kilwarlin.* — The parishes of Blaris (outside Lisburn), Drumbeg, Hillsborough, and Lambeg, in the present county of Down. Population, 11,075; Protestants, 10,296.

30. 7. *Dromara.*—The parishes of Annahilt and Drom-ara; the five townlands of Ballykeel, Drumlough, Growell, Kinallen, and Lappoges, in the parish of Dromore; the townlands of Ballycreen and Lower Ballykine (north half), in the parish of Magheradrool; and the townlands of Bally-kine and Burren, in the parish of Magherahamlet. Popula-tion, 8351; Protestants, 6679.

31. 8. *Moira.*—The parishes of Magheralin (in county Down) and Moira; the parish of Donaghcloney, except the townlands of Corcreeny and Cornreany. Population, 9292; Protestants, 7854.

32. 9. *Dromore.*—The parish of Dromore, except the five townlands included in the barony of Dromara; the five townlands of Carnew, Enagh, Fedany, Garvaghy, and Tulli-nisky, in the parish of Garvaghy. Population, 10,135; Protestants, 8752.

33. 10. *Banbridge.*—The parishes of Magherally and Seapatrick; the townland of Lenaderg, in the parish of Tullylish. Population, 11,242; Protestants, 8994.

34. 11. *Lower Iveagh.*—The parish of Annaclone; the parish of Drumgooland, except the six townlands of Backa-derry, Ballymaginahy, Ballymagreehan, Legananny, Leitrim, and Magheramayo; the parish of Garvaghy, except the five townlands included in the barony of Dromore; the six town-lands of Annahunshigo, Ballybrick, Ballyroney, Lackan, Lis-navahrog, and Seafin, in the parish of Drumballyroney; and

the townland of Shanaghan, in the parish of Newry. Population, 9785; Protestants, 5916.

35. 12. *Upper Iveagh.*—The parish of Clonduff; the parish of Drumballyroney, except the six townlands included in the barony of Lower Iveagh; the parish of Drumgath, except the four townlands of Ballydoo, Ballykeel, Carnany, and Drumgath. Population, 11,080; Protestants, 5918.

36. 13. *West Iveagh.*—The parishes of Aghaderg and Donaghmore; the rural part of Newry, except the eight townlands of Ballyholland, Upper and Lower, Benagh, Crobane, Derryleckagh, Edenmore, Greenan, and Shanaghan; the five townlands of Bavan, Cabragh, Carrickcrossan, Croan, and Cullion, in the parish of Clonallan; and the four townlands of Ballydoo, Ballykeel, Carnany, and Drumgath, in the parish of Drumgath. Population, 11,603; Protestants, 6132.

37. 14. *Rosstrevor.*—The parishes of Kilbroney and Warrenpoint; the parish of Clonallan, except the five townlands included in the barony of West Iveagh; the seven townlands of Ballyholland, Upper and Lower, Benagh, Crobane, Derryleckagh, Edenmore, and Greenan, in the parish of Newry. Population, 10,030; Protestants, 2871.

38. 15. *Mourne.*—The present barony of Mourne. Population, 11,691; Protestants, 5362.

39. 16. *Castlewellan.*—The parishes of Ballykinler, Kilcoo, and Maghera; the parish of Kilmegan, except the four townlands of Ballywillwill, Clonvaraghan, Drumanaquoile, and Slievenisky; and the three townlands of Ballymaginahy, Ballymagrechan, and Magheramayo, in the parish of Drumgooland. Population, 10,968; Protestants, 4379.

40. 17. *Kinelarty.*—The parish of Loughinisland; the parish of Magheradrool, except the four townlands and a half included in the baronies of Dromara and Upper Castlereagh; the parish of Magherahamlet, except the two townlands included in the barony of Dromara; the four townlands of Ballywillwill, Clonvaraghan, Drumanaquoile, and Slievenisky, in the parish of Kilmegan; the three townlands of Backaderry, Legananny, and Leitrim, in the parish of Drumgooland; and the townland of Magheralone, in the parish of Kilmore. Population, 10,777; Protestants, 6282.

41. 18. *Dufferin.*—The parish of Killyleagh, except the townland of Mullagh; the parish of Kilmore, except the three townlands of Magheralone, Murvaclogher, and Ross-connor; the parish of Killinchy, except the seven townlands included in the barony of Upper Castlereagh; and the town-land of Lisowen, in the parish of Saintfield. Population, 11,478; Protestants, 9112.

42. 19. *Upper Lecale.*—The parishes of Inch and Saul; the parish of Down, except the six townlands of Bally-donnell, Ballystrew, Corbally, Grangicam, Marshallstown, and Tobercorran; the three townlands of Carrownacaw, Loughmoney, and Slievenagriddle, in the parish of Ballee; the five townlands of Audleystown, Ballintlieve, Castleward, Raholp, and Tullyratty, in the parish of Ballyculter; the townlands of Murvaclogher and Rossconnor, in the parish of Kilmore; and the townland of Mullagh, in the parish of Killyleagh. Population, 9060; Protestants, 4774.

43. 20. *Lower Lecale.*—The parishes of Ardglass, Bright, Dunsfort, Kilchief, Rathmullan, and Tyrella; the parish of Ballee, except the three townlands included in the barony of Upper Lecale; the parish of Ballyculter, except the five townlands included in the said barony; and the six town-lands of Ballydonnell, Ballystrew, Corbally, Grangicam, Marshallstown, and Tobercorran, in the parish of Down. Population, 8149; Protestants, 2670.

44. 21. *Upper Ards.*—The present barony of Upper Ards, except the parish of Ballywalter. Population, 9709; Protestants, 5447.

IV.—County Armagh.

45. 1. *Clancann.*—The parish of Killyman (in Armagh); the parish of Tartaraghan, except the townlands of Derrin-raw and Derrykeeran; the five townlands of Annaghnaboe, Aughamullan, Derryloughan, Derrytresk, and Drummurrer, in the parish of Clonoe; the eight townlands of Cannagola

Beg, Cannagola More, Canoneill, Derrylettif, Drumlellum, Roughan, Timulkenny, and Unshinagh, in the parish of Drumcree; the three townlands of Annaghmore, Ardress East, and Derrycoose, in the parish of Loughgall. Population, 9351; Protestants, 5708.

46. 2. *Clanbrassil.*—The parish of Montiaghs; the parish of Drumcree, except the town of Portadown, and the twenty-one townlands included in the baronies of Portadown and Clancann; and the townlands of Derrinraw and Derrykeeran, in the parish of Tartaraghan. Population, 8927; Protestants, 5145.

47. 3. *Portadown.*—In the parish of Drumcree, the town of Portadown, and the thirteen townlands of Annagh, Astabrackagh, Ballyworkan, Baltylum, Clownagh, Corcrain, Drumnakelly, Drumnasoo, Garvaghy, Kilmoriarty, Maghon, Mullantine, and Tavanagh; in the parish of Seagoe, the town of Portadown, and the townlands of Edenderry and Levaghery; in the parish of Kilmore, the townland of Ballintaggart. Population, 10,628; Protestants, 8078.

48. 4. *O'Neilland, East.*—The parish of Shankill (in Down and Armagh), except the town of Lurgan; the parish of Magheralin (in Armagh); the parish of Seagoe, except the town of Portadown and the townlands of Edenderry and Levaghery. Population, 10,286; Protestants, 7815.

49. 5. *Gilford.*—The parish of Tullylish, except the townland of Lenaderg; the townlands of Corcreeny and Cornreany, in the parish of Donaghcloney. Population, 10,352; Protestants, 7802.

50. 6. *Lower Orior.*—The parish of Ballymore; that part of the parish of Kilmore which lies within the present barony of Lower Orior, except the townland of Cornascreeb; that part of the parish of Loughgilly which lies within the present barony of Lower Orior, except the nine townlands of Corrinure, Crankey, Drumcrow, Drummond, Keady Beg, Lesh, Lisnalee, Maytone, and Rathcarbry; and the townlands of Cabragh and Drumart, in the parish of Mullaghbrack. Population, 10,339; Protestants, 8136.

51. 7. *Middle Orior.*—The parish of Killevy, except the twenty-four townlands included in the new barony of Upper Orior; the parish of Newry, except the town of Newry, and the four townlands of Upper and Lower Fathom and Upper and Lower Grange; the ten townlands of Crankey, Creggan Lower, Drumharriff, Drummond, Keady Beg, Lesh, Lisadian, Lisnalee, Rathcarbry, and Tullywinny in the parish of Lough-gilly; the townland of Lisnalee, in the parish of Forkhill. Population, 11,697; Protestants, 6002.

52. 8. *Lower Fews.*—The parishes of Ballymyre and Kilclooney; the parish of Mullaghbrack, except the eighteen townlands of Ballygroobany, Ballynewry, Cabragh, Carrow-money, Corry, Drumart, Drumman, Drumnagloy, Drumorgan, Hamilton's Bawn, Johnstown, Killyruddan, Macantrim, Mar-lacoo Beg, Marlacoo More, Mullaghbane, Rocks, and Teemore, and the town of Hamilton's Bawn; the town of Glenanne, and the fifteen townlands of Belleek, Carrickananny, Carrick-gallogly, Carrowmannan, Creggan Upper, Counagh, Derlett, Drumgane, Drumnahoney, Drumnahunshin, Greybillan, Lis-drumchor, Upper and Lower, Lurgyross, and Tullyah, in the parish of Loughgilly. Population, 10,863; Protestants, 6471.

53. 9. *O'Neilland, West.*—The parish of Kildarton; that part of the parish of Kilmore which lies in the present barony of O'Neilland West, except the townland of Ballin-taggart; also the townland of Cornascreeb, in the same parish; the sixteen townlands of Ballygroobany, Ballynewry, Carrow-money, Corry, Drumman, Drumnagloy, Drumorgan, Hamil-ton's Bawn, Johnstown, Killyruddan, Macantrim, Marlocoo Beg, Marlocoo More, Mullaghbane, Rocks, and Teemore, and the town of Hamilton's Bawn, in the parish of Mullaghbrack; the townlands of Upper and Lower Grange, in the parish of Newry; and the townlands of Drumnasoo and Turcarra, in the parish Loughgall. Population, 8864; Protestants, 7231.

54. 10. *Charlemont.* — The parishes of Cloufeacle and Grange; the parish of Eglish, except the townlands of Aughrafin and Navan; the parish of Loughgall, except the five townlands of Annaghmore, Ardress East, Derrycoose,

Drummasoo, and Turcarra; the townlands of Killuney and Tullyworgle, in the parish of Armagh. Population, 10,434; Protestants, 5885.

55.   11. *Armagh.*—The parish of Armagh, except the townlands of Killuney and Tullyworgle; the six townlands of Ballyheridan, Ballynahonebeg, Cavanacaw, Farmacaffy, Kennedies, and Moneypatrick, in the parish of Lisnadill; and the townland of Navan, in the parish of Eglish. Population, 11,817; Protestants, 6042.

56.   12. *Tiranny.*—The parish of Tynan; the parish of Derrynoose, except the townland of Drumherney; the twelve townlands of Aghavilly, Ballyards, Ballycoffey, Baltarran, Enagh, Killynure, Lisbanoe, Lisdrumard, Lislea, Magherarville, Moneyquin, and Tirearly, in the parish of Lisnadill; the townland of Aughrafin, in the parish of Eglish; and the townlands of Brackley and Crossnamoyle, in the parish of Keady. Population, 10,242; Protestants, 4475.

57.   13. *Keady.*—The parish of Keady, except the townlands of Brackley and Crossnamoyle; the parish of Lisnadill, except the part included in the present barony of Armagh, and the new baronies of Armagh and Tiranny; the townland of Drumherney, in the parish of Derrynoose. Population, 10,702; Protestants, 4842.

58.   14. *Middle Fews.*—The parishes of Muckno and Newtown-Hamilton; the five townlands of Cullyhanna, Big and Little, Drumlougher, Teer, and Teer Island, in the parish of Creggan; and the four townlands of Annahale, Conera, Corragarta, and Drumcrew, in the parish of Clontibret. Population, 11,476; Protestants, 4826.

V.—COUNTY TYRONE.

59.   1. *Lower Tirkeeran.*—The parishes of Clondermot (outside the city of Londonderry) and Faughanvale; the parish of Lower Cumber, except the ten townlands of Ardground, Brackfield, Gosheden, Kildoag, Killaloo, Lackagh, Legaghory, Lettermire, Oughtagh, and Toneduff. Population, 11,209; Protestants, 6664.

60. 2. *Upper Tirkeeran.*—The parishes of Banagher, Upper Cumber, and Learmount (in Tyrone and Londonderry); the ten townlands of Ardground, Brackfield, Gosheden, Kildoag, Killaloo, Lackagh, Legaghory, Lettermire, Oughtagh, and Toneduff, in the parish of Lower Cumber; the three townlands of Ballymoney, Farkland, and Muldonagh, in the parish of Bovevagh; and the townland of Ovil, in the parish of Dungiven. Population, 10,812; Protestants, 4344.

61. 3. *Upper Keenaght.*—The parishes of Balteagh and Carrick; the parish of Dungiven, except the townland of Ovil; and the parish of Bovevagh, except the three townlands of Ballymoney, Farkland, and Muldonagh. Population, 9154; Protestants, 4829.

62. 4. *Lower Keenaght.* — The parishes of Aghanloo, Drumachose, Magilligan, and Tamlaght-Finlagan. Population, 10,980; Protestants, 6929.

63. 5. *Coleraine.*—The present barony of the North-east Liberties of Coleraine. Population, 10,233; Protestants, 9063.

64. 6. *Creeve or Clankane.*—The parishes of Agivey, Dunboe, Formoyle, Killowen, and Macosquin; the twenty-eight townlands of Ballinrees, Ballybritain, Ballycaghan, Ballyclough, Ballydevitt, Ballylintagh, Ballywillin, Clarehill, Clintagh, Collins, Cornamucklagh, Craiglea Glebe, Crevolea, Crosscanley Glebe, Crossmakeever, Culdrum, Cullycapple, Drumsteeple, Glenkeen, Keely, Killengae, Knockaduff, Lisnamuck, Managher, Moneybrannon, Mullan, Rusky, and Scalty, in the parish of Aghadowey. Population, 11,231; Protestants, 9407.

65. 7. *Garvagh.* — The parishes of Desertoghill and Errigal; and the parish of Aghadowey, except the twenty-eight townlands included in the barony of Creeve. Population, 9682; Protestants, 6236.

66. 8. *Clandonnel.*—The parishes of Kilrea and Tamlaght O'Crilly; the five townlands of Ballymacombs Beg and More, and Ballyncase (Helton, Macpeake, and Strain), in Ballyscullion; and the townland of Ballymacpeake, in the parish of Maghera. Population, 10,736; Protestants, 5943.

67. 9. *Maghera.*—The parish of Killelagh ; the parish of
Maghera, except the four townlands of Ballymacpeake,
Drumlamph, Rocktown, and Toberhead ; and the parish
of Termoneeny, except the three townlands of Broagh,
Cabragh, and Lemnaroy. Population, 11,156 ; Protestants,
4022.

68. 10. *Loughinsholin.*—The parishes of Ballynascreen
and Kilcronaghan ; the parish of Desertmartin, except the
townlands of Gortanewry and Tirgan. Population, 11,795 ;
Protestants, 3886.

69. 11. *Moyola.*—The parish of Magherafelt, except the
townlands of Ballymoghan Beg and More ; the parish of Ballyscullion, except the five townlands included in the barony of
Clandonnell ; the six townlands of Aughrim, Ballymaguigan,
Ballynagarve, Carraloan, Derrygarve, and the Creagh, in the
parish of Artrea ; the townlands of Ballycomlargy, and Lisalbanagh, in the parish of Desertlyn ; the three townlands
of Drumlamph, Rocktown, and Toberhead, in the parish of
Toberhead ; and the three townlands of Broagh, Cabragh,
and Lemnaroy, in the parish of Termoneeny. Population,
13,298 ; Protestants, 7555.

70. 12. *Killetragh.*—The parish of Desertlyn, except the
townlands of Ballycomlargy and Lisalbanagh ; the parish of
Lissan (in Armagh and Londonderry), except the three townlands of Broughderg and Upper and Lower Davagh ; the
six townlands of Ballindrum, Ballydawley, Ballygruby,
Doluskey, Maghadone, and Moneymore, with the town of
Moneymore, in the parish of Artrea ; the townlands of
Annahavil and Moneyhaw, in the parish of Arboe ; the
parish of Derryloran (in Londonderry), except the townlands of Cloghog and Terressan ; also the fourteen townlands of Ballymenagh, Ballynasollus, Claggan, Cluntydoon,
Coolreaghs, Craigs, Cranfield, Drumearn, Drumgarrell, Fee-
garran, Gortin, Killycurragh, Tullycall, and Tullygare, in
the parish of Derryloran (County Tyrone); and the nine
townlands of Ballynasollus, Beltonanean, Corvanaghan,
Doons, Drumnaglogh, Drumnamalta, Muntober, Tirmac-

shane, and Tulnacross, in the parish of Kildress. Population, 9128; Protestants, 5436.

71. 13. *Ballinderry.*—The parishes of Ballinderry and Tamlaught (in Londonderry and Tyrone); the parish of Artrea, in Londonderry, except the twelve townlands included in the baronies of Killetragh and Moyola; the parish of Artrea, in Tyrone, except the four townlands of Dufless, Knockanroe, Lurganboy, and Tullyconnell; the parish of Arboe, in Londonderry, except the townlands of Annahavil and Moneyhaw; and the eleven townlands of Annaghmore, Anneeter Beg and More, Ardean, Ballynargan, Cluntoe Quin, Drumenny (Conyngham, and Stewart), Kinturk, Mullaghwotragh, and Sessia, in the parish of Arboe (County Tyrone. Population, 9824; Protestants, 5399.

72. 14. *Mountjoy.*—The parish of Arboe (in Tyrone), except the eleven townlands included in the barony of Ballinderry; the parish of Clonoe, except the five townlands transferred to County Armagh (barony of Clancann); the parish of Donaghenry, except the eight townlands of Donaghey, Highcross, Lurgy, Roughan, Rousky, Sherrigrim, Tullagh Beg, and Tullagh More; and the three townlands of Creenagh, Gortgonis and Gortnaskea, with the town of Coal Island, in the parish of Tullyniskan; the parish of Bally-clog. Population, 10,514; Protestants, 4143.

73. 15. *Tullaghoge.* — The parish of Derryloran (in Tyrone), except the fourteen townlands included in the barony of Killetragh; the four townlands of Dufless, Knockanroe, Lurganboy, and Tullyconnell, in the parish of Artrea (County Tyrone); the thirty-six townlands of Annaghanam, Annaghmore, Annaghteige, Ballymully Glebe, Cady, Cross Glebe, Desertcreat, Donaghrisk, Downs, Drumraw, Gortacar (Doris, and Glassy), Gortagowan, Gortavilly, Gortfad, Grange, Killycolp, Killygarvan, Killyneedan, Kiltyclay, Kiltyclogher, Knockavaddy, Legacurry, Loughry Demesne, Low-Cross, Mullaghshantullagh, Rockdale, Sessiagh (Lindsay), Shivey, Skenarget, Tirnaskea (Bayly), Tullaghoge, Tully, Tullyard, Tullylagan, and Tullyodonnell, in the parish of Desertcreat; the twenty-four townlands of Clare, Clonty-feragh, Corchoney, Corkhill, Derrinleagh, Drum, Drumnacross, Upper and Lower, Glasmullagh, Glenarny, Gortin and Gortnagross, Kildress, Upper and Lower, Legnacash, Mackenny, Oaklands, Oritor, Strews, Tamlaght, Tamnaskeeny, Tattykeel, Terrywinny, and Tullyroan, in the parish of Kildress; the townland of High Cross, in the parish of Donaghenry; and the townlands of Cloghog and Terressan, in the parish of Derryloran (County Londonderry). Population, 9113; Protestants, 5828.

74. 16. *Upper Dungannon.*—The parish of Donaghmore, except the town of Granville, and the twenty-nine townlands included in the baronies of Lower Dungannon, Caledon, Aughnacloy, and Pomeroy; the parish of Tullyniskan, except the three townlands of Creenagh, Gortgoins, and Gortnaskea, and the town of Coal Island; the seven townlands of Donaghey, Lurgy, Roughan, Rousky, Sherrigrim, Tullagh Beg, and Tullagh More, in the parish of Donaghenry; the sixteen townlands of Annaghquin, Annahavil, Ballynacroy, Ballynakilly, Derryraghan, Drumballyhugh, Drumnillard, Finvey, Gortavale, Gortfad Glebe, Lammy, Lisnanane, Moree, Moynagh, Oughterard, and Tolvin, in the parish of Desertcreat; the twelve townlands of Congo, Creevagh Upper, Derraghadoan, Killybrackey, Killylack Glebe, Lurgaboy, Ranaghan, Ross Beg, Ross More, Tullycullion, Tullygun, and Tullyodonnell, in the parish of Drumglass; and the thirteen townlands of Claggan, Coolnaghry, Corkhill, Creeve, Crossdermot, Curlonan, Drumconnor, Drummond, Lisnagleer, Mulnagore, Skea, Thornhill Glebe, and Tullnagall, in the parish of Pomeroy. Population, 10,300; Protestants, 5000.

75. 17. *Lower Dungannon.* — The parish of Killyman; the parish of Drumglass, except the twelve townlands included in the barony of Upper Dungannon; the seventeen townlands of Alnavannog, Coolcush, Cormullagh, Derrycreevy (Knox), Donnydeade, Drumgormal, Dunscark, Killybracken, Lisdermot, Lismulrevy, Lissan, Moygashel, Mul-

boy, Mullaghdaly, Mullybrannon, Mullycarnon, and Staug-
more (Knox), in the parish of Clonfeacle ; and the nine
townlands of Ballysaggart, Cottagequinn, Derryveen, Esk-
ragh, Killymaddy (Knox), Killyquinn, Lisnahull, Mullagh-
adrolly, and Mullaghanagh, and the town of Granville, in
the parish of Donaghmore.　Population, 10,192 ; Protestants, 5446.

　　76.　18. *Caledon.*—The parish of Aghaloo, except the
eight townlands of Annagh, Annaghmore, Drumearn, Drummond, Edenageeragh, Glencrew, Mullaghmore West, and
Mulnahorn ; the parish of Clonfeacle, except the seventeen
townlands included in the barony of Lower Dungannon ;
the three townlands of Cullenramer, Reaskmore, and Derry-
hoar, in the parish of Donaghmore ; and the townlands of
Edentiloan, and Reskatirriff, in the parish of Carnteel.
Population, 10,297 ; Protestants, 6189.

　　77.　19. *Aughnacloy.*—The parish of Carnteel, except
the three townlands of Edentiloan, Reskatirriff, and Tulnavern (upper fragment); the parish of Killeeshill, except the
townlands of Ballynahaye and Cranlome ; the parish of
Errigal Keerogue, except the fifteen townlands included in
the new baronies of Clogher and Six Mile Cross ; the nine
townlands of Aghintober, Dristernan and Dredoit, Gorey,
Gortlenaghan and Derrykeel, Killylevin, Killymaddy (Evans),
Killymoyle, Lisgallon, Mullaghbane, and Tullyallen, in the
parish of Donaghmore ; and the eight townlands of Annagh,
Annaghmore, Drumearn, Drummond, Edenageeragh, Glencrew, Mullaghmore West, and Mulnahorn, in the parish of
Aghaloo.　Population, 10,152 ; Protestants, 5635.

　　78.　20. *Clogher.*—The parish of Clogher, except the
townland of Mount Stewart ; the parish of Aghalurcher (in
Tyrone); the nine townlands of Altcloghfin, Brackagh,
Culnaha, Errigal, Garvaghy, Gort, Kilgreen, Upper and
Lower, and Rarogan, in the parish of Errigal Keerogue.
Population, 11,745 ; Protestants, 5506.

　　79.　21. *Fintona.*—The parish of Donacavey, except the
eleven townlands of Attaghmore, Baronagh, Blackfort, Dun-

namona, Edenafogry, Fallaghearn, Glennan, Killymoonan, Mullawinny, Skreen, and Tattymulmona; the parish of Dromore, except the townlands of Aghadulla (Harper), and Corrasheskin; and the townland of Mount Stewart, in the parish of Clogher. Population, 11,867; Protestants, 4278.

80. 22. *West Omagh.*—The parishes of East and West Longfield, except the seven townlands of the latter included in the new barony of Glenderg; the parish of Drumragh, except the thirty-nine townlands included in the new barony of East Omagh; and the townlands of Aghadulla (Harper), and Corrasheskin, in the parish of Dromore. Population, 11,633; Protestants, 4792.

81. 23. *East Omagh.*—The parish of Clogherney, except the townland of Mullaghslin Glebe; that part of the parish of Cappagh, which lies in the present barony of East Omagh; the sixteen townlands of Ballynamullan, Ballynaquilly, Boheragh, Cloghfin, Cranny, Crosk, Glencordial, Killybrack, Killyclogher, Killycurragh, Lisanelly, Lisnamallard, Maine, Mullaghmore, Racolpa, and Tirquin, with the towns of Lisnamallard, and Omagh (small part), in the parish of Cappagh and present barony of Upper Strabane; the thirty-nine townlands of Ballynahatty, Beagh, Blacksessagh, Coolnagard, Upper and Lower, Creevangar (Alexander, and White), Creevanmore (Crosby, and Hunter), Crucknamona, Dergmoney, Upper and Lower, Doogary, Drudgeon, Drum, Drumconnelly, Drumragh (Caldwell, J. MacCausland, and P. MacCausland), Drumshanly, Edergoole, Upper and Lower, Fireagh (Cochrane, and Gardiner), Freughmore, Gammy, Kiltamnagh, Kivlin, Lissan, Loughmuck (Alcorn, and Wallace), Meetinghouse-hill, Rakeeragh, Relaghdooey, Rylands, Sedannan, Stroancarbadagh, Tattykeel, and Tattyreagh Glebe, in the parish of Drumragh; the eleven townlands of Attaghmore, Baronagh, Blackfort, Dunnamona, Edenafogry, Fallaghearn, Glennan, Killymoonan, Mullawinny, Skreen, and Tattymulmona, in the parish of Donacavey; and the townlands of Baneran, and Deroran, in the parish of Termon Maquirk. Population, 10,613; Protestants, 5706.

K

82. 24. *Six Mile Cross.*—The parish of Termon Maquirk, except the townlands of Bancran and Deroran; the five townlands of Aghalane, Faccarry, Fernagh, Inisclan, and Killins, in the parish of Cappagh; the townland of Mullaghslin Glebe, in the parish of Clogherney; the six townlands of Altamooskan, Dunmoyle, Fallaghearn, Foremass, Upper and Lower, and Lurganboy, in the parish of Errigal Keerogue; and the townland of Tulnavern (upper fragment), in the parish of Carnteel. Population, 10,372; Protestants, 2512.

83. 25. *Pomeroy.*—The parish of Pomeroy, except the thirteen townlands included in the barony of Upper Dungannon; the fifteen townlands of Cavanoneill, Cloghfin, Drumshanbo Glebe, Dunnamore, Evishacrancussy, Evishanoran, Gortaclady, Gortreagh, Keenaghan, Killeenan, Killucan, Knockaleary, Magheraglass, Moboy, and Murnells, in the parish of Kildress; the seventeen townlands of Allen, Bardahessiagh, Carnenny, Derrygortanea, Derrylnash, Edendoit, Galcussagh, Gortindarragh, Limehill, Moneygaragh, Moymore, Mullynure, Pomeroy, Sessiagh (Scott), Skenahergney, Tirnaskea, and Tullyreavy, in the parish of Desertcreat; the eight townlands of Aghnagar, Altaglushan, Clonavaddy, Dernaseer, Derryalskea, Moghan, Reclain, and Toomog, in the parish of Donaghmore; and the townlands of Ballynahaye and Cranlome, in the parish of Killeeshill. Population, 10,028; Protestants, 2710.

84. 26. *Munterlony.*—The parishes of Bodoney, Upper and Lower; the eight townlands of Balix, Upper and Lower, Carrickayne, Clogherney, Doorat, Glengarrow, Legnagappoge, and Stroanbrack, in the parish of Donaghedy; the ten townlands of Breagh, More and Beg, Beleevna, More and Beg, Dungate, Evishbrack, Kinnagillian, Meenanea, Meenascallagh, and Teebane, in the parish of Kildress; and the three townlands of Broughderg, and Davagh, Upper and Lower, in the parish of Lissan. Population, 12,671; Protestants, 3092.

85. 27. *Ardstraw.*—That part of the parish of Ardstraw which lies within the present barony of Lower Strabane, except the twenty-two townlands included in the new baronies of Glenderg and Upper Strabane; that part of the parish of Cappagh which lies in the present barony of Upper Strabane, except the twenty-one townlands included in the new baronies of East Omagh and Six Mile Cross. Population, 11,945; Protestants, 6560.

86. 28. *Glenderg.*—The parish of Termonamongan, and those parts of the parishes of Ardstraw and Urney which lie in the present barony of West Omagh; the six townlands of Ballyfolliard, Dunrevan, Erganagh, Listymore, Lurganboy, and Priestsessagh, in the parish of Ardstraw and present barony of Lower Strabane; and the seven townlands of Aghakinmart, Bullock Park, Drumgallan, Ednashanlaght, Kilmore (Irvine, and Robinson), and Meencargagh, in the parish of West Longfield. Population, 11,209; Protestants, 5019.

87. 29. *Upper Strabane.*—The parish of Camus; the parish of Urney (in Tyrone and Donegal), except that part which lies within the present barony of West Omagh; the sixteen townlands of Ballought, Beagh, Breen, Clady (Blair, Halliday, Hood, and Johnston), Concess, Knockiniller, Ligfordrum, Liscreevaghan, Mulvin, Skinboy, Skinboy Mountain, Stonewalls, and Stonyfalls, in the parish of Ardstraw and present barony of Lower Strabane; the thirty-three townlands of Ballybun, Blairstown, Carranadore, Carrick, Carricknashane, Cashelin, Castlefinn, Cloghard, Corcullion, Demesne, Donaghmore Glebe, Drummurphy, Dungorman, Gortfad, Gortnamuck, Grahamsland, Knockrawe, Leaght, Liscooly, Lisnamulligan, Magheraboy, Magherareagh, Meenavoney, Mullanboy, Raws, Upper and Lower, Scotland, Sessiagh (Allison), Sessiagh (Long), Stranamuck, Tawnacrom, Tirinisk, and Tirnagushope, with the town of Castlefinn, in the parish of Donaghmore (in Donegal). Population, 13,565; Protestants, 5487.

88. 30. *Lower Strabane.*—The parish of Leckpatrick; the parish of Donaghedy, except the eight townlands included in the barony of Munterlony. Population 10,418; Protestants, 5685.

89. 31. *Portlough.*—The parishes of All Saints, Burt, Killea, and Muff; the parish of Templemore outside the city of Londonderry; and the nine townlands of Birdstown, Carnashannagh, Crislaghmore, Drumadooey, Fahan Level, Garvary, Gortnaskea, Moureagh, and Tievebane, in the parish of Upper Fahan. Population, 12,314; Protestants, 6789.

90. 32. *Raphoe.*—The parishes of Clonleigh, Raymoghy, and Taughboyne; the parish of Raphoe, except the four townlands of Blackrepentance, Carrickbrack, and Upper and Lower Rousky; the six townlands of Breaghy, Carnowen, Dooghan, Lisnabert, Magherashanvally, and Sessiagh, in the parish of Donaghmore (Donegal); and the three townlands of Calhame, Cornagillagh, and Treanboy, in the parish of Convoy, Population, 13,437; Protestants, 7323.

VI.—COUNTY OF TYRCONNEL.

91. 1. *Glenfinn.*—The parish of Donaghmore (in Donegal), except the forty-two townlands included in the new baronies of Upper Strabane, Raphoe, and Donegal; the parish of Stranorlar, except the three townlands of Cashelnavean, Meencargagh, and Meencrumlin; the parish of Convoy, except the four townlands of Calhame, Cark, Cornagillagh, and Treanboy; and the four townlands of Blackrepentance, Carrickbrack, and Upper and Lower Rousky, in the parish of Raphoe. Population, 11,847; Protestants, 3802.

92. 2. *Glenswilly.*—The parishes of Gartan and Leck; the parish of Conwal, except the twenty-six townlands included in the barony of Kilmacrenan; the thirteen townlands of Cloghroe, Cottian, Edenacarnan, North and South, Garrowcarry, Glenkeo, Gortnacorrib, Keenaghan, Killydesert, Legnahoory, Rathdonnell, Sockar, and Tirargus, in the parish of Kilmacrenan; and the townland of Cark, in the parish of Convoy. Population, 12,097; Protestants, 3507.

93. 3. *Kilmacrenan.*—The parish of Aghanunshin; the parish of Aughinish, except the townlands of Glenalla and Ray; the parish of Tullyfern, except the nine townlands of

Carrowkeel, Cratlagh, Drumatrumman, Dunmore, Garrymore, Gortcally, Gortnavern, Ranny, and Tirhomin; the twenty-six townlands of Ards, Big and Little, Ballaghderg, Ballyboe Lisnenan, Barrack, Bohirril, Bohirril Park, Booragh, Breaghy, Carnamogagh, Upper and Lower, Carnisk, Coolboy, Big and Little, Curraghlea, Ellistrin, Big and Little, Fallard, Gortnavern, Knocknamona, Lisnenan, Meenatole, Race End, Sallaghagrane, Windyhall, and Woodtown, in the parish of Conwal; and the twenty-five townlands of Aghawoney, Ballykeeran, Ballyscanlan, Upper and Lower, Bellanascaddan, Carrickybressil, Cashelgay, Court, Drumabodan, Glasnaut, Gortmacall, Beg and More, Gortnaskeagh, Grovehall, Kilconnell, Kilmacrenan, Letter, Massreagh, Portleen, Procklis, Ray, Skerry, and Tawny, Upper, Middle, and Lower, with the town of Kilmacrenan, in the parish of Kilmacrenan. Population, 8792; Protestants, 4355.

94. 4. *East Innishowen.* — The parishes of Upper and Lower Moville, and the ten townlands of Aghaglassan, Aghatubrid, Ballycharry, Ballymagaraghy, Dristernan, Drumaville, Drumlee, Kindroghed, Leitrim, and Moneydarragh, in the parish of Culdaff. Population, 9967; Protestants, 2274.

95. 5. *North Innishowen.* — The parishes of Clonca and Donagh; and the parish of Culdaff, except the ten townlands included in the barony of East Innishowen. Population, 12,120; Protestants, 1758.

96. 6. *West Innishowen.* — The parishes of Clonmany, Desertegny, Fahan Lower, Inch, and Mintiaghs; and the fourteen townlands of Annaslee, Ballynahone, Carrontlieve, Carrowmullin, Castlequarter, Craigtown, Crislaghkeel, Figary, Glebe, Large Glebe, Letter, Lisfanan, Magherabeg, and Roosky, in the parish of Upper Fahan. Population, 12,657; Protestants, 1168.

97. 7. *Fanad.* — The parishes of Clondavaddog and Killygarvan; the townlands of Glenalla and Ray, in the parish of Aughinish; the nine townlands of Carrowkeel, Cratlagh, Drumatrumman, Dunmore, Garrymore, Gortcally, Gortnavern, Ranny, and Tirhomin, in the parish of Tullyfern; and the

seven townlands of Carmoney, Cool, Upper and Lower, Cran-
ford, Drummacaladdery, and Woodquarter, in the parish of
Kilmacrenan. Population, 10,237; Protestants, 1786.

98. 8. *Doc.*—The parishes of Clondahorkey and Mevagh ;
and the thirty-one townlands of Ballybuninabber, Barnes,
Upper and Lower, Carrownaganonagh, Carrownasaul, Cashel,
Casheleenan, Clonkilly, Beg and More, Currin, Derriscligh,
Doon, Drumbrick, Drumdeevin, Drumlurgagh, Drumoghill,
Fawans, Golan, Goldrum, Gortalaban, Gortnalaragh, Killough-
carran, Knocknabollan, Letterfad, Loughaskerry, Meenbunone,
Meenreagh, Skreen, Upper and Lower, Stragraddy, and Tir-
killin, in the parish of Kilmacrenan. Population, 11,523 ;
Protestants, 2221.

99. 9. *Cloghaneely.*—The parishes of Raymunterdonny
and Tullyhobegly. Population, 11,489 ; Protestants, 467.

100. 10. *North Boylagh.*—The parish of Templecrone.
Population, 11,525 ; Protestants, 388.

101. 11. *South Boylagh.*—The parish of Lettermacward :
the parish of Lower Killybegs, except the townland of Glengesh ; that part of the parish of Inishkeel which lies within
the present barony of Boylagh. Population, 12,682 ; Protestants, 1006.

102. 12. *Outer Banagh.*—The parishes of Glencolumbkill,
Kilcar, and Upper Killybegs ; that part of the parish of
Inishkeel which lies in the present barony of Banagh ; the
townland of Glengesh in the parish of Lower Killybegs, and
the townland of Meentullynagarn in the parish of Killaghtee.
Population, 12,964 ; Protestants, 1120.

103. 13. *Inner Banagh.* — The parishes of Inver and
Killaghtee (except the townland of Meentullynagarn in the
latter) ; the townland of Croankeeran, in the parish of Killymard. Population, 11,734 ; Protestants, 2443.

104. 14. *Donegal.*—The parishes of Donegal and Kiltee-
vogue ; the parish of Killymard, except the townland of
Croankeeran ; the three townlands of Cashelnavean, Meencargagh, and Meencrumlin, in the parish of Stranorlar ; the
three townlands of Croaghonagh, Meenbog, and Taughboy, in

the parish of Donaghmore; and the three townlands of Barnesyneilly, Copany, and Straness, in the parish of Drumhome. Population, 12,751; Protestants, 3201.

II.—COUNTY OF BELFAST.

105. 3. *Ballyshannon.* — The parishes of Belleek and Kilbarron; the town of Ballyshannon and the seven townlands of Ardloughill, Ballyhanna, Ballymunterhiggin, Carrickboy, Dummuckrum, Finner, and Portnason, in the parish of Innismacsaint (in Donegal); also the twenty-seven townlands of Ardees, Upper and Lower, Ardgart, Barr of Slawin, Brollagh, Callagheen, Carran, Beg and More, Carrigolagh, Corgary, Cornahaltie, Corry, Derrynacross, Derrynames, Drumataffan, Drumbadreevagh, Drumlisaleen, Farrancassidy, Fassagh, Gortnalee, Killy Beg, Laughill, Lergan, Manger, Moneendogue, Rosscor, and Slawin, with the adjacent islands of Lough Erne, in the parish of Innismacsaint (County Fermanagh). Population, 11,026; Protestants, 1974.

VII.—COUNTY OF FERMANAGH.

106. 1. *Tirhugh.*—The parish of Drumhome, except the three townlands of Barnesyneilly, Copany, and Sraness; the parish of Templecarn (in Donegal); and the parish of Templecarn (in Fermanagh), except the three townlands of Drumlongfield, Dreenan, and Mullans, with Lustymore and the other islands in Lough Erne. Population, 9317; Protestants, 4405.

107. 2. *Lury.*—The parishes of Drumkeeran and Magheraculmoney; the twenty-eight townlands of Ballymactaggart, Bunaninver, Carranboy, Coolaness, Coolisk, Cullaghmore, Dromore, Drumadravy, Drumaran, Drumasky, Drumbulcan, Drumduff, Drummonaghan, Drumpeen, Drumshane, Drumskool, Duross, Glenkeen, Keeran, Knockroe (Archdall), Moneykee, North Moynaghan, Mullies, Rahall, Rossachrin, Rossmore, Shallany, and Whitehill North, in the parish of Derryvullan; and the three townlands of Drumlongfield,

Dreenan, and Mullans, with Lustymore and the other islands of the parish of Templecarn. Population, 9215; Protestants, 4975.

108. 3. *Tirkennedy.*—The parish of Kilskeery; the parish of Magheracross (in Tyrone and Fermanagh), except the townland of Ballydoolagh; the parish of Trory, except the seven townlands of Conerick, Derryargon, Derrygore, Derryinch, Drumcoo, Kilmacormick, and Ring; that part of the parish of Derryvullan which lies in the present barony of Lurg, except the twenty-eight townlands included in the new barony of Lurg. Population, 10,151; Protestants, 5593.

109. 4. *Enniskillen.*—Those parts of the parishes of Cleenish, Derryvullan, and Enniskillen, which lie in the present barony of Tirkennedy, except the island of Knock; the seven townlands of Conerick, Derryargon, Derrygore, Derryinch, Drumcoo, Kilmacormick, and Ring, in the parish of Trory; the townlands of Ballyreagh and Largy, in the parish of Derrybrusk; and the townland of Ballydoolagh, in the parish of Magheracross. Population, 11,507; Protestants, 6206.

110. 5. *Magherastephana.*—The present barony of Magherastephana. Population, 12,131; Protestants, 6591.

111. 6. *Clanawley.*—The parish of Killesher; the parish of Rossorry, except the nine townlands included in the new barony of Magheraboy; that part of the parish of Enniskillen which lies in the present barony of Magheraboy; that part of the parish of Derrybrusk which lies in the present barony of Tirkennedy, except the townlands of Ballyreagh and Largy; the sixty-three townlands of Abocurragh, Abohill, Aghannagh, Ardtonnagh, Ballysooragh, Bellanaleck, Bohevney, Brockagh, Carneyhill, Cloonatrig, Cloonaveel, Coolyermer, Cornahawla, Corraderrybrock, Corraglass, Corrateskin, Crockareddy, Derreens East, Derryaghna, Derrychurra, Derrycormick, Derrygiff, Derryhowlaght West, Derryinch, Derryleck, Derryscobe, Drumageever, Drumane, Drumbargny, Drumcolgny, Drumconlan East, Drumderg, Drumlaghy, Drumrainy, Drumsroohill, Gardrum, Gortadrehid, Gortahurk East, Gortdonaghy,

Greenwoodhill, Killywillin, Lanaghran, Leam Beg, Leam More, Letterbreen, Lisbofin, Moybane, Moybrone, Mullaghmaddy, Mullymesker, Oakfield, Point, Ross, Rossavalley, Rossdoney, Rushin East, Sessiagh West, Skea, Skreen, Tonyloman, Tonyteige, Trillick, and Tully, in the parish of Cleenish and present barony of Clanawley; and the islands of Cleenish and Knock, in the parish of Derryvullan. Population, 10,534; Protestants, 5277.

112. 7. *Magheraboy.*—The parish of Devenish, except the eighteen townlands excluded from the Grand Duchy; the parish of Boho, except the three townlands of Agho, Ross, and Tullygerravra; the parish of Innismacsaint (in Fermanagh), except the fifteen townlands excluded from the Grand Duchy, and the twenty-seven townlands included in the new barony of Ballyshannon; that part of the parish of Cleenish which lies in the present barony of Clanawley, except the sixty-three townlands included in the new barony of Clanawley; the nine townlands of Bowara, Brughas, Cloghanagh, Croaghrim, Dinnydoon, Drumsillagh, Killycat, Kilnaloo, and Moyglass, in the parish of Rossorry; and the townland of Lurgandarragh, in the parish of Cleenish and present barony of Magheraboy. Population, 8975; Protestants, 3510.

VIII.—COUNTY OF MONAGHAN.

113. 1. *Coole.*—The parish of Galloon, except the three townlands of Carrowmaculla, Derrysteaton, and Galloon; the parish of Drummully (in Fermanagh and Monaghan), except the four townlands of Derrykerrib, Drumboghanagh Glebe, Goladuff, and Gubdoo; the twelve townlands of Clonagam, Clonatty, Clonfad, Clonfeile, Clonmackan, Clontivim, Drumera, Drumharriff, Drumrainy, Gowny, Kilroosky, and Summerhill, in the parish of Clones (County Fermanagh); also the town of Clones and the thirty-one townlands of Altartate Glebe, Annaghkilly, Burdautien, Carn, Carney's Island, Cladowen, Clonavilla, Clonboy, Cloncallick, Cloncumber, Cloncurrin, Clonedergole, Clonkeen (Cole, and Lucas), Clonkirk, Clonmore, Clontibret, Clontreat, Crossmoyle, Drumard, Drumeru

(Dickson), Glear, Largy, Legarhill, Liseggerton, Lisnaroe, (Far, and Near), Mullanamoy, Munnilly, Teehill, and Tirnahinch Near, in the parish of Clones (County Monaghan). Population, 10,269 ; Protestants, 4516.

114. 2. *Clankelly.*—The parish of Clones (in Fermanagh and Monaghan), except the town of Clones and the forty-six townlands included in the new baronies of Coole and Monaghan ; the parish of Drumsnat ; the thirty-two townlands of Aghnaskea, Annamakiff, Boughill, Carnowen, Cashlan, Cavanavally, Cloghernagh, Coaghen, Conaghy, Corlat, Cornawall, Derryleggan, Doosky, Drumcaw, Drumguilly, Drumhilly, Drumleny, Dyan, Edenagoash, Glasdrummond, Golanmurphy, Killycronaghan, Killyfuddy, Killygorman, Killykeskeame, Kilnamaddy, Lecklevera, Lisarrilly, Listellan, Roosky, Tattynagall, and Tiredigan, in the parish of Killeevan ; the six townlands of Aghagaw, Allagesh, Corrinshigo, Formoyle, Killydonnelly, and Mullatigorry, in the parish of Tedavnet ; and the townland of Carrowmaculla, in the parish of Galloon. Population, 11,804 ; Protestants, 3283.

115. 3. *Monaghan.*—The parish of Tedavnet, except the six townlands included in the new barony of Clankelly ; the town of Monaghan, and the eighteen townlands of Camla, Coolshannagh, Cornecassa, Crover, Gallanagh, Gortakeeghan, Killyconigan, Killygowan, Kilnacloy, Knockroe, Mullaghadun, Mullaghcroghery, Mullaghmatt, Mullaghmonaghan, Roosky, Tirkeenan, Tully, and Tullygrimes, in the parish of Monaghan ; the eighteen townlands of Aghaboy, Aghalisk, Annaghervy, Annagola, Ballyleck, Brandrum, Clonavarn, Corcreeghy, Drumacaslan, Drumaconnor, Killyleen, Kilnahaltar, Lisbane, Mullynahinch Point, Rossafield, Tirnadown, and Tullybryan, in the parish of Kilmore ; and the three townlands of Derryarrit, Dundrumman, and Skeatry, in the parish of Clones. Population, 11,404 ; Protestants, 2942.

116. 4. *Trough.*—The parishes of Donagh and Errigal Trough (in Monaghan and Tyrone) ; the nineteen townlands of Corbeg, Cornahoe, Corvalley, Creighans, Crowey, Crumlin, Drumacruttan, Drumagelvin, Drumgoole, Knockacunnier,

Leitrim, Seaveagh, Shelvins, Skinnagin, Templetate, Terry-caffe, Tiravera, Tuckmilltate, and Tullygoney, in the parish of Tehallan. Population, 10,579; Protestants, 2884.

117. 5. *Rossmore.*—The parish of Monaghan, except the town and the eighteen townlands included in the new barony of Monaghan; the parish of Kilmore, except the eighteen townlands included in that barony, and the two included in the new barony of Ballybay; the parish of Tehallan, except the nineteen townlands included in the new barony of Trough; the twelve townlands of Braddocks, Cordevlis North, Corfad, Corlongford, Corraviller, Corvally, Cussaboy, Derrylusk, Kilnacran, Kilnamaddy, Shanmullagh, and Terrygeely, in the parish of Tullycorbet; and the sixty-six townlands of Aghnameal, Annaglogh, Annahuby, Annaseeragh, Arclintagh, Avalbane, Avalreagh, Ballygreany, Bryanlitter, Carrickaderry, Carrickamure, Cashel, Cavancreavy, Clerran, Coolartragh, Corcaskea, Corlagan North, Cornabrandy, Corlahoe, Upper and Lower, Cornamucklagh North, Creeve, Crossaghy, Crossmore, Derryarrelly, Doosky, Down, Dromore, Drumbeo, Drumgallan, Drumgolat, Drumnart, Drumneill, Ennis, Feddans, Fintully, Gallagh, Glasdrumman, East and West, Glennyhorn, Greenmount, Kilcrow, Killymonaghan, Latnakelly, Lemgare, Letteragh, Letterbane, Lisaginny, Lisdrumgormly, Lisglassan, Lisnagreeve, Listinny, Listroar, Moy Etra, Moy Otra, Moysnaght, Mullagarry, Mullans, Pullans, Shanmullagh, Tassan, Tattyreagh North, Tirmacmoe, Tonagh, Tullybuck, and Tullycunaskey, in the parish of Clontibret. Population, 11,160; Protestants, 3296.

118. 6. *Ballybay.*—The parish of Ballybay; the parish of Clontibret, except the sixty-six townlands included in the new barony of Rossmore, the four townlands transferred to County Armagh (barony of Middle Fews), and the eleven townlands transferred to the county of Oriel (barony of Farney); the parish of Tullycorbet, except the twelve townlands included in the barony of Rossmore; the townlands of Aghnaclea and Ballynagarry, in the parish of Kilmore; and the twenty townlands of Aghnamullen, Anny, Bowelk, Cordevlis, Corfad, Corkecran, Corraskea, Corryhagan, Cumry, Derryroosk, Drumfaldra, Drumskelt, Keenogbane, Keenog-duff, Lisgillan, Lisgorran, Monintin, Mullanagore, Mullanary Glebe, and Tamlat, in the parish of Aghnamullan. Population, 11,090; Protestants, 3410.

119. 7. *Dartrey.*—The parishes of Aghabog, Ematris, and Currin (Fermanagh and Monaghan); the townlands of Clos-sagh Beg and Clossagh More, in the parish of Aghnamullan; the parish of Killeevan, except the thirty-nine townlands included in the new barony of Clankelly. Population, 11,871; Protestants, 5435.

IX.—County of East Breffney or Cavan.

120. 1. *Tullygarvey.*—The parish of Drumgoon, except the twenty-seven townlands included in the new barony of Clankee in the county of Oriel; the parish of Kildrumsher-dan, except the three townlands of Drumnatread, Ratrussan, and Tievenanass; the eighteen townlands of Clonacullion, Cormeen, Corsilloga, Cortannel, Drumlood, Edenbrone, Gort-lanna, Killyliss, Leagh, Lisnagalliagh, Lisnalong, Money, Mountain Lodge, Mount Carmel, Moylemore, Moylemuck, Raw, and Tattybrack, in the parish of Aghnamullen; the thirty-four townlands of Ballyhally, Bracklagh, Bunnoe, Corcraff, Cornagarron, Corrakeeran, Corravogy, Corrinshigo, Devally, Drumacleeskin, Drumbrollisk, Drumcor, Drum-herriff, North and South, Drumskelt, Duncollog, Dunmurry, Killyrue, Lattacapple, Lisarney, Lisboduff, Lisbree, Longfield, Magherintemple, Nutfield, Pottle East, Rahoran, Rakenny, Ronard, See, Tullavally, Tullyalt, Tullybrick, and Tullyna-cross, in the parish of Drung; the eighteen townlands of Ardglushin, Brockly, Claragh, Conaghoo, Corcraff, Drum-avrack, Drumbartagh, Drumbo, Drumcarn, Drumconra, Drumeenagh, Keelagh, Kilnacross, Kivvy, Mullacroghery, Mullalougher, Neddaiagh, and Treehoo, in the parish of Annagh. Population, 11,752; Protestants, 3254.

121. 2. *Stradone.*—The parish of Larah; the parish of

Lavey, except the thirteen townlands excluded from Ulster; the parish of Drung, except the thirty-four townlands included in the new barony of Tullygarvey; the three townlands of Drumnatread, Ratrussan, and Tievenanass, in the parish of Kildrumsherdan; the three townlands of Ardamagh, Coolcanadass, and Dresternagh, in the parish of Annagh; the nine townlands of Aghalackan, Drumoghra, Edenticlare, Glasdrumman, Lismullig, Poles, Pottle, and Shankill, Upper and Lower, in the parish of Annagelliff; the twenty-two townlands of Carrickateane, Castleterra, Clonconor Glebe, Clonervy, Corcloghan, Corranure, Corratober, Corravarry, Creeve, Cullentragh, Drumohan, Drumryan, Fartan, Upper and Lower, Heney, Keadew, Killygarry, Lisdeegin, Lisdunvis Glebe, Lisnacark, Shantemon, and Unshinagh, in the parish of Castleterra; and the five townlands of Banagher, Corraweelis, Crumlin, Gallon Glebe, and Pollakeel, in the parish of Denn. Population, 10,750; Protestants, 1149.

122. 3. *Belturbet or Lower Loughtee.* — The parish of Drumlane; the parish of Annagh, except the twenty-one townlands included in the new baronies of Stradone and Tullygarvey; the parish of Tomregan (in Cavan), except the townland of Berrymount; the twelve townlands of Brandrum, Carn, Cloncose, Clooneen, Cormeen, Drumcase, Drumerdannan, Glasstown, Gorteen, Gortnacleigh, Kilnacross, and Listiernan, in the parish of Kildallan; the six townlands of Bofealan, Crossmakelagher, Drumane, Killynaff, Lecharrownahone, and Tonyrevan, in the parish of Templeport; the eight townlands of Bunn, Derrylina, Putiaghan, Upper and Lower, Rivory, Urney, Inishmore, and Inishmuck, in the parish of Urney; the four townlands of Derrykerrib, Drumboghanagh Glebe, Goladuff, and Gubdoo, in the parish of Drummully; and the townlands of Derrysteaton and Galloon, in the parish of Galloon. Population, 11,660; Protestants, 3253.

123. 4. *Knockninny.* — The parish of Kinawley (in Cavan and Fermanagh), except the four townlands of Dummakeever,

Eshveagh, Tonanilt, and Tullycrafton, excluded from Ulster ; and the parish of Tomregan (in Fermanagh). Population, 10,775 ; Protestants, 2740.

124. 5. *Carrigallen.*—The parish of Killashandra ; the parish of Kildallan, except the twelve townlands included in the new barony of Belturbet ; the parish of Carrigallen, except the townlands of Gortermone and South Tully ; the three townlands of Burren, Coologe, and Toberlyan (Duffin), in the parish of Templeport ; the townland of Berrymount, in the parish of Tomregan ; and the seven townlands of Cordalea, Derries, Upper and Lower, Gartnanoul, Snakeel, Eonish Island, and Inch Island, in the parish of Kilmore. Population, 13,009 ; Protestants, 4604.

125. 6. *Cavan or Upper Loughtee.*—The parish of Annagelliff, except the nine townlands included in the barony of Stradone ; the parish of Castleterra, except the twenty-two townlands included in the barony of Stradone ; the parish of Kilmore, except the seven townlands included in the new barony of Carrigallen ; the parish of Urney, except the eight townlands included in the barony of Belturbet ; the townlands of Coolnacarrick and Rabrackan, in the parish of Ballintemple ; the five townlands of Aghaconny, Cashel, Gortachurk, Kilmainham, and Mullaghkeel, in the parish of Crosserlough ; the townland of Aghadreenagh, and the eleven townlands of the parish of Denn, which lie in the present barony of Clanmahon. Population, 12,522 ; Protestants, 3132.

X.—COUNTY OF ORIEL.

126. 1. *Cremorne.*—The parish of Aghnamullan, except the forty townlands included in the new baronies of Ballybay, Dartry, and Tullygarvey ; the townlands of Lower and Middle Bocks, in the parish of Donaghmoyne ; the twenty-two townlands of Ardragh, Cargaghmore, Cargaghoge, Carrickadooey, Coraghy, Corcreeghagh, Corduff, Cornasassonagh, Corrinenty, Corvally, Faraghy, Greaghlane, Greaghlatacapple, Lisacullion, Lisdrumturk, Lisirril, Mullaghcroghery, Ouvry, Raferagh, Shanco, Sreenty, and Ummera-

free, in the parish of Magheross. Population, 10,264; Protestants, 1240.

127. 2. *Clankee.*—The parish of Knockbride; the parish of Shercock, except the townlands of Crossmakeelan and Nolagh (half); the townlands of Derrynure and Killan, in the parish of Bailieborough, the twenty-seven townlands of Ardmone, Barnagrow, Cashel, Corcloghan, Corleckduff, Coskemduff, Doohallat, Dooreagh, Drokaghbane, Drumaveil South, Drumcondra, Drumlumman, Drutamon, Gallonreagh, Killycleare, Knappagh, Knocknashammer, Larawechan, Lisclogher, Lisdoagh, Lisnaclea, Lurganboy, Moyduff, Mullaghard, Mullan, Ralaghan, and Tonyhull, in the parish of Drumgoon. Population, 9327; Protestants, 2468.

128. 3. *Bailieborough.*—The parish of Bailieborough, except the townlands of Derrynure and Killan; the parish of Killinkere, except the townlands of Drumfomina and Drummallaght; the parish of Moybolgue (in Cavan), and the four townlands of Agheragh, Corgreagh, Lisnaboy, and Teevurcher, in the parish of Moybolgue (in Meath); the eight townlands of Carrigagh, Cormeen, Cornaville, North and South, Drumaneber, Fertagh, Leitrim, Upper and Lower, in the parish of Moynalty; and the townlands of Crossmakeelan, and Nolagh (half), in the parish of Shercock. Population, 11,217; Protestants, 3065.

129. 4. *Morgallion.*—The barony of Morgallion, except the six townlands of the parish of Enniskeen included in the new barony of Kingscourt; the barony of Lower Slane, except the parish of Ardagh; the parish of Rathkenny, in the barony of Upper Slane; in the barony of Lower Kells, the parishes of Cruicetown, Enniskeen (except the three townlands included in the new barony of Kingscourt), Kilbeg (except the town and townland of Carlanstown), Kilmainham, Moybolgue (except the four townlands included in the new barony of Bailieborough), Nobber and Staholmog; also in the same barony the sixteen townlands of Aghancane, Ballymakane, Carrickspringan, Coolnahnich, Corboggy, Feagh, Golashane, Quigelagh, Rathmanoo, Screehoge, Skearke, Trohanny, Tullyarran, Tullyattin, Tullypole, and Ughtyneill, in the parish of Moynalty. Population, 11,590; Protestants, 422.

130. 5. *Kingscourt.*—The parish of Enniskeen (in Cavan); the nine townlands of Boynabought, Cornacarrow, Cornahoova, Corrakerran, Corratober, Drumgill, Dunheeda, Kilnalun, and Rolagh, in the parish of Enniskeen (in Meath); the parish of Ardagh (in Meath), except the townland of Cloghreagh; the six townlands of Crowmartin, Knockaboys, Lagan, Mullabane, Rathgeenan, and Tully, in the parish of Clonkeen (in Louth); the townland of Calga, in the parish of Philipstown (barony of Ardee in Louth); the parish of Killanny (in Louth); the parish of Killanny (in Monaghan), except the twelve townlands included in the new barony of Farney; the parish of Magheracloone; the five townlands of Corduff (Kelly), Derrylavan, Drumgoan, Latinalbany, and Magheraboy, in the parish of Magheross. Population, 11,796; Protestants, 1070.

131. 6. *Farney.* — The parish of Donaghmoyne, except the townlands of Lower and Middle Bocks; the parish of Magheross, except the twenty-seven townlands included in the new baronies of Cremorne and Kingscourt; the twelve townlands of Annacroff, Ballingarry, Coolaha, Coolreagh, Coolremony, Dunelty, Garlegobban, Kinallybane, Kinallyduff, Lisnakelly, Radrumskean, and Stradeen, in the parish of Killanny (County Monaghan); the eleven townlands of Annadrumman, Annagleve, Annalittin, Carrickagarvan, Cavanaguillagh, Clonavogy, Cornalough, Formil, Knockavolis Mullaghanee, and Tullyvin, in the parish of Clontibret. Population, 12,946; Protestants, 863.

132. 7. *Upper Orior.*—The parish of Jonesborough (in Louth and Armagh); the parish of Forkill, except the townland of Lisnalee; the twenty-four townlands of Aghadavoyle, Aghayalloge, Aghmakane, Annaghcloghmullin, Annahaia, Ballard, Ballinliss, Ballintemple, Ballynalack, Ballymacdermot Carrickbroad, Carricknagalliagh, Carrivemaclone, Cloghoge, Clonlum, Cloutygora, Drumintee, Ellisholding, Killeen,

Lislea, Meigh, Newtown, Seafin, and Tamnaghbane, in the parish of Killevy; and the townlands of Upper and Lower Fathom, in the parish of Newry. Population, 12,781; Protestants, 792.

133. 8. *Upper Fews.*—The parish of Creggan (in Armagh), except the five townlands of Cullyhanna, Big and Little, Drumlougher, Teer, and Teer Island; the parishes of Kane and Roche; and the townlands of Dungooly and Lurgankeel in the parish of Faughart. Population, 9900; Protestants, 538.

134. 9. *Carlingford.*—The parishes of Carlingford and Ballyboys; the parish of Ballymascanlan, except the sixteen townlands included in the barony of East Louth; and the townland of Bellurgan, in the parish of Castletown. Population, 10,288; Protestants, 1006.

135. 10. *East Louth.*—The parishes of Ballybarrack, Castletown (except the townland of Bellurgan), Clonkeehan, Darver, Dromiskin, Dunbin, Dundalk (outside the town), Hoggardstown, Haynestown (except the townland of Rathroal), and Mansfieldstown; the parish of Faughart, except the two townlands included in the new barony of Upper Fews; the sixteen townlands of Aghaboys, Aghnaskeagh, Ballymascanlan, Broughattin, Carrickaneena, Culfore, Drumnacarra, Drumnasillagh, Faughart, Upper and Lower, Kilcurry, Monascreebe, Navan, Proleek, Proleek Acres, and Whitemill, in the parish of Ballymascanlan; and the townlands of Newtownfane and Rossmakay, in the parish of Louth. Population, 8775; Protestants, 576.

136. 11. *West Louth.*—The parishes of Barronstown, Creggan (in Louth), Innishkeen (in Louth and Monaghan), Killincoole, Louth (except the townlands of Newtownfane and Rossmakay), Philipstown in Louth barony, Philipstown in Ardee barony (except the townland of Calga), and Tallanstown; also the townland of Rathroal, in the parish of Haynestown. Population, 9477; Protestants, 385.

137. 12. *Ardee.*—The parishes of Ardee, Cappoge, Charlestown, Collon, Dromin, Gernonstown, Kildemock, Kilsaran, Mapastown, Mosstown, Richardstown, Shanlis, Smar-

more, Stabannan, and Stickillin ; and the parish of Clonkeen
except the six townlands of Crowmartin, Knockaboys, Lagan,
Mullaghbane, Rathgeenan, and Tully. Population, 11,060;
Protestants, 776.

138. 13. *Ferrard.*—The present barony of Drogheda ; the
present barony of Ferrard, excluding the parish of Collon,
and the parish of Tullyallen (except the townland of Newtown
Stalaban) ; the parish of Drumcar, in the present barony of
Ardee. Population, 11,109 ; Protestants, 532.

XI.—COUNTY OF FINGAL.

139. 1. *Slane.*—The barony of Upper Slane, except the
parish of Rathkenny ; the parishes of Ardmulchan, Athlum-
ney, Brownstown, Danestown, Dowdstown, Follistown, Kil-
carn, Lismullin, Monkstown, Skreen, Staffordstown, Tara, and
Templekeeran, in the barony of Skreen ; in the barony of
Lower Duleek, the parishes of Danestown, Donore (except
the townland of Cruicerath), Fennor, Kentstown, Knock-
common, and Painestown, with the seven townlands of
Corballis, Drumman, Kellystown, Lougher, Rahill, Red-
mountain, and Roughgrange, in the parish of Duleek ; in the
barony of Lower Navan, the parish of Dunmoe and the parish
of Donaghmore, except the town of Navan and the three townlands of Nevinstown, Rathaldron, and Windtown ; in the
county of Louth the parish of Tullyallen, except the townland
of Newtown Stalaban. Population, 10,663 ; Protestants, 735.

140. 2. *Duleek.* — The barony of Upper Duleek ; the
barony of Lower Duleek, except the parts included in the new
barony of Slane ; the parishes of Cushinstown, Kilmoon,
Macetown, Rathfeigh, and Timoole, in the barony of Skreen ;
and the parishes of Ballymadun and Garristown, in the barony
of Balrothery West. Population, 10,104 ; Protestants, 438.

141. 3. *Balrothery.*—The present barony of Balrothery
East, except the twenty-four townlands of the parish of Lusk
included in the new barony of Nethercross ; and the parishes
of Grallagh, Hollywood, and Naul, in the barony of Balrothery
West. Population, 11,666 ; Protestants, 893.

142. 4. *Nethercross.*—The present barony of Nethercross; in the barony of Balrothery West, the parishes of Ballyboghil, Clonmethan, Palmerstown, and Westpalstown; in the barony of Balrothery East the twenty-four townlands of Annsbrook, Balleally, East and West, Bettyville, Bridetree, Broomfield, Coldwinters, Colecot, Corduff, Corduff Common, Corduff Hall, Corduff (Hackett), Deanestown, Gracedieu, Irishtown, Newhaggard, Newtowncorduff, Richardstown, Staffordstown, Staffordstown Turvey, Thomondtown, Turvey, Wimbletown, and Woodpark, in the parish of Lusk; in the present barony of Coolock, the parishes of Baldoyle, Balgriffin, Cloghran, Kinsaley, Malahide, Portmarnock, St Margaret's and Swords, with the parish of Santry, except the four townlands included in the new barony of Coolock; in the barony of Castleknock, the parish of Ward; the three townlands of Hunstown, Johnstown, and Mitchelstown, in the parish of Castleknock; and the ten townlands of Baleskin, Bishopswood, Broghan, Charlestown, Coldwinters, Glebe, Kilshane, Poppintree, Shallon, and Stockens, in the parish of Finglas. Population, 9833; Protestants, 1090.

143. 5. *Dunboyne.*—The present baronies of Dunboyne and Ratoath; the barony of Upper Deece, except the parishes of Agher and Rathcore; in the barony of Lower Deece, the parishes of Derrypatrick, Kiltale, and Knockmark; in the barony of Skreen, the parishes of Dunsany, Killeen, and Trevet; in the barony of Castleknock, the parishes of Clonsilla, Cloghran, and Mulhuddart; the townland of Cruiserath in the parish of Finglas; and the parish of Castleknock, except the six townlands included in the baronies of Kilmainham and Nethercross. Population, 11,804; Protestants, 934.

144. 6. *Kilmainham.*—In the barony of Castleknock, the parishes of Chapelizod, St James, and St Jude, the parish of Finglas, except the eleven townlands included in the new baronies of Dunboyne and Nethercross; and the three townlands of Cabragh, Pelletstown, and Phœnix Park, in the parish of Castleknock; in the barony of Uppercross, the parishes of St Catherine, St James, and St Jude; in the barony of Coolock, the parish of Grangegorman, and the six townlands of Botanic Garden, Prospect, Slutsend, Tolka Park, and Violethill, Great and Little, in the parish of Glasnevin. Population, 14,500; Protestants, 4360.

145. 7. *Coolock or Howth.* — In the present barony of Coolock, the parishes of Artaine, Clontarf, Coolock, Howth, Kilbarrack, Killester, and Raheny; the parish of Clonturk, excluding the town of Drumcondra; the parish of Glasnevin excluding the town of Drumcondra and the six townlands included in the new barony of Kilmainham; and in the parish of Santry, the four townlands of Balbutcher, Santry, Santry Demesne, and Stormanstown. Population, 10,205; Protestants, 2869.

WARDS OF THE COUNTY AND BOROUGH OF NEW DUBLIN.

1. *Rathmines.*—Those parts of the parishes of Rathfarnham, St Nicholas, and St Peter, which lie in the township of Rathmines and Rathgar. Population, 22,795; Protestants, 11,953.

2. *Donnybrook.* — The parishes of St Bartholomew and Donnybrook (outside Dublin Harbour Parliamentary Division); that part of St Peter's which lies within Pembroke Township; and so much of Taney as lies within the Grand Duchy. Population, 19,632; Protestants, 8781.

3. *Kingstown.*—The parishes of Booterstown, Dalkey, Kilmacud, Monkstown, and Stillorgan; those parts of the parish of Kill which lie within the townships of Dalkey and Kingstown; and the townlands of Galloping Green North, and Newtownpark, also in the parish of Kill. Population, 32,696; Protestants, 11,016.

WARDS OF THE CITY OF LONDONDERRY.

1. *East.*—The present East Ward. Population, 8755; Protestants, 4411.

2. *North.*—The present North Ward. Population, 9238; Protestants, 4011.

3. *South.*—The present South Ward. Population, 11,169; Protestants, 4667.

WARDS OF THE CITY OF BELFAST.

1. *Cromac.* — The present Cromac Ward (12 members). Population, 49,916 ; Protestants, 39,616.

2. *Dock.*—The present Dock Ward (6 members). Population, 32,523 ; Protestants, 21,860.

3. *St Anne's.*—The present St Anne's Ward (12 members). Population, 50,204 ; Protestants, 39,481.

4. *St George's.*—The present St George's Ward (10 members). Population, 45,125 ; Protestants, 27,306.

5. *Smithfield.*—The present Smithfield Ward (6 members). Population, 30,354 ; Protestants, 19,884.

6. *Lisburn.*—The town of Lisburn (2 members). Population, 10,755 ; Protestants, 8450.

7. *Lurgan.*—The town of Lurgan (2 members). Population, 10,135 ; Protestants, 6651.

8. *Newry.*—The town of Newry (2 members). Population, 14,808 ; Protestants, 4998.

9. *Dundalk.*—The town of Dundalk (2 members). Population, 11,913 ; Protestants, 2058.

10. *Drogheda.*—The county of the town of Drogheda (2 members). Population, 12,297 ; Protestants, 984.

SUMMARY OF ULSTER.

		POPULATION.	ROMAN CATHOLICS.	PRO-TESTANTS.
Antrim,	North	75,144	22,879	52,265
	Middle	67,799	13,840	53,959
	South	74,825	11,671	63,154
		217,768	48,390	169,378
Down,	North	69,759	5,405	64,354
	West	73,167	26,730	46,437
	South or East	71,832	33,806	38,026
		214,758	65,941	148,817

		POPULATION.	ROMAN CATHOLICS.	PRO- TESTANTS.
Armagh,	East . .	71,580	22,894	48,686
	West . .	74,398	34,626	39,772
		145,978	57,520	88,458
Tyrone,	North .	71,317	35,559	35,758
	East . .	78,131	32,019	46,112
	South . .	79,520	36,449	43,071
	Middle . .	78,929	50,333	28,596
	West . .	72,888	36,025	36,863
		380,785	190,385	190,400
Tyrconnel,	North or Lower	77,536	60,467	17,069
	South or Upper	84,992	72,565	12,427
		162,528	133,032	29,496
Oriel,	Upper	67,256	58,128	9,128
	Lower	73,390	68,785	4,605
		140,646	126,913	13,733
East Brefney .		70,468	52,336	18,132
Fermanagh .		71,576	35,322	36,254
Monaghan .		78,177	52,498	25,679
Fingal . .		78,775	67,458	11,317
Belfast,	North	73,778	22,935	50,843
	East	79,247	35,314	43,933
	South	72,925	22,694	50,231
	West	75,479	28,289	47,190
		301,429	109,232	192,187
New Dublin .	.	75,123	43,373	31,750

Note.—The numbers of Roman Catholics and Protestants are only approximate in most cases, but the limits of possible variation are very narrow.

SCHEDULE III.

NEW COUNTIES.

1. *Antrim.*—(*a*) The present county, excluding the municipal boroughs of Belfast and Lisburn, the parish of Drumbeg, and that part of the parish of Shankill which lies in the barony of Upper Belfast.

(*b*) The county of the town of Carrickfergus.

Population, 217,768; Protestants, 169,378.

2. *Armagh.*—(*a*) The present county, excluding the parish of Creggan (except the five townlands of Cullyhanna, Big and Little, Drumlougher, Teer, and Teer Island), the parish of Forkill (except the townland of Lisnalee), the parish of Jonesborough, the townlands of Upper and Lower Fathom in the parish of Newry, the twenty-four townlands of Aghadavoyle, Aghayalloge, Aghmakane, Annaghcloghmullin, Annahaia, Ballard, Ballinliss, Ballintemple, Ballymacdermot, Ballynalack, Carrickbroad, Carricknagalliagh, Carrivemaclone, Cloghoge, Clonlum, Clontygora, Drumintee, Ellisholding, Killeen, Lislea, Meigh, Newtown, Seafin, and Tamnaghbane, in the parish of Killevy, and the municipal boroughs of Lurgan and Newry.

(*b*) In the county of Down, the parish of Shankill, the parish of Tullylish (except the townland of Lenaderg), and the townlands of Corcreeny and Cornreany, in the parish of Donaghcloney.

(*c*) In the county of Tyrone, the five townlands of Annaghnaboe, Aughamullan, Derryloughan, Derrytresk, and Drummurrer, in the parish of Clonoe.

(*d*) In the county of Monaghan, the parish of Muckno, and the four townlands of Annahale, Conera, Corragarta, and Drumcrew, in the parish of Clontibret.

Population, 145,978; Protestants, 88,458.

3. *Belfast.*—(*a*) The municipal borough of Belfast.

(*b*) The towns of Dundalk, Lisburn, Lurgan, and Newry.

(*c*) The new barony of Ligoniel in County Antrim, comprising the parish of Drumbo, and that part of the parish of Shankill (outside the borough) which lies in the barony of Upper Belfast.

(*d*) The new barony of Holywood in County Down, comprising the parish of Holywood, except the six townlands of Ballycultan, Ballydavey, Ballygrainey, Ballymenagh, Ballyrobert, and Craigavad, and the parish of Knockbreda, except the four townlands of Ballydollaghan, Gilnahirk, Gortgrib, and Tullycarnet.

(*e*) The new barony of Ballyshannon in the counties of Donegal and Fermanagh, comprising the parishes of Belleek and Kilbarron, together with the town of Ballyshannon and the thirty-three townlands of Ardees, Upper and Lower, Ardgart, Ardloughill, Ballyhanna, Ballymunterhiggin, Barr of Slawin, Brollagh, Callagheen, Carran, Beg and More, Carrickboy, Carrigolagh, Corgary, Cornahaltie, Corry, Derrynacross, Derrynameo, Drumataffan, Drumbadreevagh, Drumlisaleen, Dunmuckrum, Farrancassidy, Fassagh, Gortnalee, Killy Beg, Laughill, Lergan, Manger, Moneendogue, Portnason, Rosscor, and Slawin, with the adjacent islands in the parish of Innismacsaint.

(*f*) The county of the town of Drogheda.
Population, 301,429; Protestants, 192,197.

4. *Down.*—The present county, excluding the parts already described as included in the new counties of Armagh and Belfast.
Population, 214,758; Protestants, 148,817.

5. *East Brefney or Cavan.*—(*a*) All that part of the present county which is included within the Grand Duchy, except the parishes of Bailieborough, Enniskeen, Killinkere, Knockbride, Moybolgue, Mullagh, and Shercock, and the twenty-five townlands of Ardmone, Barnagrow, Cashel, Cor-

cloghan, Corleckduff, Coskemduff, Doohallat, Dooreagh, Drokaghbane, Drumaveil South, Drumcondra, Drumlumman,
Drutamon, Gallonreagh, Killycleare, Knappagh, Knockna-
shammer, Larawechan, Lisclogher, Lisdoagh, Lisnaclea, Lurganboy, Moyduff, Mullaghard, Mullan, Ralaghan, and Tony-
hull, in the parish of Drumgoon, hereafter enumerated as
included in the new county of Oriel.

(b) In the county of Fermanagh, the parishes of Kinawley
and Tomregan; the four townlands of Derrykerrib, Drumboghanagh Glebe, Goladuff, and Gubdoo, in the parish of
Drummully; and the townlands of Derrysteaton and Galloon in the parish of Galloon.

(c) In the county of Monaghan, the eighteen townlands of
Clonacullion, Cormeen, Corsilloga, Cortannel, Drumlood, Edenbrone, Gortlanna, Killyliss, Leagh, Lisnagalliagh, Lisnalong,
Money, Mountain Lodge, Mount Carmel, Moylemore, Moylemuck, Raw, and Tattybrack, in the parish of Aughnamullan.

(d) In the county of Leitrim, the parish of Carrigallen,
except the townlands of Gortermone and South Tully.
Population, 70,468; Protestants, 18,132.

6. *Fermanagh.*—(a) In the present county, the entire
baronies of Magherastephana and Tirkennedy; the barony
of Lurg, except the parish of Belleek; the barony of Clanawley, except the parish of Kinawley, and the three townlands of the parish of Boho excluded from the Grand Duchy;
the barony of Magheraboy, except the portions of the parishes
of Devenish and Innismacsaint excluded from the Grand
Duchy, and except the twenty-seven townlands of Innismacsaint included in the new barony of Ballyshannon and county
of Belfast.

(b) In the county of Donegal, the parish of Templecarn,
and the parish of Drumhome, except the three townlands of
Barnesyneilly, Copany, and Sraness.

(c) In the county of Tyrone, the parishes of Kilskeery and
Magheracross.
Population, 71,576; Protestants, 36,254.

7. *Fingal.*—(*a*) In the county of Dublin, the baronies of Balrothery, East and West, Castleknock, and Nethercross: the barony of Coolock, except the township of Drumcondra; also in the barony of Uppercross, the parishes of St Catherine, St James, and St Jude.

(*b*) In the county of Meath, the baronies of Duleek, Upper and Lower, Dunboyne, Ratoath, and Skreen; the barony of Upper Slane, except the parish of Rathkenny; the barony of Upper Deece, except the parishes of Agher and Rathcore; the parishes of Derrypatrick, Kiltale, and Knockmark, in the barony of Lower Deece; and in the barony of Lower Navan, the parish of Dunmoe, and the parish of Donaghmore, except the town of Navan, and the three townlands of Nevinstown, Rathalldron, and Windtown.

(*c*) In the county of Louth, the parish of Tullyallen, except the townland of Newtown Stalaban.

Population, 78,775; Protestants, 11,317.

8. *Monaghan.*—(*a*) In the present county, the baronies of Dartrey, Monaghan, and Trough; the parish of Ballybay; the parish of Clontibret, except the fifteen townlands of Annadrumman, Annagleve, Annahale, Annalittin, Carrickagarvan, Cavanaguillagh, Clonavogy, Conera, Cornalough, Corragarta, Drumcrew, Formil, Knockavolis, Mullaghanee, and Tullyvin; also the twenty-two townlands of Aughnamullan, Anny, Bowelk, Clossagh Beg, Clossagh More, Cordevlis, Corfad, Corkeeran, Corraskea, Corryhagan, Cumry, Derryroosk, Drumfaldra, Drumskelt, Keenogbane, Keenogduff, Lisgillan, Lisgorran, Monintin, Mullanagore, Mullanary Glebe, and Tamlat, in the parish of Aughnamullan.

(*b*) In the county of Fermanagh, the baronies of Clankelly and Coole, except the townlands of Derrysteaton and Galloon, in the parish of Galloon, and the four townlands of Derrykerrib, Drumboghanagh Glebe, Goladuff, and Gubdoo, in the parish of Drummully.

(*c*) In the county of Tyrone, the parish of Errigal Trough.

Population, 78,177; Protestants, 25,679.

9. *New Dublin.*—In the county of Dublin, the parishes of Booterstown, Dalkey, Kilmacud, Monkstown, St Bartholomew, St Nicholas, St Peter, and Stillorgan; the parish of Donnybrook, except the portion included in the Dublin Harbour Parliamentary Division; in the parish of Rathfarnham, the township of Rathmines and Rathgar; in the parish of Taney, the town of Clonskeagh and the seven townlands of Friarland, Mount Anville, Mount-Merrion, Mount-Merrion South, Roebuck in Dublin Barony, Roebuck in Rathdown Barony, and Trimleston; and in the parish of Kill, the town of Kingstown, and the townlands of Galloping Green North and Newtonpark.

Population, 75,123; Protestants, 31,750.

10. *Oriel.*—(*a*) The county of Louth, excluding the town of Dundalk and the parish of Tullyallen (except the townland of Newtown Stalaban). [*N.B.*—The town of Drogheda is a county in itself not included in Louth.]

(*b*) In the county of Armagh, the parish of Jonesborough; the parish of Forkill (except the townland of Lisnalee; the parish of Creggan (except the five townlands of Cullyhanna, Big and Little, Drumlougher, Teer, and Teer Island); the townlands of Upper and Lower Fathom, in the parish of Newry; and the twenty-four townlands of Aghadavoyle, Aghayalloge, Aghmakane, Annaghcloghmullin, Annahaia, Ballard, Ballinliss, Ballintemple, Ballymacdermot, Ballynalack, Carrickbroad, Carricknagalliagh, Carrivemaclone, Cloghoge, Clonlum, Clontygora, Drumintee, Ellisholding, Killeen, Lislea, Meigh, Newtown, Scafin, and Tamnaghbane, in the parish of Killevy.

(*c*) In the county of Monaghan, the barony of Farney; the parish of Aughnamullan (except the forty townlands included in the new counties of Monaghan and East Brefney); and the eleven townlands of Annadrumman, Annagleve, Annalittin, Carrickagarvan, Cavanaguillagh, Clonavogy, Cornalough, Formil, Knockavolis, Mullaghanee, and Tullyvin, in the parish of Clontibret.

(*d*) In the county of Cavan, the parishes of Bailieborough, Enniskeen, Killinkere, Knockbride, Moybolgue, Mullagh, and Shercock, so far as included in the Grand Duchy; and the twenty-seven townlands of Ardmone, Barnagrow, Cashel, Corcloghan, Corleckduff, Coskemduff, Doohallat, Dooreagh, Drokaghbane, Drumaveil South, Drumcondra, Drumlumman, Drutamon, Gallonreagh, Killycleare, Knappagh, Knockna-shammer, Larawechan, Lisclogher, Lisdoagh, Lisnaclea, Lur-ganboy, Moyduff, Mullaghard, Mullan, Ralaghan, and Tony-hull, in the parish of Drumgoon.

(*e*) In the county of Meath, the baronies of Morgallion and Lower Slane, and so much of the barony of Lower Kells as is included in the Grand Duchy; also the parish of Rath-kenny in the barony of Upper Slane.

Population, 140,646; Protestants, 13,733.

11. *Tyrone.*—(*a*) The present county of Tyrone, except the parishes of Errigal Trough, Kilskeery, and Magheracross; and the five townlands of Annaghnaboe, Aughnamullan, Derryloughan, Derrytresk, and Drummarrer, in the parish of Clonoe.

(*b*) The entire county of Londonderry.

(*c*) In the county of Donegal, the barony of North Raphoe (except the parish of Leck, and the four townlands of Black-repentance, Carrickbrack, and Rousky, Upper and Lower); in the barony of South Raphoe, the parish of Urney, the three townlands of Calhame, Cornagillagh, and Treanboy, in the parish of Convoy, and the town of Castlefinn, with the thirty-nine townlands of Ballybun, Blairstown, Breaghy, Carn-owen, Carranadore, Carrick, Carricknashane, Cashelin, Castle-finn, Cloghard, Corcullin, Demesne, Donaghmore Glebe, Dooghan, Drummurphy, Dungorman, Gortfad, Gortnamuck, Grahamsland, Knockrawe, Leaght, Liscooly, Lisnabert, Lis-namulligan, Magheraboy, Magherareagh, Magherashanvally, Meenavony, Mullanboy, Raws, Upper and Lower, Scotland, Sessiagh, Sessiagh (Allison), Sessiagh (Long), Stranammuck, Tawnacrom, Tirinisk, and Tirnagushhoge, in the parish of

Donaghmore; and in the the barony of Innishowen West, the parishes of Burt and Muff and the nine townlands of Birdstown Demesne, Carnashannagh, Crislaghmore, Drumadooey, Fahan Level,Garvady, Gortnaskea, Monreagh, and Tievebane, in the parish of Upper Fahan.

Population, 380,785; Protestants, 190,400.

12. *Tyrconnel.*—The present county of Donegal, except the portions included in the new counties of Belfast, Fermanagh, and Tyrone.

Population, 162,528; Protestants, 29,496.

13. *Annaly.*—(*a*) The present county of Longford, except the parish of Mohill.

(*b*) In the county of Cavan, the parishes of Drumlumman and Scrabby; the parish of Ballintemple, except the townlands of Coolnacarrick and Rabrackan; and the seven townlands of Clonmult, Drumakineo, Drumnalaragh, Keelderry, and Tedeehan Upper, Middle, and Lower, in the parish of Crosserlough.

(*c*) In the county of Leitrim, the townlands of Gortermone and South Tully, in the parish of Carrigallen.

(*d*) In the county of Westmeath, the barony of Kilkenny West; the parish of Ballymore; and the town of Ballymore in the parish of Killare.

Population, 77,868; Protestants, 6506.

14. *Carlow.*—(*a*) The present county, except the barony of Lower St Mullins.

(*b*) In the county of Kildare, the barony of Kilkea and Moone; the parishes of Moone, Tankardstown, Timolin, and Usk; the parish of Narraghmore, so far as contained in the barony of Narragh and Reban East; and the townlands of Ballintoggart and Colbinstown, in the parish of Davidstown.

(*c*) In Queen's County, the barony of Slievemargy; and the parishes of Killabban, Monksgrange, Rathaspick, and Tankardstown, in the barony of Ballyadams.

(*d*) In the county of Wexford and barony of Scarawalsh, the parishes of Ballycarney, Kilrush, Moyacomb, Newtownbarry, Templeshanbo, and Monart (except the six townlands of Carrigabruse, Cherryorchard, Daphney, Forgelands, Lyre, and Shingann); and the nine townlands of Askinvillar, Upper and Lower, Ballinlug, East and West, Bantry Commons ($\frac{1}{4}$), Blackstairs Commons ($\frac{1}{2}$), Greenan, Springmount, and Woodbrook Demesne, in the parish of Killann and barony of Bantry.

(*c*) In the county of Wicklow, the barony of Upper Talbotstown; the parishes of Aghowle, Ardoyne, Crecrin, Donard, Dunlavin, Liscolman, and Moyacomb; the three townlands of Ballingate, and Ballingate, Upper and Lower, in the parish of Carnew; and the townland of Lower Mullycagh, in the parish of Hollywood.

Population, 82,814; Protestants, 10,486.

15. *Kildare.*—(*a*) In the present county, the baronies of Clane, Connell, Ikeathy, and Oughterany, Kilcullen, Naas, North and South, and Salt, North and South; the barony of East Offaly, except the parishes of Cloncurry, Grangeclare, Lullymore, Rathangan, and Thomastown, and the three townlands of Knocknagalliagh, Moorestown, and Rathwalkin, in the parish of Kildare; in the barony of West Offaly, the parishes of Ballyshannon, Fontstown, Kilrush, and Nurney, the townland of Clarey in the parish of Harristown, and the townland of Lower Walterstown in the parish of Walterstown; in the barony of Narragh and Reban West, the parish of Narraghmore; in the barony of Narragh and Reban East, the parishes of Fontstown, and of Davidstown (except the townlands of Ballintaggart and Colbinstown).

(*b*) In the present county of Dublin, the barony of Newcastle; the barony of Uppercross, except the parishes of Donnybrook, St Catherine, St James, St Jude, St Nicholas, and St Peter; in the barony of Rathdown, the parish of Whitechurch, and the parishes of Rathfarnham and Taney, so far as not included in the county of New Dublin.

(*c*) In the present county of Wicklow, the barony of Lower Talbotstown, except the parishes of Donard and Dunlavin, and the townland of Lower Mullycagh in the parish of Hollywood.

Population, 76,608; Protestants, 11,410.

16. *Kinsellagh.*—(*a*) In the present county of Wexford, the baronies of Ballaghkeen South, Bantry, Bargay, Shelburne, and Shellmalier, East and West; the barony of Forth, except the municipal borough of Wexford; the barony of Bantry, except the nine townlands of the parish of Killann included in the county of Carlow; and in the barony of Scarawalsh, the parishes of Enniscorthy and Templeshannon, and the six townlands of Carrigbruse, Cherryorchard, Daphney, Forgelands, Lyre, and Shingaun, in the parish of Monart.

(*b*) In the county of Carlow, the barony of Lower St Mullins.

Population, 81,418; Protestants, 5033.

17. *King's County.*—(*a*) In King's county, the present baronies of Ballyboy, Ballybrit, Eglish, Garrycastle, and Kilcoursey; the barony of Clonlisk, except the parish of Borrisnafarney; in the barony of Ballycowan, the parish of Rahan, and the townland of Doory in the parish of Durrow.

(*b*) In Queen's County (present), the parish of Kilmanman.

(*c*) In the present county of Roscommon, the town of Athlone.

(*d*) In the present county of Tipperary, the parishes of Aglishcloghane, Ardcrony, Ballingarry, Borrisokane, Cloghprior, Dorrha, Finnoe, Kilbarron, Lorrha, Loughkeen, Modreeny, Terryglass, and Uskane, in the barony of Lower Ormond; also the parishes of Corbally, Cullenwaine, Rathnaveoge, and Roscrea; the parish of Bourney, except the townlands of Borrisnoe and Coolgarran, and the townland of Gortnagowna, in the parish of Killavinoge, all in the barony of Ikerrin.

(*e*) In the county of Westmeath, the baronies of Brawny and Clonlonan ; and the parish of Kilcumreragh, in the parish of Moycashel.

Population, 82,605 ; Protestants, 10,488.

18. *Meath.*—(*a*) The present county, except the parts included in the new counties of Fingal and Oriel ; and the parishes of Ballyboggan, Castlejordan, Clonard, and Killyon, in the barony of Upper Moyfenrath (transferred to the new county of Westmeath).

(*b*) In the present county of Cavan, the entire parishes of Ballymachugh, Castlerahan, Kilbride, Loughan, Lurgan, and Munterconnaught ; and the parishes of Crosserlough, Denn, Killinkere, Lavey, and Mullagh, so far as not included in the new counties of Annaly, East Brefney, and Oriel.

(*c*) In the present county of Westmeath, the baronies of Delvin and Fore, excluding the parish of Mayne, and all the townlands of the parish of Faughalstown except Ballybeg and Derrynagarragh.

Population, 80,094 ; Protestants, 7001.

19. *Ossory.*—The present county, except the municipal borough of Kilkenny, and the parishes of Abbeyleix, Attanagh, Durrow, Kilmenan, and Rosconnel.

Population, 86,332 ; Protestants, 4021.

20. *Queen's County.*—(*a*) The present county, except the barony of Slievemargy ; the parishes of Killalban, Monksgrange, Rathaspick, and Tankardstown, in the barony of Ballyadams ; and the parish of Kilmanman in the barony of Tinnahinch.

(*b*) In King's County (present), the barony of Upper Philipstown, and the parish of Clonsast.

(*c*) In the present county of Kildare, the barony of Narragh and Reban West, except the parish of Narraghmore ; the barony of West Offaly, except the parishes of Ballyshannon, Fontstown, Kilrush, and Nurney, the townland of

Clarey, in the parish of Harristown, and the townland of Lower Walterstown, in the parish of Walterstown; also in the barony of East Offaly, the parishes of Cloncurry, Grangeclare, Lullymore, Rathangan, and Thomastown; and the three townlands of Knocknagalliagh, Moorestown, and Rathwalkin, in the parish of Kildare.

(*d*) In the present county of Kilkenny, the parishes of Abbeyleix, Attanagh, Durrow, Kilmenan, and Rosconnel. Population, 83,658; Protestants, 10,085.

21. *Westmeath.*—(*a*) The present county, except the parts included in the new counties of Annaly, King's County, and Meath.

(*b*) In the present King's County, the baronies of Geashill, Lower Philipstown, and Warrenstown; the barony of Ballycowan, except the parish of Rahan, and the townland of Doory in the parish of Durrow.

(*c*) In the present county of Meath, the barony of Moyfenrath, except the parish of Castlerickard.

(*d*) In the present county of Kildare, the barony of Carbury.
Population, 72,306; Protestants, 5792.

22. *Wicklow.*—(*a*) The present county, except the baronies of Upper and Lower Talbotstown; and the parishes of Aghowle, Ardoyne, Crecrin, Liscohnan, and Moyacomb, with the three townlands of Ballingate, and Ballingate, Lower and Upper in the parish of Carnew, all in the barony of Shillelagh.

(*b*) In the present county of Wexford, the baronies of Gorey and North Ballaghkeen; and the parishes of Carnew, Clone, Ferns, Kilbride, Kilcomb, and Toome, in the barony of Scarawalsh.

(*c*) In the present county of Dublin, all that part of the barony of Rathdown which lies outside the new county and borough of New Dublin, and the new county of Kildare— viz., the parishes of Kilgobbin, Killiney, Kiltiernan, Old-

M

connaught, Rathmichael, and Tully, and so much of the parish of Kill as lies outside New Dublin.
Population, 87,774; Protestants, 17,657.

23. *Dublin.* — (*a*) The present municipal borough of Dublin.

(*b*) The township of Drumcondra Glasnevin and Clonliffe.

(*c*) The parish of St Mark outside the city, and that part of the parish of Donnybrook which lies within the Dublin Harbour Parliamentary Division.
Population, 259,914; Protestants, 51,132.

24. *Kilkenny.*—(*a*) The present county of the city.
Population, 12,299; Protestants, 1348.

25. *Wexford.*—(*a*) The present municipal borough.
Population, 12,163; Protestants, 800.

26. *Waterford.*—(*a*) The present county of the city, and the barony of Kilculliheen.
Population, 23,332; Protestants, 2256.

27. *Clonmel.*—(*a*) The present municipal borough, with the parish of St Mary (Clonmel) in the county of Tipperary.
Population, 10,769; Protestants, 1275.

28. *Queenstown.* — (*a*) The present township, with the remaining portions of the parishes of Clonmell and Templerobin, and the townland of Foaty, in the parish of Carrigtohill.
Population, 13,555; Protestants, 2589.

29. *Barrymore.*—(*a*) In the county of Cork, the baronies of Imokilly and Kinnattalloon; the barony of Barrymore, excluding Foaty Island and Great Island (with the town of Queenstown); the barony of Kerricurrihy, except the parish of Ballinaboy; the parishes of Carrigaline and Killanully, in

the barony of Cork; and the parishes of Carrigaline and Kilpatrick, in the barony of Kinnalea.

(*b*) In the county of Waterford, the parishes of Kilcockan, Kilwatermoy, Tallow, and Templemichael.

Population, 74,680; Protestants, 5281.

30. *Carbery, East.*—(*a*) In the county of Cork, the baronies of Carbery East (2), Courceys, Ibane and Barryroe, Kinalmeaky, and Kinsale; the barony of Kinnalea, except the parishes of Ballinaboy, Carrigaline, Kilpatrick, and Knockavilly; the six townlands of Annaghbeg, Bawngoula, Coolsheeskin, Rigsdale, Skehanagh, and Tooreen, in the parish of Dunderrow, and the three townlands of Annaghmore, Curra, and Killeen, in the parish of Innishannon; and in the barony of West Carbery, the parishes of Drinagh, Kilmacabea, and Myross.

Population, 85,633; Protestants, 10,622.

31. *Carbery, West.*—(*a*) In the county of Cork the baronies of Bantry and Bere; and the barony of West Carbery, (both divisions), except the parishes of Drinagh, Kilmacabea, and Myross.

(*b*) In the present county of Kerry, the barony of Glanarought; the barony of South Dunkerron, except the parish of Knockane; in the barony of Iveragh, the parish of Dromod; and in the barony of North Dunkerron, the townlands of Bealdarrig and Graignagrane, in the parish of Templenoe.

Population, 91,756; Protestants, 6906.

32. *Decies.* — (*a*) The present county of Waterford, excluding the baronies of Coshmore and Coshbride, Glenahirey, and Kilcullicheen; and the parish of Killaloan, in the barony of Upperthird.

Population, 67,786; Protestants, 2565.

33. *Desmond.*—(*a*) In the county of Cork, the baronies of Condons and Clangibbon, Duhallow, Fermoy, and Orrery and Kilmore; the parish of Mourne Abbey, in the barony of

Barretts ; and the parishes of Drishane and Kilcorney, in the barony of West Muskerry.

(*b*) In the county of Limerick, the baronies of Coshlea and Kilmallock, and the parishes of Effin, Hackmys, Kilbreedy Minor, and Tankardstown, in the barony of Coshma.

(*c*) In the county of Waterford, the parishes of Leitrim and Lismore and Mocollop.

(*d*) In the present county of Kerry, the parish of Nohavaldaly.

(*e*) In the present county of Tipperary, the townland of Barnahown in the parish of Templetenny, and the townlands of Doon, Flemingstown (southern half), and Shanrahan (southern third), in the parish of Shanrahan.

Population, 142,872 ; Protestants, 6309.

34. *Kerry.*—(*a*) The present county, except the seven parishes of Dromod, Kenmare, Kilcrohane, Kilcaskan, Kilgarvan, Templenoe, and Tuosist, included in the new county of West Carbery ; the seven parishes of Annagh, Ballymacelligott, Ballyseedy, Clogherbrien, O'Brennan, Ratass, and Tralee, included in the new county of Tralee ; and the parish of Nohavaldaly, included in the new county of Desmond.

Population, 154,012 ; Protestants, 4405.

35. *Muskerry or Clancarty.*—In the county of Cork, the barony of East Muskerry ; the barony of West Muskerry, except the parishes of Drishane and Kilcorney ; the barony of Cork, except the parishes of Carrigaline and Killanully ; the barony of Barrett's, except the parish of Mourne Abbey ; the parishes of Ballinaboy and Knockavilly ; the six townlands of Annaghbeg, Bawngoula, Coolsheskin, Rigsdale, Skehanagh, and Tooreen, in the parish of Dunderrow ; and the three townlands of Annaghmore, Curra, and Killeen, in the parish of Innishannon, all in the barony of Kinnalea ; and in the barony of Kerrycurrihy, the parish of Ballinaboy.

Population, 72,960 ; Protestants, 4499.

36. *Ormond.*—(*a*) The present county of Tipperary, excluding the portions included in the new counties of Clonmel, Desmond, Thomond, and King's County.

(*b*) In the county of Waterford, the barony of Glenahircy, and the parish of Killaloan, in the barony of Upperthird.

Population, 138,464; Protestants, 5512.

37. *Thomond.*—(*a*) The present county of Limerick, except the parts included in the new county of Desmond, and the barony of North Liberties.

(*b*) In the present county of Tipperary, the baronies of Upper Ormond and Owney and Arra; the parishes of Dromineer, Killodiernan, Kilruane, Knigh, Monsea, and Nenagh, in the barony of Lower Ormond; the parishes of Cullen, Emly, Glenbane, Kilcornan, and Templebredon, in the barony of Clanwilliam; and the parish of Borrisnafarney, in the barony of Ikerrin.

(*c*) In the present King's County, the parish of Borrisnafarney.

Population, 152,106; Protestants, 5338.

38. *Cork.*—(*a*) The county of the city of Cork.

Population, 80,124; Protestants, 11,469.

39. *Limerick.*—(*a*) The county of the city of Limerick, and the barony of North Liberties.

Population, 41,115; Protestants, 4811.

40. *Tralee.*—(*a*) The township of Tralee and the parishes of Annagh, Ballymacelligott, Ballyseedy, Clogherbrien, O'Brennan, Ratass, and Tralee.

Population, 19,798; Protestants, 1780.

41. *Clare.*—(*a*) The present county of Clare.

(*b*) In the present county of Galway, the barony of Kiltartan; and in the barony of Loughrea, the parish of Kilthomas; the six townlands of Boleyneendorrish, Kinmona, North and

South, Rathanlan, Reaskgarriff, and Tullira, in the parish of
Ardrahan; the seven townlands of Bohaboy, Derrybrien, East,
North, South, and West, Funshadaun, and Toormacnevin, in
the parish of Killeenadeema; and the townland of Kilbeg, in
the parish of Killinan.

Population, 154,920; Protestants, 3213.

42. *Clanricarde.*—(*a*) In the present county of Galway,
the baronies of Clonmacnowen, Killian, Leitrim, and Longford; the barony of Kilconnell, except the parishes of Grange,
Kilimordally, Kiltullagh, and Monivea; in the barony of
Tiaquin, the parishes of Killoscobe and Killosolan, the
parish of Ballymacward (except the townlands of Glennamucka and Gorteen); and the ten townlands of Annaghmore,
East and West, Castlebellew, Cloncalloga, Cloonoran, Marlay,
Moylough, Moylough More, Patch, and Tomree, in the parish
of Moylough; also in the barony of Loughrea, the parishes of
Kilmeen, Killaan, and Kilteskill, and the three townlands of
Boleybeg, Coppanagh, and Drummin, in the parish of Killeenadeema.

(*b*) In the present county of Roscommon, the baronies of
Moycarn and North and South Athlone (except the parish of
Fuerty and town of Athlone).

Population, 79,249; Protestants, 2634.

43. *Galway.*—(*a*) The present county, excluding the parts
included in the new counties of Clare, Clanricarde, Mayo, and
Roscommon.

Population, 145,419; Protestants, 5239.

44. *Mayo.*—(*a*) The present county of Mayo.

(*b*) The barony of Ross in the present county of Galway.

(*c*) In the present county of Roscommon, the twenty-one
townlands of Attishane, Ballinross, Benmore, Carrowreagh,
Cloonfad, East and West, Cornabanny, Culkeen, Curragh,
Fiddaun, Gortamarle, Gorteenacammadill, Hundred Acres,
Meeltraun, (Wills), Moigh, Lower and Upper, Mount Delvin,

Pollanalty, East and West, Pollaphuca, and Swinefield, in the parish of Killultagh.

(*d*) In the present county of Sligo, the barony of Leyney, except the parishes of Ballysadare, Killoran, and Kilvarnet; and the barony of Tireragh, except the parishes of Dromard and Skreen; and the ten townlands of Aughris, Ballyforis, Carrownacreevy, Cartronofarry, East, South, and West, Corcoran's Acres, Corkagh, Beg and More, and Garryduff, in the parish of Templeboy.

Population, 292,896; Protestants, 9289.

45. *Moylury.*—(*a*) In the present county of Roscommon the baronies of Boyle and French Park; in the barony of North Ballintober, the parish of Kilmore; in the barony of Roscommon, the parish of Aughrim, and the fourteen townlands of Athroe, Ballyroddy, Barrinagh, Brackloon, Currigeen, Carrownamorheeny, Cartonagor, Cloonyeffer, Corry, East and West, Edenan, and Kinclare, Kilnamaryall, Kinclare, and Rathroe, in the parish of Shankill; and in the barony of Castlereagh, the four townlands of Ballaghcullia, Ballynahowna, Cashel, and Derreen, in the parish of Kilcorkey.

(*b*) In the present county of Sligo, the barony of Coolavin; the barony of Corran, except the four townlands of Doorly, Drumfin, Knocknagroagh, and Lackagh, in the parish of Kilmorgan; in the barony of Tirerril, the parishes of Aghanagh, Killadoon, Kilmactranny, and Shancough; the parish of Tawnagh, except the four townlands of Behy, Emlagh, Murilly-roe, and Whitehill; the six townlands of Ardlee, Bricklieve, Coolboy, Coolskeagh, Lecarrow, and Treanmacmurtagh, in the parish of Drumcolumb; and the seven townlands of Annagheor, Bellanacorrigeeny, Bellarush, Brickeen, Cleavry, Drumderry, and Sheerevagh, in the parish of Kilmacallan.

Population, 73,003; Protestants, 3161.

46. *Roscommon.*—(*a*) The present county of Roscommon, so far as not included in the new counties of Clanricarde, King's County, Mayo, and Moylurg.

(*b*) In the present county of Galway, the barony of Bally-moe, except the parishes of Tuam and Kilcrerrin, the twenty-one townlands of Ballyedmond, Brackloon, Claddagh, East and West, Clonbern, Cloonagawnagh, Cloonarkan, Cornaminaun, Fortbrown, Garraunbaun, Garrauns, Gortagarraun, Kead, Kilmorry, Knockroe, Laughil, Lenaboy, Lomanagh, Bawn and Roe, Mahanagh, and Meelickbeg, in the parish of Clonbern, and the sixteen townlands of Ballywataire, Bannoges, North and South, Breanra, Carrowkeel, Carrownagur, Carrowntryla, Carrowroe, East and West, Cloonagh, Cloonboo, Beg and More, Dunblaney, Gaterstreet, Killuney, and Meelickmore, in the parish of Dunmore.

Population, 75,100; Protestants, 1070.

47. *Sligo.*—(*a*) The present county of Sligo, so far as not included in the new counties of Mayo and Moylurg.

(*b*) The parishes of Cloonclare, Cloonlogher, Drumlease, Killasnet, Killanummery, and Rossinver in the present county of Leitrim.

(*c*) In the present county of Fermanagh, those parts of the parishes of Boho, Devenish, and Innismacsaint which are excluded from the Grand Duchy of Ulster.

(*d*) In the county of Donegal, that part of the parish of Innismacsaint which is excluded from the Grand Duchy of Ulster.

Population, 80,566; Protestants, 10,805.

48. *West Brefney.*—(*a*) The present county of Leitrim, except those parts which are included in the new counties of Annaly, East Brefney, and Sligo.

(*b*) In the present county of Cavan, the parishes of Drumreilly and Killinagh, and the parish of Templeport, except the nine townlands of Bofealan, Burren, Coologe, Crossmakelagher, Drumane, Killynaff, Lecharrownahone, Toberlyan Duffin, and Tonyrevan; and the four townlands of Dunmakeever, Eshveagh, Tonanilt, and Tullycrafton, in the parish of Kinawley.

(*c*) In the present county of Longford, the parish of Mohill.
Population, 72,358; Protestants, 5531.

SCHEDULE IV.

NEW PARLIAMENTARY DIVISIONS

(OTHER THAN SINGLE COUNTIES).

1. *Antrim, North.*—The new baronies of Broughshane, Cary, Dunluce, Lower and Upper, Glenarm, Kilconway, and Route, as described in Schedule II. Population, 75,144; Protestants, 52,265.

2. *Antrim, Middle.*—The new baronies of Antrim, Ballymena, Clandeboye, Lower, Middle, and Upper, Connor, and Toome. Population, 67,799; Protestants, 53,959.

3. *Antrim, South.*—The new baronies of Carnmoney, Carrickfergus, Killultagh, Larne, Massereene, Lower and Upper, and Moylinny. Population, 74,825; Protestants, 63,154.

4. *Belfast, North.*—St Anne's Ward, the town (and new ward) of Dundalk, and the new barony of Ligoniel. Population, 73,778; Protestants, 50,843.

5. *Belfast, East.*—Dock Ward, the towns (and new wards) of Lisburn, Lurgan, and Newry, and the new barony of Ballyshannon. Population, 79,247; Protestants, 43,933.

6. *Belfast, West.*—St George's Ward and Smithfield Ward. Population, 75,479; Protestants, 47,190.

7. *Belfast, South.*—Cromac Ward, the town (and new ward) of Drogheda, and the new barony of Holywood. Population, 72,925; Protestants, 50,231.

8. *Down, North.*—The new baronies of Lower Ards, Newtown Ards, Bangor, Castlereagh, Lower and Upper,

Dromara, and Kilwarlin. Population, 69,759; Protestants, 64,354.

9. *Down, West.*—The new baronies of Banbridge, Dromore, Iveagh, Lower, Upper, and West, Moira, and Rosstrevor. Population, 73,167; Protestants, 46,437.

10. *Down, East.*—The new baronies of Ards Upper, Castlewellan, Dufferin, Kinelarty, Lecale, Lower and Upper, and Mourne. Population, 71,832; Protestants, 38,026.

11. *Armagh, East.*—The new baronies of Clanbrassil, Clancann, Gilford, O'Neilland East, Orior, Lower and Middle, and Portadown. Population, 71,508; Protestants, 48,686.

12. *Armagh, West.*—The new baronies of Armagh, Charlemont, Fews, Lower and Middle, Keady, O'Neilland West, and Tiranny. Population, 74,398; Protestants, 39,772.

13. *Tyrone, North.*—The city of Londonderry, and the new baronies of Keenaght, Lower and Upper, and Tirkeeran, Lower and Upper. Population, 71,317; Protestants, 35,758.

14. *Tyrone, East.*—The new baronies of Clandonnell, Coleraine, Creeve or Clankane, Garvagh, Loughinsholin, Maghera, and Moyola. Population, 78,131; Protestants, 46,112.

15. *Tyrone, South.*—The new baronies of Aughnacloy, Ballinderry, Caledon, Dungannon, Lower and Upper, Killetragh, Mountjoy, and Tullaghoge. Population, 79,520; Protestants, 43,071.

16. *Tyrone, Middle.*—The new baronies of Clogher, Fintona, Munterlony, Omagh, East and West, Pomeroy, and Six Mile Cross. Population, 78,929; Protestants, 28,596.

17. *Tyrone, West.*—The new baronies of Ardstraw, Glenderg, Portlough, Raphoe, and Strabane, Lower and Upper. Population, 72,888; Protestants, 36,863.

18. *Tyrconnell, Lower.*—The new baronies of Doe, Fanad, Glenswilly, Innishowen, East, North, and West, and Kilmacrenan. Population, 77,536; Protestants, 17,069.

19. *Tyrconnell, Upper.* — The new baronies of Banagh,

Inner and Outer, Boylagh, North and South, Cloghaneely, Donegal, and Glenfinn. Population, 84,992; Protestants, 12,427.

20. *Oriel, Upper.*—The new baronies of Bailieborough, Clankee, Cremorne, Farney, Kingscourt, and Morgallion. Population, 67,256; Protestants, 9128.

21. *Oriel, Lower.*—The new baronies of Ardee, Carlingford, Ferrard, Fews Upper, Louth East, Louth West, and Orior Upper. Population, 73,390; Protestants, 4605.

22. *Dublin, North.*—The parishes of Clonturk, Glasnevin, St George, St Mary, and St Thomas, so far as contained in the new county. Population, 85,604; Protestants, 18,064.

23. *Dublin, South.* — The parishes of Donnybrook, St Andrew, St Anne, St Bridget, St Mark, and St Peter, so far as contained in the new county. Population, 83,348; Protestants, 21,174.

24. *Dublin, West.*—The remainder of the city (and new county). Population 90,962; Protestants, 11,894.

25. *Desmond, Upper.* — The baronies of Duhallow, and Orrery, and Kilmore; those parts of the baronies of Barretts, West Muskerry, and Magunihy (Kerry), which lie within the new county; the parish of Hackmys in the barony of Coshma (Limerick); and the six parishes of Ballyhay, Caherduggan, Carrigleamleary, Imphrick, Mallow, and Rahan, in the barony of Fermoy. Population, 71,248; Protestants, 2235.

26. *Desmond, Lower.*—The remainder of the new county. Population, 71,624; Protestants, 4074.

27. *Kerry, North.* — The baronies of Clanmaurice and Iraghticonnor; the barony of Corkaguiny, except the parish of Annagh; and in the barony of Trughenacmy, the parishes of Ardfert, Ballynahaglish, Brosna, and Fenit; the ten townlands of Ballinard, Coollegrean, Knockachur, Knocknadarriv, Lackabane, Lackbrooder, Lyre, Reacaslagh, Tooreenagowan, and Tooreennaserty, in the parish of Ballincuslane; and the sixteen townlands of Ahane, Ahaneboy (north half), Ballyduff, Beheenagh, Broughane, Feavautia, Gortroe, Knock-

nariddera, Knocknagashel, East and West, Meenbannivane, Meenleitrim, North and South, Muingvautia, Tooreenard, and Tooreenmore, in the parish of Castleisland. Population, 79,696; Protestants, 2665.

28. *Kerry, South.*—The remainder of the new county. Population, 74,316; Protestants, 1736.

29. *Ormond, East.*—The baronies of Eliogarty and Slieve-ardagh; the barony of Ikerrin, so far as contained in the new county; the barony of Iffa and Offa, East, except the parish of St Mary, Clonmel, the nine townlands of Black-castle, Clashavaddra, Clonmore, Correnstown, Decoy, Kil-molash, Upper, Moorestown, Shanballyard, and Woodrooff, in the parish of Inishlounaght, and the townlands of Graigne and Woodrooff, in the parish of Newchapel; the barony of Middlethird, except the parishes of Ardmayle, Boytourath, Dangandargan, Dogstown, Killeenasteena, Knockgraffon, Oughteragh, and Relickmurry and Athassel; and in the barony of Upper Kilnamanagh, the parish of Ballycahill. Population, 68,597; Protestants, 2863.

30. *Ormond, West.*—The remainder of the new county. Population, 69,767; Protestants, 2649.

31. *Thomond, West.*—The present baronies of Connello, Lower and Upper, Glenquin, Kenry, and Shanid; the barony of Coshma, except the parishes of Bruff, Tullabrocky, and Uregare; and the six townlands of Ballingayrour, Ballinlee, North and South, Ballinrea, Garbally, and Parkroe, in the parish of Dromin; also in the barony of Pubblebrien, the parishes of Croom, Kilkeedy, and Killonahan, and the town-land of Ballymacsradeen, West, in the parish of Monaster-anenagh; also in the barony of Small County, the townlands of Crean and Drumbeg, in the parish of Glenogra. Popula-tion, 73,138; Protestants, 2233.

32. *Thomond, East.*—The remainder of the new county. Population, 78,968; Protestants, 3105.

33. *Waterford Group.*—The united counties of Waterford, Clonmel, Kilkenny, Queenstown, and Wexford. Population, 72,118; Protestants, 8268.

34. *Limerick and Tralee.*—The united counties of Limerick and Tralee. Population, 60,913 ; Protestants, 6592.

35. *Galway, West.*—The baronies of Aran, Ballynahinch, and Moycullen, and the county of the town of Galway. Population, 70,313 ; Protestants, 3657.

36. *Galway, East.*—The remainder of the new county. Population, 75,106 ; Protestants, 1582.

37. *Clare, West.*—The present baronies of Clonderalow, Corcomroe, Ibrickan, and Moyarta ; the barony of Islands, except the parish of Clare Abbey, the town of Ennis, and the seventeen townlands of Ballymacaula, Cahircalla Beg, Cahircalla More, Claureen, Cloghleagh, Clonroad Beg, Clonroad More, Drumbiggil, Drumcaran Beg, Drumcaran More, Drumcliff, Fountain, Keelty, Kilnacally, Lifford, Loughvella, and Shanvogh, in the parish of Drumcliff; and in the barony of Inchiquin, the parishes of Inagh and Kilnamona, and the seven townlands of Carrowvere, Drinagh, Loughnagowan, Martry, Moanreel, North and South, and Ratline, in the parish of Rath. Population, 75,655 ; Protestants, 1268.

38. *Clare, East.*—The remainder of the new county. Population, 79,265 ; Protestants, 1945.

39. *Mayo, North.*—The present barony of Tireragh, so far as contained in the new county ; the present barony of Tirawley, except the parish of Addergoole ; the present barony of Erris, except the thirty-seven townlands of Aughness, Bellagarvaun, Bellaveeny, Bunmore, East and West, Castlehill, Claggan, Claggan Mountain, Croaghaun, Doona, Dooreel, Drumgollagh, Drumsleed, Essaun, Fahy, Gortbrack South, Greenaun, Kildun, Knockmoyleen, Lagduff Beg, Lagduff More, Lettera, Lurgandarragh, Maumaratta, Muingnanarnad, Owenduff, Owenglass, Scardaun, Sheeanmore, Srahduggaun, Srahederdaowen, Srahnamangagh, Tallagh, Tarsaghaun Beg, North and South, Tarsaghaun More, and Tawnanasheffin, together with the five islands of Annagh, Glassillan, Illaneroagh, Inishaghoo, and Inishbiggle, in the parish of Kilcommon ; and in the barony of Gallen, the parishes of Attymass and Kilgarvan. Population, 70,636 ; Protestants, 4080.

40. *Mayo, East.*—The barony of Leyney, so far as contained in the new county; the barony of Gallen, except the parishes of Attymass and Kilgarvan; and in the barony of Costello, the parishes of Castlemore, Kilbeagh, Kilcolman, and Kilturra, with the twenty-one townlands of Ballinrumpa, Ballyglass, Carrownlacka, Cashelnahenny, Clooncasha, Cloonierin, Cloon-amna, Corgarriff, Culliagh, Kilcashel, Killaclare, Kilmovee, Leveelick, Magheraboy, Raherolus, Ranagissanns, Rusheens, East and West, Skeheen, Sraheens, and Uggool, in the parish of Kilmovee. Population, 74,803; Protestants, 912.

41. *Mayo, South.*—The baronies of Clanmorris and Kilmaine; the barony of Costello, so far as not included in East Mayo; the parishes of Burriscarra, Drum, Manulla, Rosslee, and Tonaghty, in the barony of Carra; also the parish of Kiltullagh (in Roscommon), so far as comprised in the new county of Mayo. Population, 72,324; Protestants, 1092.

42. *Mayo, West.*—The remainder of the new county. Population, 75,133; Protestants, 3205.

SCHEDULE V.

SHORT LIST OF NEW BARONIES IN LEINSTER.

ANNALY.

1. Ardagh (Edgeworthstown).[1]
2. Clanhugh (Drumlish, Ballinamuck).
3. Clanmahon (Scrabby, Kilgolagh).
4. Granard.
5. *Longford* [2] (Ballinalee, Castle Forbes).
6. Moydow (Cloondara, Lanesborough).
7. Shrule (Ballymahon, Glassan, Lissoy).

[1] The names in brackets are those of towns or other notable places included in the barony.

[2] The names in italics are those of baronies where 15 per cent of the population are Protestant, exclusive of troops.

CARLOW.

1. *Carlow.*
2. Idrone (Bagenalstown, Borris).
3. *Imaile* (Baltinglass, Donard).
4. Moone (Castledermot, Ballitore, Dunlavin).
5. Scarawalsh (Newtown-Barry).
6. Slievemargy (Ballickmoyler, Old Leighlin).
7. *Tullow* (Tullowphelim, Clonegall, Myshall).

KILDARE.

1. Clane (Robertstown, Prosperous).
2. Kildare (Kilcullen).
3. Naas (Newbridge).
4. *Rathfarnham* (Crumlin, Dundrum).
5. Salt (Celbridge, Cloncurry, Leixlip, Maynooth).
6. Talbotstown or Blessington (Ballymore Eustace, Hollywood).
7. Upper Cross (Lucan, Chapelizod, Newcastle, Tallaght).

KING'S COUNTY.

1. Athlone or Calry.
2. *Ely O'Carroll, East* (Parsonstown, Kinnitty).
3. *Ely O'Carroll, West* (Cloghjordan, Borrisokane).
4. Fircall (Frankford).
5. Garrycastle (Banagher, Clonmacnoise, Ferbane).
6. Kilcoursie (Clara, Moate).
7. *Roscrea or Clonlisk.*

KINSELLAGH.

1. Ballaghkeen (Castlebridge).
2. Bargay.
3. Enniscorthy.
4. Forth.
5. New Ross.
6. Saint Mullins (Castleboro).
7. Shelburne (Duncannon).
8. Shelmalier (Taghmon, Adamstown).

MEATH.

1. Castlerahan (Virginia).
2. Delvin (Athboy).
3. Fore (Oldcastle, Castlepollard).
4. Kells.
5. Kilnaleck (Mount Nugent).
6. Lune (Trim).
7. Navan.

Ossory.

1. Callan.
2. Crannagh (Kilkenny).
3. Fassadineen (Castlecomer).
4. Galmoy (Freshford, Urlingford).
5. Gowran.
6. Knocktopher (Thomastown, Inistiogue).
7. Ida (Piltown).
8. Iverk (Rosbercon, Mullinavat).

Queen's County.

1. *Clanmalier* (Portarlington, Clonygowan).
2. Clarmallagh (Rathdowney).
3. Cullenagh (Abbeyleix, Durrow).
4. Leix (Athy, Stradbally).
5. Offaly (Monasterevan, Rathangan, Clonbulloge).
6. *Tinnahinch* (Maryborough, Mountmellick).
7. *Upper Ossory* (Mountrath, Castletown, Coolrain).

Westmeath.

1. Clancolman (Mullingar).
2. Corkaree (Street, Ballynacarrigy).
3. Fartullagh (Edenderry, Philipstown, Rochfortbridge).
4. Moycashel or Rathconrath (Kilbeggan, Loughanavally).
5. Moyfenrath or Farbill (Johnstown, Killucan, Kinnegad).
6. Tullamore (Geashill).

Wicklow.

1. *Arklow.*
2. *Fercullen* (Bray, Enniskerry, Delgany).
3. *Ferns* (Monamolin, Ballycanew, Ford).
4. *Gorey* (Coolgreany, Killenagh).
5. Ranelagh or Ballinacor (Rathdrum, Glendalough).
6. *Rathdown* (Killiney, Carrickmines, Little Bray).
7. *Shillelagh* (Carnew, Tinahely).
8. *Wicklow* (Wicklow, Newtown-Mount-Kennedy).

PRINTED BY WILLIAM BLACKWOOD AND SONS.

CATALOGUE

OF

MESSRS BLACKWOOD & SONS'

PUBLICATIONS.

CATALOGUE

OF

MESSRS BLACKWOOD & SONS

PUBLICATIONS.

——✦——

ALISON. History of Europe. By Sir ARCHIBALD ALISON, Bart.,
D.C.L.

  1. From the Commencement of the French Revolution to the
Battle of Waterloo.
LIBRARY EDITION, 14 vols., with Portraits. Demy 8vo, £10, 10s.
ANOTHER EDITION, in 20 vols. crown 8vo, £6.
PEOPLE'S EDITION, 13 vols. crown 8vo, £2, 11s.

  2. Continuation to the Accession of Louis Napoleon.
LIBRARY EDITION, 8 vols. 8vo, £6, 7s. 6d.
PEOPLE'S EDITION, 8 vols. crown 8vo, 34s.

  3. Epitome of Alison's History of Europe. Twenty-ninth
Thousand, 7s. 6d.

  4. Atlas to Alison's History of Europe. By A. Keith Johnston.
LIBRARY EDITION, demy 4to, £3, 3s.
PEOPLE'S EDITION, 31s. 6d.

—— Life of John Duke of Marlborough. With some Account
of his Contemporaries, and of the War of the Succession. Third Edition,
2 vols. 8vo. Portraits and Maps, 30s.

—— Essays: Historical, Political, and Miscellaneous. 3 vols.
demy 8vo, 45s.

ACTA SANCTORUM HIBERNIÆ ; Ex Codice Salmanticensi.
Nunc primum integre edita opera CAROLI DE SMEDT et JOSEPHI DE BACKER,
e Soc. Jesu, Hagiographorum Bollandianorum ; Auctore et Sumptus Largiente
JOANNE PATRICIO MARCHIONE BOTHAE. In One handsome 4to Volume, bound
in half roxburghe, £2, 2s. ; in paper wrapper, 31s. 6d.

AIRD. Poetical Works of Thomas Aird. Fifth Edition, with
Memoir of the Author by the Rev. JARDINE WALLACE, and Portrait.
Crown 8vo, 7s. 6d.

ALLARDYCE. The City of Sunshine. By ALEXANDER ALLAR-
DYCE. Three Vols. post 8vo, £1, 5s. 6d.

—— Memoir of the Honourable George Keith Elphinstone,
K.B., Viscount Keith of Stonehaven, Marischal, Admiral of the Red. 8vo,
with Portrait, Illustrations, and Maps, 21s.

ALMOND. Sermons by a Lay Head-master. By HELY HUTCHIN-
SON ALMOND, M.A. Oxon., Head-master of Loretto School. Crown 8vo, 5s.

ANCIENT CLASSICS FOR ENGLISH READERS. Edited by
Rev. W. LUCAS COLLINS, M.A. Price 2s. 6d. each. *For list of Volumes, see page 2.*

AYTOUN. Lays of the Scottish Cavaliers, and other Poems. By
W. EDMONDSTOUNE AYTOUN, D.C.L., Professor of Rhetoric and Belles-Lettres
in the University of Edinburgh. New Edition, printed from a new type,
and tastefully bound. Fcap. 8vo, 3s. 6d.
Another Edition, being the Thirtieth. Fcap. 8vo, cloth extra, 7s. 6d.
Cheap Edition. Fcap. 8vo. Illustrated Cover. Price 1s.

—— An Illustrated Edition of the Lays of the Scottish Cavaliers.
From designs by Sir NOEL PATON. Small 4to, in gilt cloth, 21s.

—— Bothwell : a Poem. Third Edition. Fcap., 7s. 6d.

—— Poems and Ballads of Goethe. Translated by Professor
AYTOUN and Sir THEODORE MARTIN, K.C.B. Third Edition. Fcap., 6s.

—— Bon Gaultier's Book of Ballads. By the SAME. Fifteenth
and Cheaper Edition. With Illustrations by Doyle, Leech, and Crowquill.
Fcap. 8vo, 5s.

—— The Ballads of Scotland. Edited by Professor AYTOUN.
Fourth Edition. 2 vols. fcap. 8vo, 12s.

—— Memoir of William E. Aytoun, D.C.L. By Sir THEODORE
MARTIN, K.C.B. With Portrait. Post 8vo, 12s.

BACH. On Musical Education and Vocal Culture. By ALBERT
B. BACH. Fourth Edition. 8vo, 7s. 6d.

—— The Principles of Singing. A Practical Guide for Vocalists
and Teachers. With Course of Vocal Exercises. Crown 8vo, 6s.

—— The Art of Singing. With Musical Exercises for Young
People. Crown 8vo, 3s.

BALLADS AND POEMS. By MEMBERS OF THE GLASGOW
BALLAD CLUB. Crown 8vo, 7s. 6d

BANNATYNE. Handbook of Republican Institutions in the
United States of America. Based upon Federal and State Laws, and other
reliable sources of information. By DUGALD J. BANNATYNE, Scotch Solicitor,
New York ; Member of the Faculty of Procurators, Glasgow. Cr. 8vo, 7s. 6d.

BELLAIRS. The Transvaal War, 1880-81. Edited by Lady BEL-
LAIRS. With a Frontispiece and Map. 8vo, 15s.

—— Gossips with Girls and Maidens, Betrothed and Free.
New Edition. Crown 8vo, 5s.

BESANT. The Revolt of Man. By WALTER BESANT, M.A.
Eighth Edition. Crown 8vo. 3s. 6d.

—— Readings in Rabelais. Crown 8vo, 7s. 6d.

BEVERIDGE. Culross and Tulliallan; or Perthshire on Forth. Its
History and Antiquities. With Elucidations of Scottish Life and Character
from the Burgh and Kirk-Session Records of that District. By DAVID
BEVERIDGE. 2 vols. 8vo, with Illustrations, 42s.

—— Between the Ochils and the Forth ; or, From Stirling
Bridge to Aberdour. Crown 8vo, 6s.

BLACK. Heligoland and the Islands of the North Sea. By
WILLIAM GEORGE BLACK. Crown 8vo, 4s.

BLACKIE. Lays and Legends of Ancient Greece. By JOHN
STUART BLACKIE, Emeritus Professor of Greek in the University of Edinburgh. Second Edition. Fcap. 8vo. 5s.

—— The Wisdom of Goethe. Fcap. 8vo. Cloth, extra gilt, 6s.

—— Scottish Song : Its Wealth, Wisdom, and Social Significance. Crown 8vo. With Music. 7s. 6d.

—— A Song of Heroes. Crown 8vo, 6s.

BLACKWOOD'S MAGAZINE, from Commencement in 1817 to
October 1889. Nos. 1 to 888, forming 144 Volumes.

—— Index to Blackwood's Magazine. Vols. 1 to 50. 8vo, 15s.

BLACKWOOD. Tales from Blackwood. Forming Twelve Volumes of Interesting and Amusing Railway Reading. Price One Shilling each, in Paper Cover. Sold separately at all Railway Bookstalls.
They may also be had bound in cloth, 18s., and in half calf, richly gilt, 30s. Or 12 volumes in 6, roxburghe, 21s., and half red morocco, 28s.

—— Tales from Blackwood. New Series. Complete in Twenty-four Shilling Parts. Handsomely bound in 12 vols., cloth, 30s. In leather back, roxburghe style, 37s. 6d. In half calf, gilt, 52s. 6d. In half morocco, 55s.
In course of Publication.

—— Tales from Blackwood. Third Series. In Parts. Each price 1s.   [*Nos. I. to VI. now ready.*
In course of Publication.

—— Travel, Adventure, and Sport. From 'Blackwood's Magazine.' In Parts. Uniform with 'Tales from Blackwood.' Each price 1s.
[*Nos. I. to V. now ready.*

—— Standard Novels. Uniform in size and legibly Printed. Each Novel complete in one volume.
FLORIN SERIES, Illustrated Boards. Or in New Cloth Binding, 2s. 6d.

TOM CRINGLE'S LOG. By Michael Scott.	PEN OWEN. By Dean Hook.
THE CRUISE OF THE MIDGE. By the Same.	ADAM BLAIR. By J. G. Lockhart.
CYRIL THORNTON. By Captain Hamilton.	LADY LEE'S WIDOWHOOD. By General Sir E. B. Hamley.
ANNALS OF THE PARISH. By John Galt.	
THE PROVOST, &c. By John Galt.	SALEM CHAPEL. By Mrs Oliphant.
SIR ANDREW WYLIE. By John Galt.	THE PERPETUAL CURATE. By Mrs Oliphant.
THE ENTAIL. By John Galt.	
MISS MOLLY. By Beatrice May Butt.	MISS MARJORIBANKS. By Mrs Oliphant.
REGINALD DALTON. By J. G. Lockhart.	JOHN: A Love Story. By Mrs Oliphant.

SHILLING SERIES, Illustrated Cover. Or in New Cloth Binding, 1s. 6d.

THE RECTOR, and THE DOCTOR'S FAMILY. By Mrs Oliphant.	SIR FRIZZLE PUMPKIN, NIGHTS AT MESS, &c.
THE LIFE OF MANSIE WAUCH. By D. M. Moir.	THE SUBALTERN.
	LIFE IN THE FAR WEST. By G. F. Ruxton.
PENINSULAR SCENES AND SKETCHES. By F. Hardman.	VALERIUS: A Roman Story. By J. G. Lockhart.

BLACKMORE. The Maid of Sker. By R. D. BLACKMORE, Author of 'Lorna Doone,' &c. New Edition. Crown 8vo, 6s.

BLAIR. History of the Catholic Church of Scotland. From the Introduction of Christianity to the Present Day. By ALPHONS BELLESHEIM, D.D., Canon of Aix-la-Chapelle. Translated, with Notes and Additions, by D. OSWALD HUNTER BLAIR, O.S.B., Monk of Fort Augustus. To be completed in 4 vols. 8vo. Vols. I. and II. 25s. Vol. III. 12s. 6d.

BOSCOBEL TRACTS. Relating to the Escape of Charles the Second after the Battle of Worcester, and his subsequent Adventures. Edited by J. HUGHES, Esq., A.M. A New Edition, with additional Notes and Illustrations, including Communications from the Rev. R. H. BARHAM, Author of the 'Ingoldsby Legends.' 8vo, with Engravings, 16s.

BROOKE, Life of Sir James, Rajah of Saráwak. From his Personal Papers and Correspondence. By SPENSER ST JOHN, H.M.'s Minister-Resident and Consul-General Peruvian Republic ; formerly Secretary to the Rajah. With Portrait and a Map. Post 8vo. 12s. 6d.

BROUGHAM. Memoirs of the Life and Times of Henry Lord Brougham. Written by HIMSELF. 3 vols. 8vo, £2, 8s. The Volumes are sold separately, price 16s. each.

BROWN. The Forester: A Practical Treatise on the Planting, Rearing, and General Management of Forest-trees. By JAMES BROWN, LL.D., Inspector of and Reporter on Woods and Forests. Fifth Edition, revised and enlarged. Royal 8vo, with Engravings, 36s.

BROWN. The Ethics of George Eliot's Works. By JOHN CROMBIE BROWN. Fourth Edition. Crown 8vo, 2s. 6d.

BRYDALL. Art in Scotland ; its Origin and Progress. By ROBERT BRYDALL, Master of St George's Art School of Glasgow. 8vo, 12s. 6d.

BROWN. A Manual of Botany, Anatomical and Physiological. For the Use of Students. By ROBERT BROWN, M.A., Ph.D. Crown 8vo, with numerous Illustrations, 12s. 6d.

BRUCE. In Clover and Heather. Poems by WALLACE BRUCE. Crown 8vo, 4s. 6d. *A limited number of Copies on large hand-made paper.*

BUCHAN. Introductory Text-Book of Meteorology. By ALEXANDER BUCHAN, M.A., F.R.S.E., Secretary of the Scottish Meteorological Society, &c. Crown 8vo, with 8 Coloured Charts and Engravings, 4s. 6d.

BUCHANAN. The Shire Highlands (East Central Africa). By JOHN BUCHANAN, Planter at Zomba. Crown 8vo, 5s.

BURBIDGE. Domestic Floriculture, Window Gardening, and Floral Decorations. Being practical directions for the Propagation, Culture, and Arrangement of Plants and Flowers as Domestic Ornaments. By F. W. BURBIDGE. Second Edition. Crown 8vo, with numerous Illustrations, 7s. 6d.

—— Cultivated Plants: Their Propagation and Improvement. Including Natural and Artificial Hybridisation, Raising from Seed, Cuttings, and Layers, Grafting and Budding, as applied to the Families and Genera in Cultivation. Crown 8vo, with numerous Illustrations, 12s. 6d.

BURTON. The History of Scotland : From Agricola's Invasion to the Extinction of the last Jacobite Insurrection. By JOHN HILL BURTON, D.C.L., Historiographer-Royal for Scotland. New and Enlarged Edition. 8 vols., and Index. Crown 8vo, £3, 3s.

—— History of the British Empire during the Reign of Queen Anne. In 3 vols. 8vo. 36s.

—— The Scot Abroad. Third Edition. Crown 8vo, 10s. 6d.

—— The Book-Hunter. New Edition. With Portrait. Crown 8vo, 7s. 6d.

BUTE. The Roman Breviary : Reformed by Order of the Holy Œcumenical Council of Trent; Published by Order of Pope St Pius V.; and Revised by Clement VIII. and Urban VIII.; together with the Offices since granted. Translated out of Latin into English by JOHN, Marquess of Bute, K.T. In 2 vols, crown 8vo, cloth boards, edges uncut. £2, 2s.

—— The Altus of St Columba. With a Prose Paraphrase and Notes. In paper cover, 2s. 6d.

BUTLER. Pompeii : Descriptive and Picturesque. By W. BUTLER. Post 8vo, 5s.

BUTT. Miss Molly. By BEATRICE MAY BUTT. Cheap Edition, 2s.

—— Eugenie. Crown 8vo, 6s. 6d.

—— Elizabeth, and Other Sketches. Crown 8vo, 6s.

—— Novels. New and Uniform Edition. Crown 8vo, each 2s. 6d. Delicia. *Now ready.*

CAIRD. Sermons. By JOHN CAIRD, D.D., Principal of the University of Glasgow. Sixteenth Thousand. Fcap. 8vo, 5s.

—— Religion in Common Life. A Sermon preached in Crathie Church, October 14, 1855, before Her Majesty the Queen and Prince Albert. Published by Her Majesty's Command. Cheap Edition, 3d.

CAMPBELL. Sermons Preached before the Queen at Balmoral. By the Rev. A. A. CAMPBELL, Minister of Crathie. Published by Command of Her Majesty. Crown 8vo, 4s. 6d.

CAMPBELL. Records of Argyll. Legends, Traditions, and Recollections of Argyllshire Highlanders, collected chiefly from the Gaelic. With Notes on the Antiquity of the Dress, Clan Colours or Tartans of the Highlanders. By LORD ARCHIBALD CAMPBELL. Illustrated with Nineteen full-page Etchings. 4to, printed on hand-made paper. £3, 3s.

CANTON. A Lost Epic, and other Poems. By WILLIAM CANTON. Crown 8vo, 5s.

CARR. Margaret Maliphant. A Novel. By Mrs COMYNS CARR, Author of 'La Fortunina,' 'North Italian Folk,' &c. 3 vols. post 8vo, 25s. 6d.

CARRICK. Koumiss; or, Fermented Mare's Milk: and its Uses in the Treatment and Cure of Pulmonary Consumption, and other Wasting Diseases. With an Appendix on the best Methods of Fermenting Cow's Milk. By GEORGE L. CARRICK, M.D., L.R.C.S.E. and L.R.C.P.E., Physician to the British Embassy, St Petersburg, &c. Crown 8vo, 10s. 6d.

CAUVIN. A Treasury of the English and German Languages. Compiled from the best Authors and Lexicographers in both Languages. By JOSEPH CAUVIN, LL.D. and Ph.D., of the University of Göttingen, &c. Crown 8vo, 7s. 6d.

CAVE-BROWN. Lambeth Palace and its Associations. By J. CAVE-BROWN, M.A., Vicar of Detling, Kent, and for many years Curate of Lambeth Parish Church. With an Introduction by the Archbishop of Canterbury. Second Edition, containing an additional Chapter on Medieval Life in the Old Palaces. 8vo, with Illustrations, 21s.

CHARTERIS. Canonicity; or, Early Testimonies to the Existence and Use of the Books of the New Testament. Based on Kirchhoffer's 'Quellensammlung.' Edited by A. H. CHARTERIS, D.D., Professor of Biblical Criticism in the University of Edinburgh. 8vo, 18s.

CHRISTISON. Life of Sir Robert Christison, Bart., M.D., D.C.L. Oxon., Professor of Medical Jurisprudence in the University of Edinburgh. Edited by his Sons. In two vols. 8vo. Vol. I.—Autobiography. 16s. Vol. II. —Memoirs. 16s.

CHURCH SERVICE SOCIETY. A Book of Common Order: Being Forms of Worship issued by the Church Service Society. Fifth Edition. 6s.

CLELAND. Barbara Allan, the Provost's Daughter. By ROBERT CLELAND, Author of 'Inchbracken,' 'True to a Type,' &c. 2 vols., 17s.

CLOUSTON. Popular Tales and Fictions: their Migrations and Transformations. By W. A. CLOUSTON, Editor of 'Arabian Poetry for English Readers,' 'The Book of Sindibad,' &c. 2 vols. post 8vo, roxburghe binding. 25s.

COBBAN. Master of his Fate. By J. MACLAREN COBBAN, Author of 'The Cure of Souls,' 'Tinted Vapours,' &c. Crown 8vo, 3s. 6d.

COCHRAN. A Handy Text-Book of Military Law. Compiled chiefly to assist Officers preparing for Examination; also for all Officers of the Regular and Auxiliary Forces. Comprising also a Synopsis of part of the Army Act. By Major F. COCHRAN, Hampshire Regiment Garrison Instructor, North British District. Crown 8vo, 7s. 6d.

COLQUHOUN. The Moor and the Loch. Containing Minute Instructions in all Highland Sports, with Wanderings over Crag and Corrie, Flood and Fell. By JOHN COLQUHOUN. Seventh Edition. With Illustrations. 8vo, 21s.

COTTERILL. Suggested Reforms in Public Schools. By C. C. COTTERILL, M.A., Assistant Master at Fettes College, Edin. Crown 8vo, 3s. 6d.

CRANSTOUN. The Elegies of Albius Tibullus. Translated into English Verse, with Life of the Poet, and Illustrative Notes. By JAMES CRANSTOUN, LL.D., Author of a Translation of 'Catullus.' Crown 8vo, 6s. 6d.

—— The Elegies of Sextus Propertius. Translated into English Verse, with Life of the Poet, and Illustrative Notes. Crown 8vo, 7s. 6d.

CRAWFORD. Saracinesca. By F. MARION CRAWFORD, Author of 'Mr Isaacs,' 'Dr Claudius,' 'Zoroaster,' &c. &c. Fourth Ed. Crown 8vo, 6s.

CRAWFORD. The Doctrine of Holy Scripture respecting the Atonement. By the late THOMAS J. CRAWFORD, D.D., Professor of Divinity in the University of Edinburgh. Fifth Edition. 8vo, 12s.

—— The Fatherhood of God, Considered in its General and Special Aspects, and particularly in relation to the Atonement, with a Review of Recent Speculations on the Subject. By the late THOMAS J. CRAWFORD, D.D., Professor of Divinity in the University of Edinburgh. Third Edition, Revised and Enlarged. 8vo, 9s.

—— The Preaching of the Cross, and other Sermons. 8vo, 7s. 6d.

—— The Mysteries of Christianity. Crown 8vo, 7s. 6d.

8 LIST OF BOOKS PUBLISHED BY

CRAWFORD. An Atonement of East London, and other Poems. By Howard Crawford, M.A. Crown 8vo, 5s.

DAVIES. Norfolk Broads and Rivers; or, The Waterways, Lagoons, and Decoys of East Anglia. By G. Christopher Davies, Author of 'The Swan and her Crew.' Illustrated with Seven full-page Plates. New and Cheaper Edition. Crown 8vo, 6s.

—— Our Home in Aveyron. Sketches of Peasant Life in Aveyron and the Lot. By G. Christopher Davies and Mrs Broughall. Illustrated with full-page Illustrations. In 1 vol. 8vo, 15s.

DAYNE. In the Name of the Tzar. A Novel. By J. Belford Dayne. Crown 8vo, 6s.

—— Tribute to Satan. A Novel. Crown 8vo, 2s. 6d.

DE LA WARR. An Eastern Cruise in the 'Edeline.' By the Countess De La Warr. In Illustrated Cover. 2s.

DESCARTES. The Method, Meditations, and Principles of Philosophy of Descartes. Translated from the Original French and Latin. With a New Introductory Essay, Historical and Critical, on the Cartesian Philosophy. By John Veitch, LL.D., Professor of Logic and Rhetoric in the University of Glasgow. A New Edition, being the Ninth. Price 6s. 6d.

DICKSON. Gleanings from Japan. By W. G. Dickson, Author of 'Japan: Being a Sketch of its History, Government, and Officers of the Empire.' With Illustrations. 8vo, 16s.

DOGS, OUR DOMESTICATED: Their Treatment in reference to Food, Diseases, Habits, Punishment, Accomplishments. By 'Magenta.' Crown 8vo, 2s. 6d.

DR HERMIONE. By the Author of 'Lady Bluebeard,' 'Zit and Xoe.' In 1 vol., crown 8vo, 6s.

DU CANE. The Odyssey of Homer, Books I.-XII. Translated into English Verse. By Sir Charles Du Cane, K.C.M.G. 8vo, 10s. 6d.

DUDGEON. History of the Edinburgh or Queen's Regiment Light Infantry Militia, now 3rd Battalion The Royal Scots; with an Account of the Origin and Progress of the Militia, and a Brief Sketch of the old Royal Scots. By Major R. C. Dudgeon, Adjutant 3rd Battalion The Royal Scots. Post 8vo, with Illustrations. 10s. 6d.

DUNCAN. Manual of the General Acts of Parliament relating to the Salmon Fisheries of Scotland from 1828 to 1882. By J. Barker Duncan. Crown 8vo, 5s.

DUNSMORE. Manual of the Law of Scotland as to the Relations between Agricultural Tenants and their Landlords, Servants, Merchants, and Bowers. By W. Dunsmore. 8vo, 7s. 6d.

DUPRE. Thoughts on Art, and Autobiographical Memoirs of Giovanni Duprè. Translated from the Italian by E. M. Peruzzi, with the permission of the Author. New Edition. With an Introduction by W. W. Story. Crown 8vo, 10s. 6d.

ELIOT. George Eliot's Life, Related in her Letters and Journals. Arranged and Edited by her husband, J. W. Cross. With Portrait and other Illustrations. Third Edition. 3 vols. post 8vo, 42s.

—— Works of George Eliot (Cabinet Edition). Handsomely printed in a new type, 21 volumes, crown 8vo, price £5, 5s. The Volumes are also sold separately, price 5s. each, viz.:—
Romola. 2 vols.—Silas Marner, The Lifted Veil, Brother Jacob. 1 vol.—Adam Bede. 2 vols.—Scenes of Clerical Life. 2 vols.—The Mill on the Floss. 2 vols.—Felix Holt. 2 vols.—Middlemarch. 3 vols.—Daniel Deronda. 3 vols.—The Spanish Gypsy. 1 vol.—Jubal, and other Poems, Old and New. 1 vol.—Theophrastus Such. 1 vol.—Essays. 1 vol.

—— George Eliot's Life. (Cabinet Edition.) With Portrait and other Illustrations. 3 vols. crown 8vo, 15s.

—— George Eliot's Life. With Portrait and other Illustrations. New Edition, in one volume. Crown 8vo, 7s. 6d.

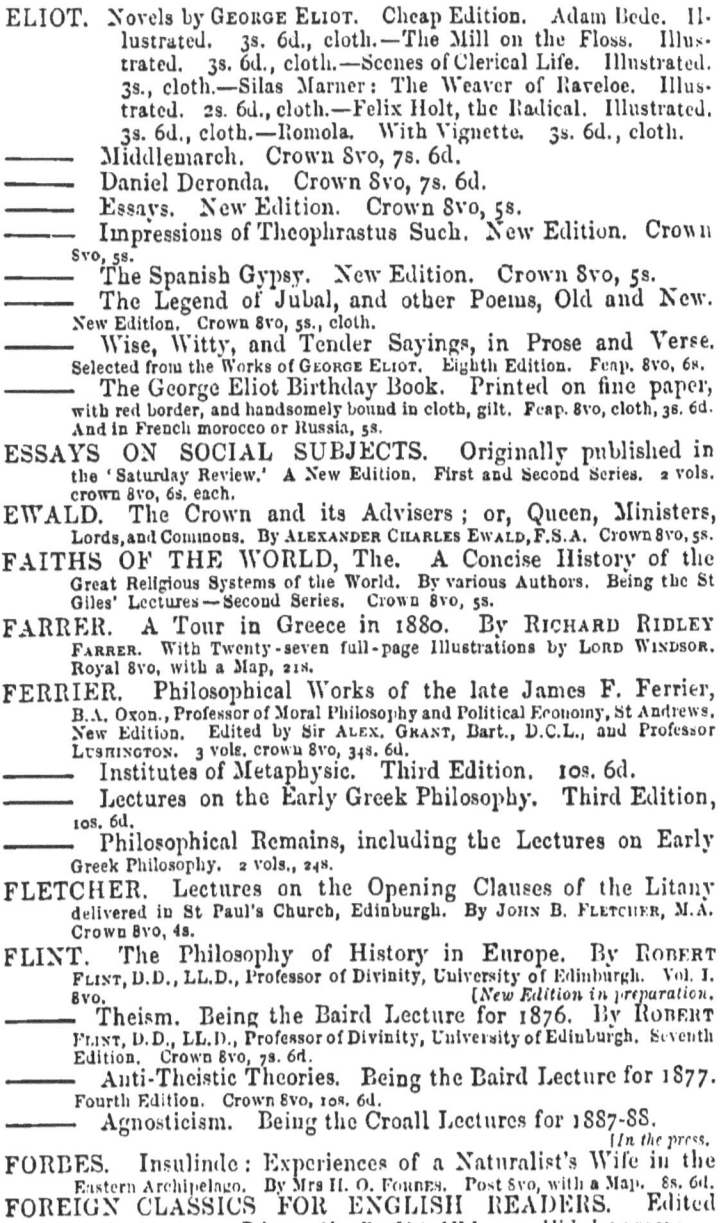

ELIOT. Novels by GEORGE ELIOT. Cheap Edition. Adam Bede. Illustrated. 3s. 6d., cloth.—The Mill on the Floss. Illustrated. 3s. 6d., cloth.—Scenes of Clerical Life. Illustrated. 3s., cloth.—Silas Marner: The Weaver of Raveloe. Illustrated. 2s. 6d., cloth.—Felix Holt, the Radical. Illustrated. 3s. 6d., cloth.—Romola. With Vignette. 3s. 6d., cloth.

———— Middlemarch. Crown 8vo, 7s. 6d.

———— Daniel Deronda. Crown 8vo, 7s. 6d.

———— Essays. New Edition. Crown 8vo, 5s.

———— Impressions of Theophrastus Such. New Edition. Crown 8vo, 5s.

———— The Spanish Gypsy. New Edition. Crown 8vo, 5s.

———— The Legend of Jubal, and other Poems, Old and New. New Edition. Crown 8vo, 5s., cloth.

———— Wise, Witty, and Tender Sayings, in Prose and Verse. Selected from the Works of GEORGE ELIOT. Eighth Edition. Fcap. 8vo, 6s.

———— The George Eliot Birthday Book. Printed on fine paper, with red border, and handsomely bound in cloth, gilt. Fcap. 8vo, cloth, 3s. 6d. And in French morocco or Russia, 5s.

ESSAYS ON SOCIAL SUBJECTS. Originally published in the 'Saturday Review.' A New Edition. First and Second Series. 2 vols. crown 8vo, 6s. each.

EWALD. The Crown and its Advisers ; or, Queen, Ministers, Lords, and Commons. By ALEXANDER CHARLES EWALD, F.S.A. Crown 8vo, 5s.

FAITHS OF THE WORLD, The. A Concise History of the Great Religious Systems of the World. By various Authors. Being the St Giles' Lectures—Second Series. Crown 8vo, 5s.

FARRER. A Tour in Greece in 1880. By RICHARD RIDLEY FARRER. With Twenty-seven full-page Illustrations by LORD WINDSOR. Royal 8vo, with a Map, 21s.

FERRIER. Philosophical Works of the late James F. Ferrier, B.A. Oxon., Professor of Moral Philosophy and Political Economy, St Andrews. New Edition. Edited by Sir ALEX. GRANT, Bart., D.C.L., and Professor LUSHINGTON. 3 vols. crown 8vo, 34s. 6d.

———— Institutes of Metaphysic. Third Edition. 10s. 6d.

———— Lectures on the Early Greek Philosophy. Third Edition, 10s. 6d.

———— Philosophical Remains, including the Lectures on Early Greek Philosophy. 2 vols., 24s.

FLETCHER. Lectures on the Opening Clauses of the Litany delivered in St Paul's Church, Edinburgh. By JOHN B. FLETCHER, M.A. Crown 8vo, 4s.

FLINT. The Philosophy of History in Europe. By ROBERT FLINT, D.D., LL.D., Professor of Divinity, University of Edinburgh. Vol. I. 8vo. [New Edition in preparation.

———— Theism. Being the Baird Lecture for 1876. By ROBERT FLINT, D.D., LL.D., Professor of Divinity, University of Edinburgh. Seventh Edition. Crown 8vo, 7s. 6d.

———— Anti-Theistic Theories. Being the Baird Lecture for 1877. Fourth Edition. Crown 8vo, 10s. 6d.

———— Agnosticism. Being the Croall Lectures for 1887-88. [In the press.

FORBES. Insulinde : Experiences of a Naturalist's Wife in the Eastern Archipelago. By Mrs H. O. FORBES. Post 8vo, with a Map. 8s. 6d.

FOREIGN CLASSICS FOR ENGLISH READERS. Edited by Mrs OLIPHANT. Price 2s. 6d. For List of Volumes published, see page 2.

FOTHERGILL. Diana Wentworth. By CAROLINE FOTHERGILL,
Author of 'An Enthusiast,' &c. 3 vols. post 8vo, 25s. 6d.

FULLARTON. Merlin : A Dramatic Poem. By RALPH MACLEOD
FULLARTON. Crown 8vo, 5s.

GALT. Annals of the Parish. By JOHN GALT. Fcap. 8vo, 2s.

——— The Provost. Fcap. 8vo, 2s.

——— Sir Andrew Wylie. Fcap. 8vo, 2s.

——— The Entail ; or, The Laird of Grippy. Fcap. 8vo, 2s.

GENERAL ASSEMBLY OF THE CHURCH OF SCOTLAND.
——— Family Prayers. Authorised by the General Assembly of
the Church of Scotland. A New Edition, crown 8vo, in large type, 4s. 6d.
Another Edition, crown 8vo, 2s.

——— Prayers for Social and Family Worship. For the Use of
Soldiers, Sailors, Colonists, and Sojourners in India, and other Persons, at
home and abroad, who are deprived of the ordinary services of a Christian
Ministry. New Edition.

——— The Scottish Hymnal Appendix. 1. Longprimer type, 1s.
2. Nonpareil type, cloth limp, 4d. ; paper cover, 2d.

——— Scottish Hymnal with Appendix Incorporated. Pub-
lished for Use in Churches by Authority of the General Assembly. 1. Large
type, cloth, red edges, 2s. 6d. ; French morocco, 4s. 2. Bourgeois type, limp
cloth, 1s.; French morocco, 2s. 3. Nonpareil type, cloth, red edges, 6d. ;
French morocco, 1s. 4d. 4. Paper covers, 3d. 5. Sunday - School Edition,
paper covers, 1d. 6. Children's Hymnal, paper covers, 1d. No. 1, bound
with the Psalms and Paraphrases, French morocco, 8s. No. 2, bound
with the Psalms and Paraphrases, cloth, 2s. ; French morocco, 3s.

GERARD. Reata : What's in a Name. By E. D. GERARD.
New Edition. Crown 8vo, 6s.

——— Beggar my Neighbour. New Edition. Crown 8vo, 6s.

——— The Waters of Hercules. New Edition. Crown 8vo, 6s.

——— The Land beyond the Forest. Facts, Figures, and
Fancies from Transylvania. By E. GERARD. In Two Volumes. With Maps
and Illustrations. 25s.

GERARD. Stonyhurst Latin Grammar. By Rev. JOHN GERARD.
Fcap. 8vo, 3s.

GILL. Free Trade : an Inquiry into the Nature of its Operation.
By RICHARD GILL. Crown 8vo, 7s. 6d.

——— Free Trade under Protection. Crown 8vo, 7s. 6d.

GOETHE'S FAUST. Translated into English Verse by Sir THEO-
DORE MARTIN, K.C.B. Part I. Second Edition. post 8vo, 6s. Ninth Edition, fcap., 3s. 6d. Part II. Second Edition, revised. Fcap. 8vo, 6s.

GOETHE. Poems and Ballads of Goethe. Translated by Professor
AYTOUN and Sir THEODORE MARTIN, K.C.B. Third Edition. fcap. 8vo, 6s.

GOODALL. Juxta Crucem. Studies of the Love that is over us.
By the late Rev. CHARLES GOODALL, B.D., Minister of Barr. With a Memoir
by Rev. Dr Strong, Glasgow, and Portrait. Crown 8vo, 6s.

GORDON CUMMING. At Home in Fiji. By C. F. GORDON
CUMMING, Author of ' From the Hebrides to the Himalayas.' Fourth Edition,
post 8vo. With Illustrations and Map. 7s. 6d.

——— A Lady's Cruise in a French Man-of-War. New and
Cheaper Edition. 8vo. With Illustrations and Map. 12s. 6d.

——— Fire-Fountains. The Kingdom of Hawaii: Its Volcanoes,
and the History of its Missions. With Map and numerous Illustrations.
2 vols. 8vo, 25s.

——— Wanderings in China. New and Cheaper Edition. 8vo,
with Illustrations, 10s.

——— Granite Crags: The Yō-semité Region of California. Illustrated with 8 Engravings. New and Cheaper Edition. 8vo, 8s. 6d.

GRAHAM. The Life and Work of Syed Ahmed Khan, C.S.I. By Lieut.-Colonel G. F. I. GRAHAM, B.S.C. 8vo, 14s.

GRANT. Bush-Life in Queensland. By A. C. GRANT. New Edition. Crown 8vo, 6s.

GRIFFITHS. Locked Up. By Major ARTHUR GRIFFITHS. Author of 'The Wrong Road,' 'Chronicles of Newgate,' &c. With Illustrations by C. J. STANILAND, R.I. Crown 8vo, 2s. 6d.

HAGGARD. Dodo and I. A Novel. By Captain ANDREW HAGGARD, D.S.O. Crown 8vo, 6s.

HALDANE. Subtropical Cultivations and Climates. A Handy Book for Planters, Colonists, and Settlers. By R. C. HALDANE. Post 8vo, 9s.

HALLETT. A Thousand Miles on an Elephant in the Shan States. By HOLT S. HALLETT, M. Inst. C.E., F.R.G.S., M.R.A.S., Hon. Member Manchester and Tyneside Geographical Societies. 8vo, with Maps and numerous Illustrations, 21s.

HAMERTON. Wenderholme : A Story of Lancashire and Yorkshire Life. By PHILIP GILBERT HAMERTON, Author of 'A Painter's Camp.' A New Edition. Crown 8vo, 6s.

HAMILTON. Lectures on Metaphysics. By Sir WILLIAM HAMILTON, Bart., Professor of Logic and Metaphysics in the University of Edinburgh. Edited by the Rev. H. L. MANSEL, B.D., LL.D., Dean of St Paul's ; and JOHN VEITCH, M.A., Professor of Logic and Rhetoric, Glasgow. Seventh Edition. 2 vols. 8vo, 24s.

—— Lectures on Logic. Edited by the SAME. Third Edition. 2 vols., 24s.

—— Discussions on Philosophy and Literature, Education and University Reform. Third Edition, 8vo, 21s.

—— Memoir of Sir William Hamilton, Bart., Professor of Logic and Metaphysics in the University of Edinburgh. By Professor VEITCH, of the University of Glasgow. 8vo, with Portrait, 18s.

—— Sir William Hamilton : The Man and his Philosophy. Two Lectures Delivered before the Edinburgh Philosophical Institution, January and February 1883. By the SAME. Crown 8vo, 2s.

HAMLEY. The Operations of War Explained and Illustrated. By Lieut.-General Sir EDWARD BRUCE HAMLEY, K.C.B., K.C.M.G., M.P. Fifth Edition, revised throughout. 4to, with numerous Illustrations, 30s.

—— National Defence ; Articles and Speeches. Post 8vo, 6s.

—— Shakespeare's Funeral, and other Papers. Post 8vo, 7s. 6d.

—— Thomas Carlyle : An Essay. Second Edition. Crown 8vo. 2s. 6d.

—— The Story of the Campaign of Sebastopol. Written in the Camp. With Illustrations drawn in Camp by the Author. 8vo, 21s.

—— On Outposts. Second Edition. 8vo, 2s.

—— Wellington's Career ; A Military and Political Summary. Crown 8vo, 2s.

—— Lady Lee's Widowhood. Crown 8vo, 2s. 6d.

—— Our Poor Relations. A Philozoic Essay. With Illustrations, chiefly by Ernest Griset. Crown 8vo, cloth gilt, 3s. 6d.

HAMLEY. Guilty, or Not Guilty? A Tale. By Major-General W. G. HAMLEY, late of the Royal Engineers. New Edition. Crown 8vo, 3s. 6d.

—— Traseaden Hall. "When George the Third was King." New and Cheaper Edition. Crown 8vo, 6s.

HARRISON. The Scot in Ulster. The Story of the Scottish Settlement in Ulster. By JOHN HARRISON, Author of 'Oure Tounis Colledge.' Crown 8vo, 2s. 6d.

HASELL. Bible Partings. By E. J. HASELL. Crown 8vo, 6s.

—— Short Family Prayers. Cloth, 1s.

HAY. The Works of the Right Rev. Dr George Hay, Bishop of Edinburgh. Edited under the Supervision of the Right Rev. Bishop STRAIN. With Memoir and Portrait of the Author. 5 vols. crown 8vo, bound in extra cloth, £1, 1s. Or, sold separately—viz. : The Sincere Christian Instructed in the Faith of Christ from the Written Word. 2 vols., 8s.—The Devout Christian Instructed in the Law of Christ from the Written Word. 2 vols., 8s.—The Pious Christian Instructed in the Nature and Practice of the Principal Exercises of Piety. 1 vol., 4s.

HEATLEY. The Horse-Owner's Safeguard. A Handy Medical Guide for every Man who owns a Horse. By G. S. HEATLEY, M.R.C.V.S. Crown 8vo, 5s.

——— The Stock-Owner's Guide. A Handy Medical Treatise for every Man who owns an Ox or a Cow. Crown 8vo, 4s. 6d.

HEDDERWICK. Lays of Middle Age ; and other Poems. By JAMES HEDDERWICK, LL.D. Price 3s. 6d.

HEMANS. The Poetical Works of Mrs Hemans. Copyright Editions.—One Volume, royal 8vo, 5s.—The Same, with Illustrations engraved on Steel, bound in cloth, gilt edges, 7s. 6d.—Six Volumes in Three, fcap., 12s. 6d. SELECT POEMS OF MRS HEMANS. Fcap., cloth, gilt edges, 3s.

HOME PRAYERS. By Ministers of the Church of Scotland and Members of the Church Service Society. Second Edition. Fcap. 8vo, 3s.

HOMER. The Odyssey. Translated into English Verse in the Spenserian Stanza. By PHILIP STANHOPE WORSLEY. Third Edition, 2 vols. fcap., 12s.

——— The Iliad. Translated by P. S. WORSLEY and Professor CONINGTON. 2 vols. crown 8vo, 21s.

HOSACK. Mary Queen of Scots and Her Accusers. Containing a Variety of Documents never before published. By JOHN HOSACK, Barrister-at-Law. A New and Enlarged Edition, with a Photograph from the Bust on the Tomb in Westminster Abbey. 2 vols. 8vo, £1, 11s. 6d.

HUTCHINSON. Hints on the Game of Golf. By HORACE G. HUTCHINSON. Fourth Edition. Fcap. 8vo, cloth, 1s. 6d.

IDDESLEIGH. Lectures and Essays. By the late EARL OF IDDESLEIGH, G.C.B., D.C.L., &c. 8vo, 16s.

INDEX GEOGRAPHICUS : Being a List, alphabetically arranged, of the Principal Places on the Globe, with the Countries and Subdivisions of the Countries in which they are situated, and their Latitudes and Longitudes. Applicable to all Modern Atlases and Maps. Imperial 8vo, pp. 676, 21s.

JAMIESON. Discussions on the Atonement : Is it Vicarious ? By the Rev. GEORGE JAMIESON, A.M., B.D., D.D., Author of 'Profound Problems in Philosophy and Theology.' 8vo, 16s.

JEAN JAMBON. Our Trip to Blunderland ; or, Grand Excursion to Blundertown and Back. By JEAN JAMBON. With Sixty Illustrations designed by CHARLES DOYLE, engraved by DALZIEL. Fourth Thousand. Cloth, gilt edges, 6s. 6d. Cheap Edition, cloth, 3s. 6d. Boards, 2s. 6d.

JENNINGS. Mr Gladstone : A Study. By LOUIS J. JENNINGS, M.P., Author of 'Republican Government in the United States,' 'The Croker Memoirs,' &c. Popular Edition. Crown 8vo, 1s.

JERNINGHAM. Reminiscences of an Attaché. By HUBERT E. H. JERNINGHAM. Second Edition. Crown 8vo, 5s.

——— Diane de Breteuille. A Love Story. Crown 8vo, 2s. 6d.

JOHNSTON. The Chemistry of Common Life. By Professor J. F. W. JOHNSTON. New Edition, Revised, and brought down to date. By ARTHUR HERBERT CHURCH, M.A. Oxon. ; Author of 'Food : its Sources, Constituents, and Uses,' &c., &c. Illustrated with Maps and 102 Engravings on Wood. Complete in one volume, crown 8vo, 7s. 6d.

——— Elements of Agricultural Chemistry and Geology. Revised, and brought down to date. By Sir CHARLES A. CAMERON, M.D., F.R.C.S.I., &c. Fifteenth Edition. Fcap. 8vo, 6s. 6d.

JOHNSTON. Catechism of Agricultural Chemistry and Geology.
An entirely New Edition, revised and enlarged, by Sir CHARLES A. CAMERON,
M.D., F.R.C.S.I.,&c. Eighty-sixth Thousand, with numerous Illustrations, 1s.

JOHNSTON. Patrick Hamilton : a Tragedy of the Reformation
in Scotland, 1528. By T. P. JOHNSTON. Crown 8vo, with Two Etchings. 5s.

KENNEDY. Sport, Travel, and Adventures in Newfoundland
and the West Indies. By Captain W. R. KENNEDY, R.N. With Illustrations
by the Author. Post 8vo, 14s.

KER. Short Studies on St Paul's Letter to the Philippians. By
Rev. WILLIAM LEE KER, Minister of Kilwinning. Crown 8vo, 5s.

KING. The Metamorphoses of Ovid. Translated in English Blank
Verse. By HENRY KING, M.A., Fellow of Wadham College, Oxford, and of
the Inner Temple, Barrister-at-Law. Crown 8vo, 10s. 6d.

KINGLAKE. History of the Invasion of the Crimea. By A. W.
KINGLAKE. Cabinet Edition, revised. Illustrated with Maps and Plans. Com-
plete in 9 Vols., crown 8vo, at 6s. each. The Vols. respectively contain : I.
THE ORIGIN OF THE WAR. II. RUSSIA MET AND INVADED. III. THE
BATTLE OF THE ALMA. IV. SEBASTOPOL AT BAY. V. THE BATTLE OF
BALACLAVA. VI. THE BATTLE OF INKERMAN. VII. WINTER TROUBLES.
VIII. and IX. FROM THE MORROW OF INKERMAN TO THE DEATH OF LORD
RAGLAN. With an Index to the Complete Work.

——— History of the Invasion of the Crimea. Demy 8vo. Vol.
VI. Winter Troubles. With a Map, 16s. Vols. VII. and VIII. From the
Morrow of Inkerman to the Death of Lord Raglan. With an Index to the
Whole Work. With Maps and Plans. 28s.

——— Eothen. A New Edition, uniform with the Cabinet Edition
of the 'History of the Invasion of the Crimea,' price 6s.

KNOLLYS. The Elements of Field-Artillery. Designed for the
Use of Infantry and Cavalry Officers. By HENRY KNOLLYS, Captain Royal
Artillery; Author of 'From Sedan to Saarbrück,' Editor of 'Incidents in the
Sepoy War,' &c. With Engravings. Crown 8vo, 7s. 6d.

LAVERGNE. The Rural Economy of England, Scotland, and Ireland. By LEONCE DE LAVERGNE. Translated from the French. With Notes
by a Scottish Farmer. 8vo, 12s.

LAWLESS. Hurrish : a Study. By the Hon. EMILY LAWLESS,
Author of 'A Chelsea Householder,' &c. Fourth Edition, crown 8vo, 6s.

LEE. A Phantom Lover : a Fantastic Story. By VERNON LEE.
Crown 8vo, 1s.

LEE. Glimpses in the Twilight. Being various Notes, Records,
and Examples of the Supernatural. By the Rev. GEORGE F. LEE, D.C.L.
Crown 8vo. 8s. 6d.

LEES. A Handbook of Sheriff Court Styles. By J. M. LEES,
M.A., LL.B., Advocate, Sheriff-Substitute of Lanarkshire. New Ed., 8vo, 21s.

——— A Handbook of the Sheriff and Justice of Peace Small
Debt Courts. 8vo 7s. 6d.

LETTERS FROM THE HIGHLANDS. Reprinted from 'The
Times.' Fcap. 8vo, 4s. 6d.

LIGHTFOOT. Studies in Philosophy. By the Rev. J. LIGHTFOOT,
M.A., D.Sc., Vicar of Cross Stone, Todmorden. Crown 8vo, 4s. 6d.

LITTLE HAND AND MUCKLE GOLD. A Study of To-day.
In 3 vols. post 8vo, 25s. 6d.

LOCKHART.- Doubles and Quits. By LAURENCE W. M. LOCK-
HART. With Twelve Illustrations. Fourth Edition. Crown 8vo, 6s.

——— Fair to See : a Novel. Eighth Edition. Crown 8vo, 6s.

——— Mine is Thine : a Novel. Eighth Edition. Crown 8vo, 6s.

LORIMER. The Institutes of Law : A Treatise of the Principles
of Jurisprudence as determined by Nature. By JAMES LORIMER, Regius
Professor of Public Law and of the Law of Nature and Nations in the University of Edinburgh. New Edition, revised and much enlarged. 8vo, 18s.

LORIMER. The Institutes of the Law of Nations. A Treatise of the Jural Relation of Separate Political Communities. In 2 vols. 8vo. Volume I. price 16s. Volume II., price 20s.

LYSTER. Another Such Victory! By ANNETTE LYSTER, Author of 'A Leal Light Heart,' 'Two Old Maids,' &c. 3 vols. crown 8vo, 25s. 6d.

M'COMBIE. Cattle and Cattle-Breeders. By WILLIAM M'COMBIE, Tillyfour. New Edition, enlarged, with Memoir of the Author. By JAMES MACDONALD, of the 'Farming World.' Crown 8vo, 3s. 6d.

MACRAE. A Handbook of Deer - Stalking. By ALEXANDER MACRAE, late Forester to Lord Henry Bentinck. With Introduction by HORATIO ROSS, Esq. Fcap. 8vo, with two Photographs from Life. 3s. 6d.

M'CRIE. Works of the Rev. Thomas M'Crie, D.D. Uniform Edition. Four vols. crown 8vo, 24s.

——— Life of John Knox. Containing Illustrations of the History of the Reformation in Scotland. Crown 8vo, 6s. Another Edition, 3s. 6d.

——— Life of Andrew Melville. Containing Illustrations of the Ecclesiastical and Literary History of Scotland in the Sixteenth and Seventeenth Centuries. Crown 8vo, 6s.

——— History of the Progress and Suppression of the Reformation in Italy in the Sixteenth Century. Crown 8vo, 4s.

——— History of the Progress and Suppression of the Reformation in Spain in the Sixteenth Century. Crown 8vo, 3s. 6d.

——— Lectures on the Book of Esther. Fcap. 8vo, 5s.

MACDONALD. A Manual of the Criminal Law (Scotland) Procedure Act, 1887. By NORMAN DORAN MACDONALD. Revised by the LORD JUSTICE-CLERK. 8vo, cloth. 10s. 6d.

MACGREGOR. Life and Opinions of Major-General Sir Charles MacGregor, K.C.B., C.S.I., C.I.E , Quartermaster-General of India. From his Letters and Diaries. Edited by LADY MACGREGOR. With Portraits and Maps to illustrate Campaigns in which he was engaged. 2 vols. 8vo, 35s.

M'INTOSH. The Book of the Garden. By CHARLES M'INTOSH, formerly Curator of the Royal Gardens of his Majesty the King of the Belgians, and lately of those of his Grace the Duke of Buccleuch, K.G., at Dalkeith Palace. 2 vols. royal 8vo, with 1350 Engravings. £4, 7s. 6d. Vol. I. On the Formation of Gardens and Construction of Garden Edifices. £2, 10s. Vol. II. Practical Gardening. £1, 17s. 6d.

MACINTYRE. Hindu Koh: Wanderings and Wild Sports on and beyond the Himalayas. By Major-General DONALD MACINTYRE, V.C., late Prince of Wales' Own Goorkhas, F.R.G.S. Dedicated to H.R.H. The Prince of Wales. 8vo, with numerous Illustrations, 21s.

MACKAY. A Manual of Modern Geography; Mathematical, Physical, and Political. By the Rev. ALEXANDER MACKAY, LL.D., F.R.G.S. 11th Thousand, revised to the present time. Crown 8vo, pp. 688. 7s. 6d.

——— Elements of Modern Geography. 53d Thousand, revised to the present time. Crown 8vo, pp. 300, 3s.

——— The Intermediate Geography. By the Rev. ALEXANDER MACKAY, LL.D., F.R.G.S. Intended as an Intermediate Book between the Author's ' Outlines of Geography' and ' Elements of Geography.' Fifteenth Edition, revised. Crown 8vo, pp. 238, 2s.

——— Outlines of Modern Geography. 186th Thousand, revised to the present time. 18mo, pp. 118, 1s.

——— First Steps in Geography. 105th Thousand. 18mo, pp. 56. Sewed, 4d.; cloth, 6d.

——— Elements of Physiography and Physical Geography. With Express Reference to the Instructions recently issued by the Science and Art Department. 30th Thousand, revised. Crown 8vo, 1s. 6d.

——— Facts and Dates; or, the Leading Events in Sacred and Profane History, and the Principal Facts in the various Physical Sciences. The Memory being aided throughout by a Simple and Natural Method. For Schools and Private Reference. New Edition. Crown 8vo, 3s. 6d.

MACKAY. An Old Scots Brigade. Being the History of Mackay's Regiment, now incorporated with the Royal Scots. With an Appendix containing many Original Documents connected with the History of the Regiment. By JOHN MACKAY (late) OF HERRIESDALE. Crown 8vo, 5s.

MACKAY. The Founders of the American Republic. A History of Washington, Adams, Jefferson, Franklin, and Madison. With a Supplementary Chapter on the Inherent Causes of the Ultimate Failure of American Democracy. By CHARLES MACKAY, LL.D. Post 8vo, 10s. 6d.

MACKENZIE. Studies in Roman Law. With Comparative Views of the Laws of France, England, and Scotland. By LORD MACKENZIE, one of the Judges of the Court of Session in Scotland. Sixth Edition, Edited by JOHN KIRKPATRICK, Esq., M.A. Cantab.; Dr Jur. Heidelb.; LL.B. Edin.; Advocate. 8vo, 12s.

MAIN. Three Hundred English Sonnets. Chosen and Edited by DAVID M. MAIN. Fcap. 8vo, 6s.

MAIR. A Digest of Laws and Decisions, Ecclesiastical and Civil, relating to the Constitution, Practice, and Affairs of the Church of Scotland. With Notes and Forms of Procedure. By the Rev. WILLIAM MAIR, D.D., Minister of the Parish of Earlston. Crown 8vo. With Supplements, 8s.

MARMORNE. The Story is told by ADOLPHUS SEGRAVE, the youngest of three Brothers. Third Edition. Crown 8vo, 6s.

MARSHALL. French Home Life. By FREDERIC MARSHALL. Second Edition. 5s.

MARSHMAN. History of India. From the Earliest Period to the Close of the India Company's Government; with an Epitome of Subsequent Events. By JOHN CLARK MARSHMAN, C.S.I. Abridged from the Author's larger work. Second Edition, revised. Crown 8vo, with Map, 6s. 6d.

MARTIN. Goethe's Faust. Part I. Translated by Sir THEODORE MARTIN, K.C.B. Second Ed., crown 8vo, 6s. Ninth Ed., fcap. 8vo, 3s. 6d.

—— Goethe's Faust. Part II. Translated into English Verse. Second Edition, revised. Fcap. 8vo, 6s.

—— The Works of Horace. Translated into English Verse, with Life and Notes. 2 vols. New Edition, crown 8vo, 21s.

—— Poems and Ballads of Heinrich Heine. Done into English Verse. Second Edition. Printed on papier vergé, crown 8vo, 8s.

—— The Song of the Bell, and other Translations from Schiller, Goethe, Uhland, and Others. Crown 8vo, 7s. 6d.

—— Catullus. With Life and Notes. Second Ed., post 8vo, 7s. 6d.

—— Aladdin : A Dramatic Poem. By ADAM OEHLENSCHLAEGER. Fcap. 8vo, 5s.

—— Correggio : A Tragedy. By OEHLENSCHLAEGER. With Notes. Fcap. 8vo, 3s.

—— King Rene's Daughter : A Danish Lyrical Drama. By HENRIK HERTZ. Second Edition, fcap., 2s. 6d.

MARTIN. On some of Shakespeare's Female Characters. In a Series of Letters. By HELENA FAUCIT, LADY MARTIN. Dedicated by permission to Her Most Gracious Majesty the Queen. Third Edition. 8vo, with Portrait, 7s. 6d.

MATHESON. Can the Old Faith Live with the New? or the Problem of Evolution and Revelation. By the Rev. GEORGE MATHESON, D.D. Third Edition. Crown 8vo, 7s. 6d.

—— The Psalmist and the Scientist ; or, Modern Value of the Religious Sentiment. Crown 8vo, 7s. 6d.

—— Sacred Songs. Crown 8vo, 5s.

MAURICE. The Balance of Military Power in Europe. An Examination of the War Resources of Great Britain and the Continental States. By Colonel MAURICE, R.A., Professor of Military Art and History at the Royal Staff College. Crown 8vo, with a Map. 6s.

MICHEL. A Critical Inquiry into the Scottish Language. With the view of Illustrating the Rise and Progress of Civilisation in Scotland. By FRANCISQUE-MICHEL, F.S.A. Lond. and Scot., Correspondant de l'Institut de France, &c. 4to, printed on hand-made paper, and bound in Roxburghe, 66s.

MICHIE. The Larch : Being a Practical Treatise on its Culture and General Management. By CHRISTOPHER Y. MICHIE. Forester, Cullen House. Crown 8vo, with Illustrations. New and Cheaper Edition, enlarged, 5s.

———— Practical Forestry. Crown 8vo, with Illustrations. 6s.

MIDDLETON. The Story of Alastair Bhan Comyn : or, The Tragedy of Dunphail. A Tale of Tradition and Romance. By the Lady MIDDLETON. Square 8vo, 10s.

MILNE. The Problem of the Churchless and Poor in our Large Towns. With special reference to the Home Mission Work of the Church of Scotland. By the Rev. ROBT. MILNE, M.A., D.D., Ardler. Crown 8vo, 3s. 6d.

MINTO. A Manual of English Prose Literature, Biographical and Critical : designed mainly to show Characteristics of Style. By W. MINTO, M.A., Professor of Logic in the University of Aberdeen. Third Edition, revised. Crown 8vo, 7s. 6d.

———— Characteristics of English Poets, from Chaucer to Shirley. New Edition, revised. Crown 8vo, 7s. 6d.

MITCHELL. Biographies of Eminent Soldiers of the last Four Centuries. By Major-General JOHN MITCHELL, Author of 'Life of Wallenstein.' With a Memoir of the Author. 8vo, 9s

MOIR. Life of Mansie Wauch, Tailor in Dalkeith. With 8 Illustrations on Steel, by the late GEORGE CRUIKSHANK. Crown 8vo, 3s. 6d. Another Edition, fcap. 8vo, 1s. 6d.

MOMERIE. Defects of Modern Christianity, and other Sermons. By ALFRED WILLIAMS MOMERIE, M.A., D.Sc., LL.D., Professor of Logic and Metaphysics in King's College, London. Third Edition. Crown 8vo, 5s.

———— The Basis of Religion. Being an Examination of Natural Religion. Second Edition. Crown 8vo, 2s. 6d.

———— The Origin of Evil, and other Sermons. Sixth Edition, enlarged. Crown 8vo, 5s.

———— Personality. The Beginning and End of Metaphysics, and a Necessary Assumption in all Positive Philosophy. Fourth Ed. Cr. 8vo, 3s.

———— Agnosticism. Second Edition. Revised. Crown 8vo, 5s.

———— Preaching and Hearing ; and other Sermons. Second Edition. Crown 8vo, 4s. 6d.

———— Belief in God. Second Edition. Crown 8vo, 3s.

———— Inspiration ; and other Sermons. Crown 8vo, 5s.

———— Church and Creed. Crown 8vo, 4s. 6d.

MONTAGUE. Campaigning in South Africa. Reminiscences of an Officer in 1879. By Captain W. E. MONTAGUE, 94th Regiment, Author of ' Claude Meadowleigh,' &c. 8vo, 10s. 6d.

MONTALEMBERT. Memoir of Count de Montalembert. A Chapter of Recent French History. By Mrs OLIPHANT, Author of the ' Life of Edward Irving.' &c. 2 vols. crown 8vo, £1, 4s

MORISON. Sordello. An Outline Analysis of Mr Browning's Poem. By JEANIE MORISON, Author of 'The Purposes of the Ages,' 'Ane Booke of Ballades,' &c. Crown 8vo, 3s.

MURDOCH. Manual of the Law of Insolvency and Bankruptcy : Comprehending a Summary of the Law of Insolvency, Notour Bankruptcy, Composition - contracts, Trust-deeds, Cessio, and Sequestrations: and the Winding-up of Joint-Stock Companies in Scotland ; with Annotations on the various Insolvency and Bankruptcy Statutes: and with Forms of Procedure applicable to these Subjects. By JAMES MURDOCH, Member of the Faculty of Procurators in Glasgow. Fifth Edition, Revised and Enlarged, 8vo, £1, 10s.

MY TRIVIAL LIFE AND MISFORTUNE: A Gossip with no Plot in Particular. By A PLAIN WOMAN. New Edition, crown 8vo, 6s.

By the SAME AUTHOR.

POOR NELLIE. New and Cheaper Edition. Crown 8vo, 6s.

NAPIER. The Construction of the Wonderful Canon of Logarithms (Mirifici Logarithmorum Canonis Constructio). By JOHN NAPIER of Merchiston. Translated for the first time, with Notes, and a Catalogue of Napier's Works, by WILLIAM RAE MACDONALD. Small 4to, 15s. *A few large paper copies may be had, printed on Whatman paper, price* 30s.

NEAVES. Songs and Verses, Social and Scientific. By an Old Contributor to 'Maga.' By the Hon. Lord NEAVES. Fifth Ed., fcap. 8vo, 4s.

—— The Greek Anthology. Being Vol. XX. of 'Ancient Classics for English Readers.' Crown 8vo, 2s. 6d.

NICHOLSON. A Manual of Zoology, for the Use of Students. With a General Introduction on the Principles of Zoology. By HENRY ALLEYNE NICHOLSON, M.D., D.Sc., F.L.S., F.G.S., Regius Professor of Natural History in the University of Aberdeen. Seventh Edition, rewritten and enlarged. Post 8vo, pp. 956, with 555 Engravings on Wood, 18s.

—— Text-Book of Zoology, for the Use of Schools. Fourth Edition, enlarged. Crown 8vo, with 188 Engravings on Wood, 7s. 6d.

—— Introductory Text-Book of Zoology, for the Use of Junior Classes. Sixth Edition, revised and enlarged, with 166 Engravings, 3s.

—— Outlines of Natural History, for Beginners ; being Descriptions of a Progressive Series of Zoological Types. Third Edition, with Engravings, 1s. 6d.

—— A Manual of Palæontology, for the Use of Students. With a General Introduction on the Principles of Palæontology. By Professor H. ALLEYNE NICHOLSON and RICHARD LYDEKKER. Third Edition. Rewritten and greatly enlarged. 2 vols. 8vo, with Engravings, £3 3s.

—— The Ancient Life-History of the Earth. An Outline of the Principles and Leading Facts of Palæontological Science. Crown 8vo, with 276 Engravings, 10s. 6d.

—— On the "Tabulate Corals" of the Palæozoic Period, with Critical Descriptions of Illustrative Species. Illustrated with 15 Lithograph Plates and numerous Engravings. Super-royal 8vo, 21s.

—— Synopsis of the Classification of the Animal Kingdom. 8vo, with 106 Illustrations, 6s.

—— On the Structure and Affinities of the Genus Monticulipora and its Sub-Genera, with Critical Descriptions of Illustrative Species. Illustrated with numerous Engravings on wood and lithographed Plates. Super-royal 8vo, 18s.

NICHOLSON. Communion with Heaven, and other Sermons. By the late MAXWELL NICHOLSON, D.D., Minister of St Stephen's, Edinburgh Crown 8vo, 5s. 6d.

—— Rest in Jesus. Sixth Edition. Fcap. 8vo, 4s. 6d.

NICHOLSON. A Treatise on Money, and Essays on Present Monetary Problems. By JOSEPH SHIELD NICHOLSON, M.A., D.Sc., Professor of Commercial and Political Economy and Mercantile Law in the University of Edinburgh. 8vo, 10s. 6d.

NICOLSON AND MURE. A Handbook to the Local Government (Scotland) Act, 1889. With Introduction, Explanatory Notes, and Index. By J. BADENACH NICOLSON, Advocate, Counsel to the Scotch Education Department, and W. J. MURE, Advocate, Legal Secretary to the Lord Advocate for Scotland. Seventh Reprint. 8vo, 5s.

OLIPHANT. Masollam: a Problem of the Period. A Novel. By LAURENCE OLIPHANT. 3 vols. post 8vo, 25s. 6d.

—— Scientific Religion ; or, Higher Possibilities of Life and Practice through the Operation of Natural Forces. Second Edition. 8vo, 16s.

18   LIST OF BOOKS PUBLISHED BY

OLIPHANT. Altiora Peto. New and Cheaper Edition. Crown
8vo, boards, 2s. 6d. Illustrated Edition. Crown 8vo, cloth, 6s.
———— Piccadilly : A Fragment of Contemporary Biography. With
Eight Illustrations by Richard Doyle. Eighth Edition, 4s. 6d. Cheap Edition,
in paper cover, 2s. 6d.
———— Traits and Travesties ; Social and Political. Post 8vo,10s.6d.
———— The Land of Gilead. With Excursions in the Lebanon.
With Illustrations and Maps. Demy 8vo, 21s.
———— The Land of Khemi. Post 8vo, with Illustrations, 10s. 6d.
———— Haifa : Life in Modern Palestine. 2d Edition. 8vo, 7s. 6d.
———— Episodes in a Life of Adventure ; or, Moss from a Rolling
Stone. Fourth Edition. Post 8vo, 6s.
———— Fashionable Philosophy, and other Sketches. In paper
cover, 1s.
———— Sympneumata : or, Evolutionary Functions now Active in
Man. Edited by LAURENCE OLIPHANT. Post 8vo, 10s. 6d.
OLIPHANT. Katie Stewart. By Mrs Oliphant. 2s. 6d.
OSBORN. Narratives of Voyage and Adventure. By Admiral
SHERARD OSBORN, C.B. 3 vols. crown 8vo, 12s.
OSSIAN. The Poems of Ossian in the Original Gaelic. With a
Literal Translation into English, and a Dissertation on the Authenticity of the
Poems. By the Rev. ARCHIBALD CLERK. 2 vols. imperial 8vo, £1, 11s. 6d.
OSWALD. By Fell and Fjord ; or, Scenes and Studies in Iceland.
By E. J. OSWALD. Post 8vo, with Illustrations. 7s. 6d.
OUTRAM. Lyrics : Legal and Miscellaneous. By the late GEORGE
OUTRAM, Esq., Advocate. New Edition, with Explanatory Notes. Edited
by J. H. Stoddart, LL.D. and Illustrated by William Ralston and A. S.
Boyd. Fcap. 8vo, 5s.
PAGE. Introductory Text-Book of Geology. By DAVID PAGE,
LL.D., Professor of Geology in the Durham University of Physical Science,
Newcastle, and Professor LAPWORTH of Mason Science College, Birmingham.
With Engravings and Glossarial Index. Twelfth Edition. Revised and En-
larged. 3s. 6d.
———— Advanced Text-Book of Geology, Descriptive and Indus-
trial. With Engravings, and Glossary of Scientific Terms. Sixth Edition, re-
vised and enlarged, 7s. 6d.
———— Introductory Text-Book of Physical Geography. With
Sketch-Maps and Illustrations. Edited by CHARLES LAPWORTH, LL.D., F.G.S.,
&c., Professor of Geology and Mineralogy in the Mason Science College, Bir-
mingham. 12th Edition. 2s. 6d.
———— Advanced Text-Book of Physical Geography. Third
Edition, Revised and Enlarged by Prof. LAPWORTH. With Engravings. 5s.
PATON. Spindrift. By Sir J. NOEL PATON. Fcap., cloth, 5s.
———— Poems by a Painter. Fcap., cloth, 5s.
PATON. Body and Soul. A Romance in Transcendental Path-
ology. By FREDERICK NOEL PATON. Third Edition. Crown 8vo, 1s.
PATTERSON. Essays in History and Art. By R. HOGARTH
PATTERSON. 8vo, 12s.
———— The New Golden Age, and Influence of the Precious
Metals upon the World. 2 vols. 8vo, 31s. 6d.
PAUL. History of the Royal Company of Archers, the Queen's
Body-Guard for Scotland. By JAMES BALFOUR PAUL, Advocate of the Scottish
Bar. Crown 4to, with Portraits and other Illustrations. £2, 2s.
PEILE. Lawn Tennis as a Game of Skill. With latest revised
Laws as played by the Best Clubs. By Captain S. C. F. PEILE, B.S.C. Fourth
Edition, fcap. cloth, 1s. 6d
PETTIGREW. The Handy Book of Bees, and their Profitable
Management. By A. PETTIGREW. Fifth Edition, Enlarged, with Engrav-
ings. Crown 8vo, 3s. 6d.

PHILOSOPHICAL CLASSICS FOR ENGLISH READERS.

Companion Series to Ancient and Foreign Classics for English Readers. Edited by WILLIAM KNIGHT, LL.D., Professor of Moral Philosophy, University of St Andrews. In crown 8vo volumes, with portraits, price 3s. 6d.
[For list of Volumes published, see page 2.

POLLOK. The Course of Time : A Poem. By ROBERT POLLOK, A.M. Small fcap. 8vo, cloth gilt, 2s. 6d. The Cottage Edition, 32mo, sewed, 8d. The Same, cloth, gilt edges, 1s. 6d. Another Edition, with Illustrations by Birket Foster and others, fcap., gilt cloth, 3s. 6d., or with edges gilt, 4s.

PORT ROYAL LOGIC. Translated from the French ; with Introduction, Notes, and Appendix. By THOMAS SPENCER BAYNES, LL.D., Professor in the University of St Andrews. Tenth Edition, 12mo, 4s.

POTTS AND DARNELL. Aditus Faciliores : An easy Latin Construing Book, with Complete Vocabulary. By A. W. POTTS, M.A., LL.D., Head-Master of the Fettes College, Edinburgh ; and the Rev. C. DARNELL, M.A., Head-Master of Cargilfield Preparatory School, Edinburgh. Tenth Edition, fcap. 8vo, 3s. 6d.

——— Aditus Faciliores Graeci. An easy Greek Construing Book, with Complete Vocabulary. Fourth Edition, fcap. 8vo, 3s.

PRINGLE. The Live-Stock of the Farm. By ROBERT O. PRINGLE. Third Edition. Revised and Edited by JAMES MACDONALD, of the 'Farming World,' &c. Crown 8vo, 7s. 6d.

PUBLIC GENERAL STATUTES AFFECTING SCOTLAND from 1707 to 1847, with Chronological Table and Index. 3 vols. large 8vo, £3, 3s.

PUBLIC GENERAL STATUTES AFFECTING SCOTLAND, COLLECTION OF. Published Annually with General Index.

RAMSAY. Rough Recollections of Military Service and Society. By Lieut.-Col. BALCARRES D. WARDLAW RAMSAY. Two vols. post 8vo, 21s.

RAMSAY. Scotland and Scotsmen in the Eighteenth Century. Edited from the MSS. of JOHN RAMSAY, Esq. of Ochtertyre, by ALEXANDER ALLARDYCE, Author of 'Memoir of Admiral Lord Keith, K.B.,' &c. 2 vols. 8vo, 31s. 6d.

RANKIN. A Handbook of the Church of Scotland. By JAMES RANKIN, D.D., Minister of Muthill ; Author of 'Character Studies in the Old Testament,' &c. An entirely New and much Enlarged Edition. Crown 8vo, with 2 Maps, 7s. 6d.

RANKINE. A Treatise on the Rights and Burdens incident to the Ownership of Lands and other Heritages in Scotland. By JOHN RANKINE, M.A., Advocate, Professor of Scots Law in the University of Edinburgh. Second Edition, Revised and Enlarged. 8vo, 45s.

RECORDS OF THE TERCENTENARY FESTIVAL OF THE UNIVERSITY OF EDINBURGH. Celebrated in April 1884. Published under the Sanction of the Senatus Academicus. Large 4to, £2, 12s. 6d.

RICE. Reminiscences of Abraham Lincoln. By Distinguished Men of his Time. Collected and Edited by ALLEN THORNDIKE RICE, Editor of the 'North American Review.' Large 8vo, with Portraits, 21s.

ROBERTSON. Orellana, and other Poems. By J. LOGIE ROBERTSON, M.A. Fcap. 8vo. Printed on hand-made paper. 6s.

ROBERTSON. Our Holiday Among the Hills. By JAMES and JANET LOGIE ROBERTSON. Fcap. 8vo, 3s. 6d.

ROSCOE. Rambles with a Fishing-rod. By E. S. ROSCOE. Crown 8vo, 4s. 6d.

ROSS. Old Scottish Regimental Colours. By ANDREW ROSS, S.S.C., Hon. Secretary Old Scottish Regimental Colours Committee. Dedicated by Special Permission to Her Majesty the Queen. Folio. £2, 12s. 6d.

RUSSELL. The Haigs of Bemersyde. A Family History. By JOHN RUSSELL. Large 8vo, with Illustrations. 21s.

RUSSELL. Fragments from Many Tables. Being the Recollections of some Wise and Witty Men and Women. By GEO. RUSSELL. Cr. 8vo, 4s. 6d.

RUSSELL. Essays on Sacred Subjects for General Readers. By the Rev. WILLIAM RUSSELL, M.A. 8vo, 10s. 6d.

RUSTOW. The War for the Rhine Frontier, 1870. By Col. W. RUSTOW. Translated from the German, by JOHN LAYLAND NEEDHAM, Lieutenant R.M. Artillery. 3 vols. 8vo, with Maps and Plans, £1, 11s. 6d.

RUTLAND. Notes of an Irish Tour in 1846. By the DUKE OF RUTLAND, G.C.B. (Lord JOHN MANNERS). New Edition. Crown 8vo, 2s. 6d.

RUTLAND. Gems of German Poetry. Translated by the DUCHESS OF RUTLAND (Lady JOHN MANNERS). New Edition in preparation.

———— Impressions of Bad-Homburg. Comprising a Short Account of the Women's Associations of Germany under the Red Cross. Crown 8vo, 1s. 6d.

———— Some Personal Recollections of the Later Years of the Earl of Beaconsfield, K.G. Sixth Edition, 6d.

———— Employment of Women in the Public Service. 6d.

———— Some of the Advantages of Easily Accessible Reading and Recreation Rooms, and Free Libraries. With Remarks on Starting and Maintaining Them. Second Edition, crown 8vo, 1s.

———— A Sequel to Rich Men's Dwellings, and other Occasional Papers. Crown 8vo, 2s. 6d.

———— Encouraging Experiences of Reading and Recreation Rooms, Aims of Guilds, Nottingham Social Guild, Existing Institutions, &c., &c. Crown 8vo, 1s.

SCHILLER. Wallenstein. A Dramatic Poem. By FREDERICK VON SCHILLER. Translated by C. G. A. LOCKHART. Fcap. 8vo, 7s. 6d.

SCOTCH LOCH FISHING. By "Black Palmer." Crown 8vo, interleaved with blank pages, 4s.

SCOUGAL. Scenes from a Silent World; or, Prisons and their Inmates. By FRANCIS SCOUGAL. Crown 8vo, 6s.

SELLAR. Manual of the Education Acts for Scotland. By ALEXANDER CRAIG SELLAR, M.P. Eighth Edition. Revised and in great part rewritten by J. EDWARD GRAHAM, B.A. Oxon., Advocate. Containing the Technical Schools Act, 1887, and all Acts bearing on Education in Scotland. With Rules for the conduct of Elections, with Notes and Cases. With a Supplement, being the Acts of 1889 in so far as affecting the Education Acts. 8vo, 12s. 6d.
[SUPPLEMENT TO SELLAR'S MANUAL OF THE EDUCATION ACTS FOR SCOTLAND. 8vo, 2s.]

SELLER AND STEPHENS. Physiology at the Farm; in Aid of Rearing and Feeding the Live Stock. By WILLIAM SELLER, M.D., F.R.S.E., and HENRY STEPHENS, F.R.S.E., Author of 'The Book of the Farm,' &c. Post 8vo, with Engravings, 16s.

SETH. Scottish Philosophy. A Comparison of the Scottish and German Answers to Hume. Balfour Philosophical Lectures, University of Edinburgh. By ANDREW SETH, M.A., Professor of Logic, Rhetoric, and Metaphysics in the University of St Andrews. Second Edition. Crown 8vo, 5s.

———— Hegelianism and Personality. Balfour Philosophical Lectures. Second Series. Crown 8vo, 5s.

SETON. A Budget of Anecdotes. Chiefly relating to the Current Century. Compiled and Arranged by GEORGE SETON, Advocate, M.A. Oxon. New and Cheaper Edition, fcap. 8vo. Boards, 1s. 6d.

SHADWELL. The Life of Colin Campbell, Lord Clyde. Illustrated by Extracts from his Diary and Correspondence. By Lieutenant-General SHADWELL, C.B. 2 vols. 8vo With Portrait, Maps, and Plans. 36s.

SHAND. Half a Century; or, Changes in Men and Manners. By ALEX. INNES SHAND, Author of 'Against Time,' &c. Second Ed., 8vo, 12s. 6d.

———— Letters from the West of Ireland. Reprinted from the 'Times.' Crown 8vo, 5s.

SHARPE. Letters from and to Charles Kirkpatrick Sharpe. Edited by ALEXANDER ALLARDYCE, Author of 'Memoir of Admiral Lord Keith, K.B.,' &c. With a Memoir by the Rev. W. K. R. BEDFORD. In two vols. 8vo. Illustrated with Etchings and other Engravings. £2, 12s. 6d.

SIM. Margaret Sim's Cookery. With an Introduction by L. B. WALFORD, Author of 'Mr Smith: A Part of His Life,' &c. Crown 8vo, 5s.

SKELTON. Maitland of Lethington ; and the Scotland of Mary Stuart. A History. By JOHN SKELTON, C.B., LL.D. Author of 'The Essays of Shirley.' Demy 8vo. 2 vols., 28s.

SMITH. Thorndale ; or, The Conflict of Opinions. By WILLIAM SMITH, Author of 'A Discourse on Ethics,' &c. New Edition. Cr. 8vo, 10s. 6d.

——— Gravenhurst ; or, Thoughts on Good and Evil. Second Edition, with Memoir of the Author. Crown 8vo, 8s.

——— The Story of William and Lucy Smith. Edited by GEORGE MERRIAM. Large post 8vo, 12s. 6d.

SMITH. Memoir of the Families of M'Combie and Thoms. Originally M'Intosh and M'Thomas. Compiled from History and Tradition. By WILLIAM M'COMBIE SMITH. 8vo.

SMITH. Greek Testament Lessons for Colleges, Schools, and Private Students, consisting chiefly of the Sermon on the Mount and the Parables of our Lord. With Notes and Essays. By the Rev. J. HUNTER SMITH, M.A., King Edward's School, Birmingham. Crown 8vo 6s.

SMITH. Writings by the Way. By JOHN CAMPBELL SMITH, M.A., Sheriff-Substitute. Crown 8vo, 9s.

SMITH. The Secretary for Scotland. Being a Statement of the Powers and Duties of the new Scottish Office. With a Short Historical Introduction and numerous references to important Administrative Documents. By W. C. SMITH, LL.B., Advocate. 8vo, 6s.

SOLTERA. A Lady's Ride Across Spanish Honduras. By MARIA SOLTERA. With Illustrations. Post 8vo, 12s. 6d.

SORLEY. The Ethics of Naturalism. Being the Shaw Fellowship Lectures, 1884. By W. R. Sorley, M.A., Fellow of Trinity College, Cambridge, and Examiner in Philosophy in the University of Edinburgh. Crown 8vo, 6s.

SPEEDY. Sport in the Highlands and Lowlands of Scotland with Rod and Gun. By TOM SPEEDY. Second Edition, Revised and Enlarged. With Illustrations by Lieut.-Gen. Hope Crealocke, C.B., C.M.G., and others. 8vo, 15s.

SPROTT. The Worship and Offices of the Church of Scotland. By GEORGE W. SPROTT, D.D., Minister of North Berwick. Crown 8vo, 6s.

STAFFORD. How I Spent my Twentieth Year. Being a Record of a Tour Round the World, 1886-87. By the MARCHIONESS OF STAFFORD. With Illustrations, crown 8vo, 8s. 6d.

STARFORTH. Villa Residences and Farm Architecture : A Series of Designs. By JOHN STARFORTH, Architect. 102 Engravings. Second Edition, medium 4to, £2, 17s. 6d.

STATISTICAL ACCOUNT OF SCOTLAND. Complete, with Index, 15 vols. 8vo, £16, 16s. Each County sold separately, with Title, Index, and Map, neatly bound in cloth, forming a very valuable Manual to the Landowner, the Tenant, the Manufacturer, the Naturalist, the Tourist, &c.

In course of publication.

STEPHENS' BOOK OF THE FARM ; detailing the Labours of the Farmer, Farm-Steward, Ploughman, Shepherd, Hedger. Farm-Labourer, Field-Worker, and Cattleman. Illustrated with numerous Portraits of Animals and Engravings of Implements. Fourth Edition. Revised, and in great part rewritten by JAMES MACDONALD, of the 'Farming World,' &c., &c. Assisted by many of the leading agricultural authorities of the day. To be completed in Six Divisional Volumes.

[Divisions I., II., and III., price 10s. 6d. each, now ready.

STEPHENS. The Book of Farm Buildings; their Arrangement and
Construction. By HENRY STEPHENS, F.R.S.E., Author of 'The Book of the
Farm;' and ROBERT SCOTT BURN. Illustrated with 1045 Plates and En-
gravings. Large 8vo, uniform with 'The Book of the Farm,' &c. £1, 11s. 6d.
——— The Book of Farm Implements and Machines. By J.
SLIGHT and R. SCOTT BURN, Engineers. Edited by HENRY STEPHENS. Large
8vo, uniform with 'The Book of the Farm,' £2, 2s.

STEVENSON. British Fungi. (Hymenomycetes.) By Rev. JOHN
STEVENSON, Author of 'Mycologia Scotia,' Hon. Sec. Cryptogamic Society of
Scotland. 2 vols. post 8vo, with Illustrations, price 12s. 6d. each.
Vol. I. AGARICUS—BOLBITIUS. Vol. II. CORTINARIUS—DACRYMYCES.

STEWART. Advice to Purchasers of Horses. By JOHN STEWART,
V.S., Author of 'Stable Economy.' New Edition. 2s. 6d.
——— Stable Economy. A Treatise on the Management of
Horses in relation to Stabling, Grooming, Feeding, Watering, and Working.
By JOHN STEWART, V.S. Seventh Edition, fcap. 8vo, 6s. 6d.

STODDART. Angling Songs. By THOMAS TOD STODDART. New
Edition, with a Memoir by ANNA M. STODDART. Crown 8vo, 7s. 6d.

STORMONTH. Etymological and Pronouncing Dictionary of the
English Language. Including a very Copious Selection of Scientific Terms.
For Use in Schools and Colleges, and as a Book of General Reference. By the
Rev. JAMES STORMONTH. The Pronunciation carefully Revised by the Rev.
P. H. PHELP, M.A. Cantab. Tenth Edition, Revised throughout. Crown
8vo, pp. 800. 7s. 6d.
——— Dictionary of the English Language, Pronouncing,
Etymological, and Explanatory. Revised by the Rev. P. H. PHELP. Library
Edition. Imperial 8vo, handsomely bound in half morocco, 31s. 6d.
——— The School Etymological Dictionary and Word-Book.
Fourth Edition. Fcap. 8vo, pp. 254. 2s.

STORY. Nero; A Historical Play. By W. W. STORY, Author of
'Roba di Roma.' Fcap. 8vo, 6s.
——— Vallombrosa. Post 8vo, 5s.
——— He and She; or, A Poet's Portfolio. Fcap. 3s. 6d.
——— Poems. 2 vols. fcap., 7s. 6d.
——— Fiammetta. A Summer Idyl. Crown 8vo, 7s. 6d.

STRICKLAND. Life of Agnes Strickland. By her SISTER.
Post 8vo, with Portrait engraved on Steel, 12s. 6d.

STURGIS. John-a-Dreams. A Tale. By JULIAN STURGIS.
New Edition, crown 8vo, 3s. 6d.
——— Little Comedies, Old and New. Crown 8vo, 7s. 6d.

SUTHERLAND. Handbook of Hardy Herbaceous and Alpine
Flowers, for general Garden Decoration. Containing Descriptions of up-
wards of 1000 Species of Ornamental Hardy Perennial and Alpine Plants;
along with Concise and Plain Instructions for their Propagation and Culture.
By WILLIAM SUTHERLAND, Landscape Gardener; formerly Manager of the
Herbaceous Department at Kew. Crown 8vo, 7s. 6d.

TAYLOR. The Story of My Life. By the late Colonel MEADOWS
TAYLOR, Author of 'The Confessions of a Thug,' &c. &c. Edited by his
Daughter. New and cheaper Edition, being the Fourth. Crown 8vo, 6s.

THE BULL I' TH' THORN. A Romance. In 3 vols. Crown
8vo, 25s. 6d.

THOLUCK. Hours of Christian Devotion. Translated from the
German of A. Tholuck, D.D., Professor of Theology in the University of Halle.
By the Rev. ROBERT MENZIES, D.D. With a Preface written for this Transla-
tion by the Author. Second Edition, crown 8vo, 7s. 6d.

THOMSON. Handy Book of the Flower-Garden: being Practical
Directions for the Propagation, Culture, and Arrangement of Plants in Flower-
Gardens all the year round. With Engraved Plans. By DAVID THOMSON,
Gardener to his Grace the Duke of Buccleuch, K.T., at Drumlanrig. Fourth
and Cheaper Edition, crown 8vo, 5s.

THOMSON. The Handy Book of Fruit-Culture under Glass: being a series of Elaborate Practical Treatises on the Cultivation and Forcing of Pines, Vines, Peaches, Figs, Melons, Strawberries, and Cucumbers. With Engravings of Hothouses, &c., most suitable for the Cultivation and Forcing of these Fruits. By DAVID THOMSON, Gardener to his Grace the Duke of Buccleuch, K.T., at Drumlanrig. Second Ed. Cr. 8vo, with Engravings, 7s. 6d.

THOMSON. A Practical Treatise on the Cultivation of the Grape-Vine. By WILLIAM THOMSON, Tweed Vineyards. Ninth Edition, 8vo, 5s.

THOMSON. Cookery for the Sick and Convalescent. With Directions for the Preparation of Poultices, Fomentations, &c. By BARBARA THOMSON. Fcap. 8vo, 1s. 6d.

THOTH. A Romance. Third Edition. Crown 8vo, 4s. 6d.
By the Same Author.
A DREAMER OF DREAMS. A Modern Romance. Second Edition. Crown 8vo, 6s.

TOM CRINGLE'S LOG. A New Edition, with Illustrations. Crown 8vo, cloth gilt, 5s. Cheap Edition, 2s.

TRANSACTIONS OF THE HIGHLAND AND AGRICULTURAL SOCIETY OF SCOTLAND. Published annually, price 5s.

TULLOCH. Rational Theology and Christian Philosophy in England in the Seventeenth Century. By JOHN TULLOCH, D.D., Principal of St Mary's College in the University of St Andrews; and one of her Majesty's Chaplains in Ordinary in Scotland. Second Edition. 2 vols. 8vo, 16s.

—— Modern Theories in Philosophy and Religion. 8vo, 15s.

—— Luther, and other Leaders of the Reformation. Third Edition, enlarged. Crown 8vo, 3s. 6d.

—— Memoir of Principal Tulloch, D.D., LL.D. By Mrs OLIPHANT, Author of 'Life of Edward Irving.' Third and Cheaper Edition. 8vo, with Portrait. 7s. 6d.

TWO STORIES OF THE SEEN AND THE UNSEEN. 'THE OPEN DOOR,' 'OLD LADY MARY.' Crown 8vo, cloth, 2s. 6d.

VEITCH. Institutes of Logic. By JOHN VEITCH, LL.D., Professor of Logic and Rhetoric in the University of Glasgow. Post 8vo, 12s. 6d.

—— The Feeling for Nature in Scottish Poetry. From the Earliest Times to the Present Day. 2 vols. fcap. 8vo, in roxburghe binding. 15s.

—— Merlin and Other Poems. Fcap. 8vo. 4s. 6d.

—— Knowing and Being. Essays in Philosophy. First Series. Crown 8vo, 5s.

VIRGIL. The Æneid of Virgil. Translated in English Blank Verse by G. K. RICKARDS, M.A., and Lord RAVENSWORTH. 2 vols. fcap. 8vo, 10s.

WALFORD. A Stiff-Necked Generation. By L. B. WALFORD, Author of 'Mr Smith,' &c. Cheap Edition. Crown 8vo, 6s.

—— Four Biographies from 'Blackwood': Jane Taylor, Hannah More, Elizabeth Fry, Mary Somerville. Crown 8vo, 5s.

WARREN'S (SAMUEL) WORKS :—
Diary of a Late Physician. Cloth, 2s. 6d.; boards, 2s.
Ten Thousand A-Year. Cloth, 3s. 6d.; boards, 2s. 6d.
Now and Then. The Lily and the Bee. Intellectual and Moral Development of the Present Age. 4s. 6d.
Essays : Critical, Imaginative, and Juridical. 5s.

WARREN. The Five Books of the Psalms. With Marginal Notes. By Rev. SAMUEL L. WARREN, Rector of Esher, Surrey; late Fellow, Dean, and Divinity Lecturer, Wadham College, Oxford. Crown 8vo, 5s.

WEBSTER. The Angler and the Loop-Rod. By DAVID WEBSTER. Crown 8vo, with Illustrations, 7s. 6d.

WELLINGTON. Wellington Prize Essays on "the System of Field Manœuvres best adapted for enabling our Troops to meet a Continental Army." Edited by Lieut.-General Sir EDWARD BRUCE HAMLEY, K.C.B. 8vo, 12s. 6d.

WENLEY. Socrates and Christ: A Study in the Philosophy of Religion. By R. M. WENLEY, M.A., Lecturer on Mental and Moral Philosophy in Queen Margaret College, Glasgow; Examiner in Philosophy in he University of Glasgow. Crown 8vo, 6s.

WERNER. A Visit to Stanley's Rear-Guard at Major Barttelot's Camp on the Aruhwimi. With an Account of River-Life on the Congo. By J. R. WERNER, F.R.G.S., Engineer, late in the Service of the Etat Independant du Congo. With Maps, Portraits and other Illustrations. 8vo, 10s.

WESTMINSTER ASSEMBLY. Minutes of the Westminster Assembly, while engaged in preparing their Directory for Church Government, Confession of Faith, and Catechisms (November 1644 to March 1649). Edited by the Rev. Professor ALEX. T. MITCHELL, of St Andrews, and the Rev. JOHN STRUTHERS, LL.D. With a Historical and Critical Introduction by Professor Mitchell. 8vo, 15s.

WHITE. The Eighteen Christian Centuries. By the Rev. JAMES WHITE. Seventh Edition, post 8vo, with Index, 6s.

———— History of France, from the Earliest Times. Sixth Thousand, post 8vo, with Index, 6s.

WHITE. Archæological Sketches in Scotland—Kintyre and Knapdale. By Colonel T. P. WHITE, R.E., of the Ordnance Survey. With numerous Illustrations. 2 vols. folio, £4, 4s. Vol. I., Kintyre, sold separately, £2, 2s.

———— The Ordnance Survey of the United Kingdom. A Popular Account. Crown 8vo, 5s.

WILLIAMSON. Poems of Nature and Life. By DAVID R. WILLIAMSON, Minister of Kirkmaiden. Fcap. 8vo, 3s. ,

WILLS AND GREENE. Drawing-room Dramas for Children. By W. G. WILLS and the Hon. Mrs GREENE. Crown 8vo, 6s.

WILSON. Works of Professor Wilson. Edited by his Son-in-Law Professor FERRIER. 12 vols. crown 8vo, £2, 8s.

———— Christopher in his Sporting-Jacket. 2 vols., 8s.

———— Isle of Palms, City of the Plague, and other Poems. 4s.

———— Lights and Shadows of Scottish Life, and other Tales. 4s.

———— Essays, Critical and Imaginative. 4 vols., 16s.

———— The Noctes Ambrosianæ. 4 vols., 16s.

———— Homer and his Translators, and the Greek Drama. Crown 8vo, 4s.

WINGATE. Annie Weir, and other Poems. By DAVID WINGATE. Fcap. 8vo, 5s.

———— Lily Neil. A Poem. Crown 8vo, 4s. 6d.

WORDSWORTH. The Historical Plays of Shakspeare. With Introductions and Notes. By CHARLES WORDSWORTH, D.C.L., Bishop of S. Andrews. 3 vols. post 8vo, each 7s. 6d.

WORSLEY. Poems and Translations. By PHILIP STANHOPE WORSLEY, M.A. Edited by EDWARD WORSLEY. Second Edition, enlarged. Fcap. 8vo, 6s.

YATE. England and Russia Face to Face in Asia. A Record of Travel with the Afghan Boundary Commission. By Captain A. C. YATE, Bombay Staff Corps. 8vo, with Maps and Illustrations, 21s.

YATE. Northern Afghanistan ; or, Letters from the Afghan Boundary Commission. By Major C. E. Yate, C.S.I., C.M.G. Bombay Staff Corps, F.R.G.S. 8vo, with Maps. 18s.

YOUNG. A Story of Active Service in Foreign Lands. Compiled from letters sent home from South Africa, India, and China, 1856-1882. By Surgeon-General A. Graham Young, Author of 'Crimean Cracks.' Crown 8vo, Illustrated, 7s. 6d.

YULE. Fortification : for the Use of Officers in the Army, and Readers of Military History. By Col. YULE, Bengal Engineers. 8vo, with numerous Illustrations, 10s. 6d.

12/89.